Personality Assessment
in Treatment Planning

Personality Assessment in Treatment Planning

Use of the MMPI-2 and BTPI

James N. Butcher
Julia N. Perry

OXFORD
UNIVERSITY PRESS

2008

OXFORD
UNIVERSITY PRESS

Oxford University Press, Inc., publishes works that further
Oxford University's objective of excellence
in research, scholarship, and education.

Oxford   New York
Auckland   Cape Town   Dar es Salaam   Hong Kong   Karachi
Kuala Lumpur   Madrid   Melbourne   Mexico City   Nairobi
New Delhi   Shanghai   Taipei   Toronto

With offices in
Argentina   Austria   Brazil   Chile   Czech Republic   France   Greece
Guatemala   Hungary   Italy   Japan   Poland   Portugal   Singapore
South Korea   Switzerland   Thailand   Turkey   Ukraine   Vietnam

Published by Oxford University Press, Inc.
198 Madison Avenue, New York, New York 10016

www.oup.com

Oxford is a registered trademark of Oxford University Press

Library of Congress Cataloging-in-Publication Data
Butcher, James Neal, 1933–
Personality assessment in treatment planning : use of the MMPI-2
and BTPI/James N. Butcher, Julia N. Perry.
     p. ; cm.
Rev. ed. of: MMPI-2 in psychological treatment / James Butcher. 1990.
Includes bibliographical references.
ISBN: 978-0-19-533097-7 (cloth)
1. Minnesota Multiphasic Personality Inventory. 2. Personality assessment.
I. Perry, Julia N. II. Butcher, James Neal, 1933-MMPI-2 in psychological treatment. III. Title.
[DNLM: 1. MMPI. 2. Personality Inventory. 3. Psychotherapy—methods.
WM 145.5.M6 B98 3p 2008]

RC473.M5B87 2008

616.89'075—dc22   2007037167

9 8 7 6 5 4 3 2 1

Printed in the United States of America
on acid-free paper

Preface

The success of psychotherapy, regardless of the theoretical orientation of the therapist or client symptoms, depends greatly upon gaining an early understanding of the extent of the client's problems, the personality characteristics of the client, the potential for changing directions that the client possesses, and the establishment of attainable treatment goals. Research has demonstrated that undertaking personality assessment, particularly when the results are shared with the client in test feedback sessions, can lead to effective client therapist collaboration and remarkably positive outcomes in the therapeutic process.

In this book, we have attempted to provide the therapist with a conceptual framework for viewing a client's personality characteristics, symptomatic status, and sources of treatment resistance, and we have suggested workable techniques for sharing needed personality information with the client. We have presented background information on two objective assessment measures, the Minnesota Multiphasic Personality Inventory (MMPI-2) and the Butcher Treatment Planning Inventory (BTPI), that can be employed in order to gain a practical understanding of a client's personality characteristics, his or her treatment attitudes, and the presence of possible sources of treatment resistance.

This volume is a revised and substantially expanded edition of an earlier work that served as a widely used resource for psychologists employing psychological assessment in treatment evaluations—namely, *The Use of the MMPI-2 in Psychological Treatment* by James Butcher, which was published in 1990, shortly after the original MMPI was revised in 1989. A great deal of research has accrued since 1990 in the area of assessment methodology and with regard to practical methods for conducting psychological test feedback with clients. This book was designed to highlight the treatment related research and review the tactics for using objective instruments for assessing clients in therapy.

The authorship on this edition of the book has been enhanced by including Julia Perry, a clinical psychologist and psychotherapy researcher at the Minneapolis Veteran's Affairs Medical Center, so as to expand the focus of the volume and to incorporate her extensive experience in using psychological assessment methods in client assessment, particularly her extensive work with the BTPI.

We would like to acknowledge the support of a number of people throughout the development of this project. First, James Butcher would like to acknowledge the continuing support of his family, his wife, Carolyn L. Williams, and three children Sherry Butcher, Janus Butcher, and Holly Butcher. Second, Julia Perry would like to acknowledge the support of her family and friends, particularly Carolyn Perry, Pamela Perry, Marjorie Rollins, Theresa Glaser, and Ken Abrams. We would also like to give thanks to the Oxford editorial staff for their guidance and assistance throughout this project, particularly Joan Bossert and Abby Gross. We would also like to thank Betty Kininiki and Holly butcher for assistance in the reference checking stage of development. Finally, we would also like to express our appreciation to two reviewers of early editions of this book who have made a number of very valuable suggestions for improving coverage.

James N. Butcher
Julia N. Perry

Contents

Personality Assessment
in Treatment Planning

1

Importance of Psychological Assessment in Treatment Planning

Psychological treatment—whether psychodynamic, behavioral, or based on some other theoretical viewpoint—proceeds best when both the therapist and the client understand the client's problems and weaknesses, resources, and strengths. The task of assessment may precede the initiation of treatment or it may be ongoing throughout therapy. Therapists of different theoretical views approach the task of assessing and evaluating the client from different avenues. Assessment can involve providing a "normative framework" within which the therapist can compare the patient's problems with others, or it may be more "idiographic," with the therapist seeking to understand the patient on his or her own terms through interview, observations, and information from others such as a spouse.

This book is devoted to appraising and understanding self-reported problems and personality factors of clients by bringing to them an objective perspective using the Minnesota Multiphasic Personality Inventory (MMPI-2), the most widely researched and most frequently used clinical assessment instrument, and the Butcher Treatment Planning Inventory (BTPI), a self-report instrument to address client problems and attitudes, treatment processes, and progress in treatment. Before delving into the applications of these instruments in treatment planning, let us explore some general issues related to the use of psychological tests in mental health evaluation.

Why Use Psychological Tests?

What benefit can a client derive from a therapist who uses psychological tests in pretreatment evaluation? A person facing the difficult task of gaining self-knowledge through therapy with an eye toward making or consolidating important changes into his or her life is committed to the task of self-scrutiny. The therapy setting itself, particularly in relationship-oriented treatment, provides an arena for personal discovery of behaviors, attitudes, and motivations that might evoke painful emotions. In the course of therapy a skillful therapist and a willing, motivated client can uncover many of the sources of difficulties that plague the patient, and they may have considerable opportunity to explore them in depth. Not all therapies, however, have the luxury of time or involve an insightful, verbally fluent patient. Psychological assessment can provide a shortcut and, at times, a clearly defined path on the way to revealing a client's problems. Psychological assessment through the use of objective tests can offer an "outside" opinion about personality maladjustment and symptomatic behavior. When personality-based information is shared with clients, a remarkable progress of change is often begun. The descriptive and predictive information obtained through a psychological measure like the MMPI-2 and BTPI can provide both therapist and patient with invaluable clues to the nature and source of problems. In addition, such information may forewarn of possibly dangerous psychological "minefields" that could impair progress as well as reveal areas of potential growth.

In most cases, psychological assessment is undertaken as a means of obtaining information that will be helpful to the client in therapy. Foremost among the benefits of pretherapy assessment is that psychological testing can provide information about motivation, fears, attitudes, defensive styles, and symptoms of which the client may be unaware. As we will see, psychological test results can provide both client and therapist with a normative framework from which such problems can be viewed. All clients need to be evaluated, understood, and at times confronted by information outside their personal awareness. They need to know how severe their problems are in comparison to those of other people. Patients seek and deserve to have personal feedback from their therapists about the nature and extent of their problems. Psychological testing provides an excellent framework within which *initial* client feedback may be provided.

Test-based descriptions and predictions, even though they may only reaffirm a person's expectations or beliefs, nevertheless serve an important function: they bring into focus important material needed for the therapeutic exchange. Moreover, through the use of the MMPI-2 validity indicators and BTPI patient attitudes scales, the individual's openness to treatment can be discerned. It is usually assumed that patients who enter therapy are motivated to seek help and are open to becoming engaged in the task of describing and relating their problems to a therapist. It is further assumed that patients, because they want to be understood, are accessible to the therapist's inquiries and will disclose problems appropriately. Unfortunately, the assumption that patients are ready to engage in the treatment process is not always well founded. The MMPI-2 and BTPI validity indicators provide a direct test of a patient's readiness for treatment. By directly assessing response attitudes, the therapist can evaluate the patient's level of cooperativeness and encourage or reinforce the willingness to engage in the task of self-disclosure. For example, patients who produce defensive, uncooperative test patterns, as reflected in the test validity scores, or those who appear to have a "closed mind" to behavioral change may be relatively inaccessible to the therapist during sessions. When the therapist has this knowledge early in the treatment process, problems of lack of trust or hesitancy to disclose personal information can be confronted.

Personality assessment instruments have three major applications in treatment planning: in pretreatment planning, in assessing progress during therapy, and in posttreatment evaluation. The functions of these assessments differ somewhat and so need to be addressed separately.

Pretreatment Planning: Obtaining an "Outside Opinion"

It may seem obvious that people in treatment need to have pertinent, objective information about themselves if they are to know what behaviors need to be changed. Thus, providing patients with objective information about themselves and their problems becomes one of the most important tasks the therapist undertakes. Psychological test results provide a valuable framework from which clients can obtain information about themselves. For example, the symptoms and problems a person is reporting can be viewed in an objective framework in comparison with thousands of other troubled individuals; clues to a person's coping strategies are also obtainable in the MMPI-2 and BTPI; and the client's need for treatment is reflected in the profiles. Normative psychological testing can provide a valuable perspective that allows a person to view his or her personal problems from a different vantage point and to obtain an objective measure of the extent of the problems.

Moreover, people who are seeking professional help to remedy psychological or interpersonal problems are usually motivated to learn all they can about themselves. Test feedback sessions can involve patients in the clinical process. And yet psychological treatment can be a difficult undertaking for the client. It is a path that may be filled with countless obstacles and deep emotional chasms; however, it promises the client help through a time of trouble. The client is faced with the task of disclosing to a stranger a great deal of personal information that may be painful to recall. It may at times seem to the client to be a hopeless mess—too difficult to sort through and even more difficult to formulate into words and sentences that can be relayed to another person.

A client's problems or beliefs may have been stored away for a long time and may only be selectively remembered. The self-expression of troubled individuals is frequently hampered by bits and pieces of memories that enter into consciousness in a random fashion. It is difficult for the therapist to know what to focus on and what to ignore. And, certainly, some of these pieces of information are believed by the client to be too dangerous to report to anyone—even to a professional who proposes to help. Therefore, early treatment sessions are frequently filled with gaps and "untold secrets," either because the client cannot accurately remember, cannot articulate well, or consciously chooses not to report.

Furthermore, many people entering treatment for the first time have an unclear or confused picture of their problems and may actually be unaware of the presence or extent of their psychological distress. Thus, it is usually valuable to provide feedback to patients early in the treatment to determine if there is any recognized or unspoken problem that requires attention. And confronting problems can be an important motivational element in the early stages of psychotherapy.

Another important benefit of using psychological tests in pretreatment evaluation is that they identify problems that are not apparent from the clinical interview. In fact, psychological test results might reveal issues or problems that the therapist and patient did not discuss in initial interviews. For example, in one case a patient failed to disclose the extent of his substance abuse and the impact it was having on his life. His MacAndrew Addiction (MAC-R) score on the MMPI-2 (an addiction proneness scale; see Chapter 5) was in the range (raw score 28) that is highly suggestive of alcohol abuse (see Craig, 2005). When the therapist discussed problems, the patient acknowledged, after an initial denial, that alcohol addiction was likely to be a factor.

Special Considerations: Treatment Receptivity Versus Resistance

One of the key considerations in carrying out psychological treatment is the degree to which resistance to treatment affects clients; see Perry (2008) for a complete review of this topic. Resistance can be present early in the psychotherapeutic process, perhaps preventing clients from getting involved in psychotherapy at all. Data suggest that perhaps half of the individuals who may need or benefit from psychological treatment never receive it, given estimates that around 14% of people meet criteria for at least one mental disorder (e.g., Regier et al., 1993) but only around 6% of Americans actually receive it (Castro, 1993). Over the past decades, a range of factors have been identified as affecting this decision, from level of education and income (Rosenthal & Frank, 1958) to race (Raynes & Warren, 1971) to traditionalism of attitudes (Brody, 1994).

In addition, research has shown that therapy is usually shorter than therapists anticipate and that a high percentage of clients terminate early, prior to achieving success in therapy (see Koss & Butcher, 1986). Recently, Connell, Grant, and Mullin (2006) found that the average "estimated" rate of unplanned endings was calculated at 50%, with a high rate determined as 58% or higher and a low rate as 38%. (For further discussion on early terminations see Arnow et al., 2007, and Lazaratou et al., 2006.)

Among the more robust predictors of resistance to psychotherapy is gender, with numerous studies demonstrating greater willingness to engage in psychotherapy among women as compared to men (e.g., Cheatham, Shelton, & Ray, 1987; Johnson, 1988; Ryan, 1969). Butcher, Rouse, and Perry (1998) looked specifically at men's and women's attitudes toward therapy within a university student sample, using a seven-item "Survey of Treatment Attitudes." The 213 women and 175 men answered such questions as, "Have you ever been in psychological counseling in the past?" and "Do you think that you would be willing to seek assistance from a psychologist or psychiatrist if you were experiencing problems in psychological adjustment?" Findings revealed that the female students were more likely than the male students to have participated in counseling. The female students were also more apt to have considered participating in some kind of psychological treatment. In addition, the women in the study reported being more willing than the men to recommend psychological interventions to a family member or friend.

In addition to "resistance" that prevents people from presenting for care, there is the "resistance" that affects ongoing psychotherapy, often operationalized in terms of poor treatment response. This form may vary depending upon diagnostic considerations or personality-related factors, sometimes being temporary and sometimes being more long-lasting (e.g., Beutler et al., 1991).

Therapy receptivity versus resistance is important to consider regardless of how these terms are conceptualized. First and foremost, some degree of shared understanding of how treatment will proceed and what benefit will look like is critical for clients and therapists. The members of this dyad need some fundamental appreciation for not only what will constitute therapeutic benefit and change but how likely these things are to take place and what factors might get in the way of them. Psychological assessment methods provide a means by which to glean some of this information objectively. They might afford client and therapist a means of comprehending why treatment may not be progressing as they had intended, uncovering potential trouble spots in psychotherapy that will need to be addressed. They also might suggest avenues for course-correcting. For example, a measure such as Prochaska, Velicer, DiClemente, and Fava's (1988) Stages of Change Questionnaire could assess a client's initial readiness to make changes so that the treatment plan can be designed accordingly. The data from this instrument could also suggest ways of helping the client move to the next stage of readiness, particularly if the current one is not conducive to making changes.

It seems clear that given the various ways in which personality measures can underscore resistance-related factors, it is advisable for therapists to employ them in the early stages of treatment and to repeat as needed throughout a course of care.

Receptivity and resistance are key issues for managed care companies and other funding sources who authorize psychological services as well. Their decisions about resource allocation can be more accurately informed with objective data than without it. The findings from psychological tests can classify clients' intervention needs in a reliable and valid manner, providing a means of justifying the need for a particular set of therapeutic strategies or a set number of sessions (Ben-Porath, 1997; Butcher, 1997a,b). Other advantages of psychological assessment methods to treatment plan formulation include the greater ease with which automated test data can be interpreted, their cost effectiveness, and the fact that automated interpretations have been demonstrated to be more valid than interpretations based upon subjective clinical judgments (Ben-Porath, 1997; Dawes, Faust, & Meehl, 1989; Grove & Meehl, 1996; Meehl, 1954).

As we will discuss in more detail later, people who seek help feel the need to be understood by the therapist; they usually appreciate the therapist's efforts to know them. Consequently, when a therapist communicates the need for pretreatment testing to gain a better understanding of a client, the client will generally recognize the therapist's purpose and will respond positively. The therapist should recognize, however, that clients who have undergone pretreatment testing feel that they have disclosed a great deal of personal information and will seek some acknowledgment of the risk they have taken. Most patients want to know their test results and would like the therapist to provide detailed feedback of what it all means.

Treatment Progress: Evaluation of Ongoing Treatment Cases

There may be more than a grain of truth in the humorously intended comment that therapy is a process by which an emotionally disturbed person gradually convinces the therapist that his or her unswerving view of the world, though bizarre, is in fact real. Therapists are notorious for their efforts to understand and accept individual idiosyncrasies and pathology. Indeed, one of the highly desirable qualities of a therapist is the ability to provide "unconditional positive regard" to an individual whose behavior is seemingly unacceptable to others. But in addition to providing much-needed support for the patient, acceptance of patient pathology can also lead to a loss of perspective on the part of the therapist. Thus, periodic psychological assessment during therapy or at its completion is an important facet of psychological treatment. Retest evaluation in the course of therapy can promote accountability and further encourage the patient's self-examination.

The use of an objective instrument like the MMPI-2 or BTPI to monitor progress in therapy can provide an external view of the patient's pathology and the progress being made in treatment. For example, a 29-year-old man (see MMPI-2 profile in Fig. 1.1) sought treatment because he was fearful that he was going to be fired from his job and so sure that things were out of his control that he was unable to go to work. In the initial therapeutic interview he appeared fearful, ruminative, tense, and anxious, and he was self-critical about being unable to perform his job. He had worked for his present company for about 5 years and had recently been promoted to a new position that required more interpersonal skill and assertiveness. He felt that he was not performing well (although his supervisors were pleased with his work) and believed that he was going to be fired because of his ineffectiveness. His high level of distress is shown in Figure 1.1 in the marked elevation on scales 2 and 7.

He was referred to a female therapist with the recommendation that the initial treatment goals might be to reduce the high levels of anxiety and to help him become effective in dealing with his immediate concerns over his job. The therapist, employing a cognitive–behavioral treatment approach, initiated efforts to reduce the work-related stress and then "inoculated" the client against a return to the level of distress he had experienced. The first eight therapeutic sessions were supportive efforts to assist him in reducing his tensions while getting him to return to work. The therapist assisted him in problem solving while providing the appropriate feedback. The client showed marked improvement at work and became confident that he would be able to perform the job satisfactorily. He was retested on the MMPI-2 after eight sessions and produced the MMPI-2 profile shown in Figure 1.2. Inspection of the profile indicates a considerable reduction in tension and anxiety, as apparent in the reduction in scale 7.

Both the client and therapist were confident that his initial goal of dealing with work stress had been met. The MMPI-2 profile, however, revealed other significant clinical problems, particularly depression, withdrawal, and social

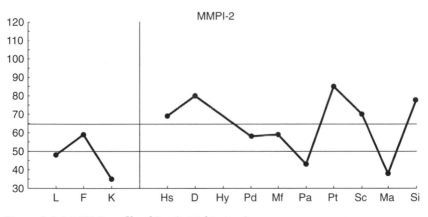

Figure 1.1. MMPI-2 profile of Jim (initial testing).

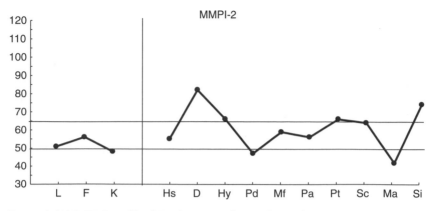

Figure 1.2. MMPI-2 profile of Jim (retesting during therapy).

isolation. In providing test feedback for the patient, the therapist was able to focus on the great success he had had in dealing with his fears and insecurities on the job. She praised him for the gains he had made in overcoming many of his problems and pointed out the need to shift the treatment goals toward reducing his depression and social isolation. In making this shift, the therapist and her client explored his unrealistic expectations and examined how these negatively affected his self-evaluations. In addition, she encouraged her client to deal with his social isolation by becoming more active and assertive in developing social relationships. In this case intermediate testing revealed the progress made and new goals to be met and was of significant value in the therapeutic outcome.

Posttreatment Evaluation

Psychological evaluation at the end of treatment can be an important aspect of the therapeutic process. It enables the client and the therapist to appraise the changes made and to gain insight into problems the client may encounter as therapy ends, as well as the resources the client can call on to meet such problems. As a result of end-of-treatment testing clients can get a sense of their progress and gain the confidence that comes from being more in control of their personal life than when treatment began.

Psychometric Factors in the Assessment of Change in the MMPI-2 Profiles

Clinicians and researchers using the personality measure in treatment evaluation have long been aware of the stability of MMPI profiles over time. Test–retest correlation among various groups has been reported to be moderate to high depending on the population studied and the retest interval used (Dahlstrom, Welsh, & Dahlstrom, 1975). Even test–retest correlations over very long retest intervals (30 years, for example; Leon et al., 1979) have reportedly been high, with some scales (Si) showing correlations as high as 0.736. One reason for the high test–retest stability is that the original MMPI contained many extreme items that draw similar endorsement, even over long periods. Studies (Goldberg & Jones, 1969; Schofield, 1950) have shown that many MMPI items, about 87%, are similarly endorsed when the test is administered on two different occasions. The MMPI-2 has included some items that may be more susceptible to change on retest; however, the heavy "trait saturation" in the item pool is likely to be characteristic of the MMPI-2 item pool as well. Although MMPI responses gravitate toward stability at retest in group studies, it is interesting that an individual, after a major traumatic event or after treatment, can display a dramatic shift from initial testing to retest.

Another factor that makes assessment of change in MMPI-2 profiles after treatment difficult is that retest profiles tend to regress toward the mean on the second testing. Profiles, for example in patient groups, are in general highly elevated at initial testing. Even without an accompanying behavioral change, profiles tend to be lower in elevation at retest. It may be difficult to know at retest how much scale elevation change to expect on the basis of the regression phenomenon. Interpretation of change in a patient's profile at retest should be made cautiously. It is clear that interpretations should not be made unless the differences exceed the standard error of measurement (SEm) for the scale (Butcher et al., 1989) and preferably are two times the SEm for conservative personality appraisal. See Jacobson and Truax (1991) for a discussion of assessing clinical significance in psychotherapy change.

Illustration of Posttreatment Change

A posttreatment evaluation can provide valuable information for the therapist because it permits assessment of the effects of the treatment on the client's personality and symptoms. It allows the therapist to determine if, for example, mood changes have occurred or if the client is experiencing problems in controlling anger. An evaluation of the individual's attitudes and behavior at this point, when one hopes that most significant issues have been resolved, can provide the therapist with insight into major unresolved issues or problems that the client is likely to face at the termination of therapy. The case that follows illustrates the use of the MMPI-2 in evaluating progress in treatment and in enabling the therapist to understand the client's psychological adjustment as he or she leaves treatment.

Illustration of a Test–Retest MMPI-2 Following Psychotherapy: A Case History

A 23-year-old man named Ed, who had recently moved to the Midwest, was referred for psychological treatment by his therapist in his hometown on the East Coast. Ed had moved to get away from his family, particularly his father, the tyrannical owner of a large manufacturing firm. Ed had been very unhappy working for his father and one day, without telling anyone his plans, left family, job, and Porsche and headed west on his motorcycle. He stopped in St. Paul, got a job as an accounting clerk, and started a new life, but he soon became dissatisfied and, at the suggestion of his previous therapist, sought psychological treatment in St. Paul.

Presenting Symptoms

Ed appeared to be depressed and anxious when he came to his first appointment. He reported that he felt pessimistic about his future and thought he might not be able to accomplish his goal of becoming independent. He was obsessive about being inadequate and unable to think for himself. He felt lonely, isolated, and very unsure of himself socially. He had particular difficulty initiating conversations, and was having trouble making new friends. Ed reported a considerable amount of anger toward his father and a sense of inadequacy and inferiority that resulted from feeling "oppressed" by his father. He also complained of physical problems—especially headaches and stomachaches when he worked for his father. He felt so depressed that he did not venture out of his rooming house in the evenings. He was inactive and stayed glued to the television because that took no energy. He knew no one in town and felt he would not be a very good friend to anyone now anyway because he was "too self-preoccupied."

Comment on the Initial MMPI-2

Ed approached the testing in a frank and open manner, producing a valid MMPI-2 profile (Fig. 1.3). He related a number of psychological adjustment problems and seemingly was seeking help in overcoming them. The MMPI-2 clinical profile highlights a number of problems and symptoms that Ed was experiencing at the time of his first treatment session. He reported being depressed and anxious about his situation and related feeling tense, lonely, and insecure. He appeared to be having great difficulty concentrating on his work and was indecisive. He had no zest for life and was preoccupied with his inability to accomplish personal goals. The relatively high score on the Psychopathic Deviate scale (Pd) reflects rebellious attitudes and family conflict (the Harris–Lingoes Family Problems Scale, Pd1, was T = 69). He

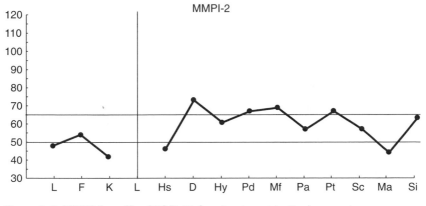

Figure 1.3. MMPI-2 profile of Ed (initial pretreatment testing).

appeared to be a somewhat passive young man who reported being shy and isolated.

Psychotherapy

Ed was seen in psychological treatment for 6 months. During the assessment phase, the therapist provided emotional support and listened to his perceptions of his problems and feeling about his family. This therapeutic approach is best described as cognitive–behavioral treatment for depression. The therapeutic goals included helping Ed to see his situation differently by exploring his expectations and providing him with positive feedback when he was able to experiment with alternative (more adaptive) approaches to a problem. For example, the therapist provided positive reinforcement by praising Ed when he began to take steps to break his isolation and meet other people. The therapist encouraged him to experiment with and adopt more effective behaviors and through role-playing provided Ed with some techniques for meeting other people and for asserting himself in appropriate ways.

Ed used the therapy hours to great advantage and implemented alternative behaviors effectively. Before long, he began developing a circle of friends and became socially active. He played in a soccer league and joined several singles groups. During the first 3 months of therapy, he avoided contact with his parents. (It is interesting that his treatment bills were paid by his father, who mailed payment to Ed's previous therapist, who then forwarded the payment to his present therapist.) During the latter period of treatment, Ed began to view his relationship with his parents in a different light. He no longer saw himself as a "helpless wimp" who had to go along with his father's wishes. He was feeling fairly comfortable with his work, even though it was "pretty boring," and began to feel that he had showed his "old man." At the termination of therapy, Ed thought that he might be able to visit his family but really felt that things were working out well where he was. He was busy every night and had no time to go home for a visit. He surmised that he might return home some-day but certainly not under the old circumstances.

Posttreatment MMPI-2 Profile

Retesting at the end of Ed's treatment showed significant changes in his self-reported symptoms and behavior as reflected by the MMPI-2. His validity scale pattern depicted a clear shift from an essentially problem-oriented pre-sentation of symptoms to one that revealed few psychological problems. As with most people who show improvement in psychological treatment, Ed's K score increased in magnitude over his initial test administration (Barron, 1953), and he reported fewer symptoms, as reflected by the lower F-scale elevation.

The most significant change in his posttreatment clinical picture (Fig. 1.4) was the overall lowering of the profile, with all scales below a T-score of 64. Most dramatic was the large drop in the Depression scale. Ed was clearly re-porting few symptoms indicative of depression. His mood had improved mark-edly, and he did not appear to be having the same problems of low self-esteem and depressed mood. Similarly, he produced a lower elevation on the Psychas-thenia scale (Pt), revealing that his morale had improved considerably since the first test administration. The anger and irritation directed at his family members, reflected in the Pd scale, were not as pronounced as they were in the initial test. Interesting shifts in two generally stable aspects of the profile occurred as well: Ed showed less elevation on the Masculinity-Femininity (Mf) and the Social Introversion (Si) scales. Both of these profile changes probably resulted, in part, from his having some changes in his day-to-day activities that altered the way he perceived himself; he became more socially active and reached out to other people more effectively. He became a member of a soccer team whose activities, on and off the field, were "macho." In addition, part of

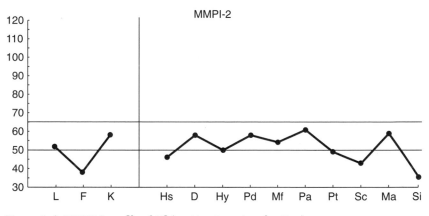

Figure 1.4. MMPI-2 profile of Ed (posttreatment evaluation).

his treatment program involved initiating social relationships with women. He began dating and found several new circles of friends, which resulted in a lessening of the social isolation he had been experiencing at initial testing.

Use of the MMPI in Treatment Evaluation Research

The MMPI has been used extensively as a criterion measure in the evaluation of treatment approaches. A detailed discussion of the use of the MMPI-2 in psychological treatment research is beyond the scope of this volume, but readers interested in research in MMPI changes following treatment would find the following studies informative:

- In general psychopathological samples, see Rouse, Sullivan, and Taylor (1997) for a description of over 1,000 studies related to the use of MMPI/ MMPI-2 in treatment planning. See also Chodzko-Zajko and Ismail, 1984; Moras and Strupp, 1982; Skoog, Anderson, and Laufer, 1984.
- In chronic pain treatment, see Brandwin and Kewman, 1982; Long, 1981; Malec, 1983; Moore, Armentrout, Parker, and Kivlahan, 1986; Oostdam, Duivenvoorden, and Pondaag, 1981; Strassberg, Reimherr, Ward, Russell, and Cole, 1981; Sweet, Breuer, Hazelwood, Toye, and Pawl, 1985; Turner, Herron, and Weiner, 1986; Uomoto, Turner, and Herron, 1988.
- In substance abuse populations, see Cernovsky, 1984; Ottomanelli, Wilson, and Whyte, 1978; Pettinati, Sugerman, and Maurer, 1982; Thurstin, Alfano, and Sherer, 1986.
- In mixed samples, see Archer, Gordon, Zillmer, and McClure, 1985; Walker, Blankenship, Ditty, and Lynch, 1987; Young, Gould, Glick, and Hargreaves, 1980.
- For summaries of the use of the MMPI in psychotherapy outcome research, mostly summarizing research on treatment of depression, see Hollon and Mandell, 1979; Klump and Butcher, 1997.

The Therapist's Role in Treatment Evaluation

The primary thesis of this book is that there is an accumulated base of knowledge about personality and its maladjustment that is pertinent to making treatment decisions about individuals in therapy. The field of personality assessment provides both methods and substantive information to support treatment-oriented evaluation (for example, see Kamphuis and Finn, 2002; Finn and Kamphuis, 2006) for discussions of using test feedback in treatment planning; see also Chapter 8 in this book for a discussion of providing test feedback to clients. Our aim is to explore the extensive base of information, particularly from the

MMPI-2, that can be applied in psychotherapeutic assessments to facilitate understanding of the patient and to appraise the effectiveness of the treatment intervention. Given that the provision of personality test feedback is an important aspect of psychological treatment, it is interesting to consider why some therapists choose not to conduct formal personality assessment of their patients before treatment begins. Psychologists and psychiatrists undergo extensive academic and practical training to gain the knowledge and experience needed to help people with psychological problems. Although the training backgrounds of mental health professionals and treatment roles differ, each professional employs skills and procedures to aid problem assessment.

Pretreatment assessment of personality seems intuitively to be a desirable if not necessary task; however, many professional therapists use little more than an intake interview before therapy is begun. Why do some therapists choose not to do a psychological assessment of patients at pretreatment? Several possible factors can be identified.

1. Some therapists, particularly those with a long-term, dynamic orientation, may approach psychological therapy with the view that the therapeutic process itself is the assessment, and they therefore may not typically engage in external or objective assessment of the client's problem or personality. In contrast, therapists with a more directive or more focused treatment approach tend to employ outside assessment procedures readily. One reason for the pretreatment evaluation is the need to move quickly in the therapeutic process. This is especially true for therapists who employ brief directive approaches.

2. Another factor that influences pretreatment assessment is the belief of some therapists that tests will bias them in their approach to the client. Consequently, they initiate treatment with little or no idea of the nature and extent of the patient's problems. A possible pitfall of this approach is that the therapist cannot determine if major blocks to treatment are likely to occur or if the treatment approach he or she is planning is the most appropriate one.

   Because many treatment effects are specific to a particular treatment rather than general to all treatments, there can be some advantage to the therapist's being aware of benefits that are likely to accrue from treatment efforts with a particular type of problem. For example, through employing objective procedures, therapists can determine if serious relationship or character flaws that would sabotage therapy are present. If so, the therapist may be able to determine more effective ways of initiating treatment. For example, a 37-year-old woman sought therapy after her second divorce. She wanted to enter long-term, dynamic therapy because she viewed her problem as "unique and difficult to understand." She "shopped" for a therapist (without disclosing this wish) by keeping the initial few appointments, during which she put the therapist to a test (which was invariably failed). She then left treatment, only to seek out yet another therapist. Her MMPI-2 profile (a 46 code; Fig. 1.5) revealed the following characteristics:

> rigid, moralistic, vindictive, aggressive, and secretive; given to hasty generalizations; shows suspicious behavior; is unchanging in the face of input; impulsive; prone to rationalize her own actions; and has difficulties in forming relationships.

Two previous therapists who had seen her in treatment, seemingly without assessment information, were apparently impressed in the initial interview with her "tendency to gain sudden insight" and her driven "desire to understand herself." However, they were probably unaware that her well-ingrained oppositional behavior led her to jump to conclusions about the therapists' intentions and competency to understand her, and thus led her to reject them.

In this case use of the MMPI-2 provided the third clinician with information about her negative attitudes toward authority figures (including therapists), her tendency to make and hold firm conclusions on the basis of little information, and her inclination to act impulsively. This information forewarned the therapist, who prepared himself and the patient for a stormy opening treatment session. The patient herself became disarmed by the early but friendly confrontation of her difficulties, particularly in forming relationships, to the point that she was challenged to stick with therapy longer than she had in the past.

3. Some therapists do not employ external assessment strategies to plan treatment or to monitor the progress of therapy. Their training in assessment methods may have been incomplete, or their professional training has led them to the view that psychological assessment is unimportant to understanding the client. Professionals trained in or exposed to one treatment model or one training setting will be shaped to do clinical work in a certain way. For most therapists, the familiar becomes "right," and other techniques are excluded from consideration.

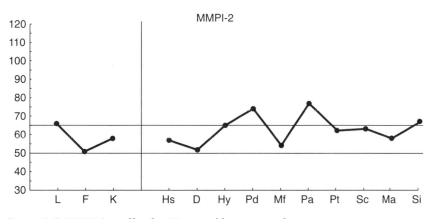

Figure 1.5. MMPI-2 profile of a 37-year-old woman seeking treatment.

Value of Assessment

An important goal for the therapist is to provide appropriate and useful feedback to the client. Approaching this task directly can help promote an atmosphere of openness in therapy that will have later benefits. The establishment of honest communication is one of the most important early goals of treatment. Indeed, the most prominent challenge in the early stages of psychotherapy is to develop a comfortable relationship that allows disclosure. Basic to productive therapeutic communication is the incorporation of a process that facilitates development of a mutually informing and constructive exploration of problems.

Most therapists, whatever their treatment orientation, are faced with a puzzle—the complicated task of understanding an individual's present difficulties in the context of past experiences, current pressures, social network, aspirations, and other life patterns, and integrating the findings and applying a workable treatment plan. It is important in the early stages of treatment to increase the flow of relevant information between the patient and the therapist and to promote communication and understanding between them. Some professionals rely more on interview and observation; others, particularly psychologists, employ standardized assessment procedures (see discussion of the costs and benefits of assessment in treatment planning in Table 1.1).

The Therapist's Assessment Task

Conducting successful psychological treatment involves more than passively listening to a person describe his or her day or early life experiences. The therapist has the responsibility of first forming a helping relationship, understanding the person's immediate problems, and appraising the person's strengths, resources, and potential, and then developing a program of intervention that will assist in alleviating the individual's problems.

Successful psychological treatment is not simply a friendly, social exchange between two people; it demands that the therapist bring the accumulated evidence of the science of psychology into the treatment setting. People who seek therapy usually view their psychotherapists as experts. Most clients expect that the therapist will apply special techniques or knowledge gained from training and experience that will aid them in resolving their problems. As they enter treatment, patients believe that the mental health specialist will use objective methods and established proven procedures. Once the therapist has established a tolerant, accepting treatment environment for the patient, it is important to assess the patient's problems and provide appropriate feedback.

The patient, however, may or may not be aware that the specific training and academic background of different professionals qualify them to apply some procedures but not others. For example, having the requisite medical background enables a psychiatrist to prescribe medications for a patient,

Table 1.1.   Costs Versus Benefits of Assessment in Treatment Planning

Klump and Butcher (1997) provided a cost–benefit analysis of using psychological tests in treatment planning. The actual cost to administer, score, and interpret psychological tests was relatively low with respect to what information they provide the therapist. However, the benefits from having assessment information available in the treatment process are great.

Costs

- Client's time: A small proportion of client therapy time is needed for the administration of a test like the MMPI-2 or BTPI.
- Little of the therapist's time is committed to administration, given the ease and quickness of objective test administration and scoring.
- The resources required include test booklets, scoring systems, and possibly computerized interpretations. As before, however, this expenditure is typically minimal.
- Facilities that allow privacy for administration and monitoring of tests are needed.

Benefits

- Increased understanding of the client.
- Provision of an objective viewpoint.
- Identification of problems not apparent from the clinical interview.
- Enhanced rapport.
- Information regarding the need for treatment.
- A mechanism for providing patient feedback early in the therapy. The provision of test feedback, as noted earlier, serves to focus the therapy on productive issues.
- Decreased therapy time.
- Establishes baseline information that can serve as a record of progress.
- Maximization of limited resources.

Adapted from Klump, K., & Butcher, J. N. (1997). Psychological tests in treatment planning: The importance of objective assessment. In J. N. Butcher (Ed.), *Personality assessment in managed care* (pp. 93–130). New York: Oxford University Press.

whereas having a background in clinical or counseling psychology may lead a clinician to use different techniques, such as psychological tests, to help understand patients' problems (although prescription privileges are available to some psychologists).

Regardless of the differences we find among various schools of psychotherapy and psychiatry, we find that patients are consistent in their desire to receive direct feedback about their problems. Feedback, which will assist in a client's recovery, thus becomes a key element in the treatment setting—a necessity at appropriate intervals in the therapeutic process.

The necessity of providing feedback, discussed in more detail in Chapter 8, is variously interpreted by different schools of psychotherapy. Some approaches to treatment give extensive and in-depth psychological feedback to the client early in therapy; others may only indirectly address the task of providing personality and interpersonal data for the patient to incorporate into his or her treatment plan. Perhaps the most extreme viewpoint is the psychoanalytic view, which follows the strategy of limited feedback (i.e., limited direction by the therapist) early in therapy. Interpretations often do not enter into treatment directly; when they do, treatment is much farther along. Other treatment orientations, such as the client-centered approach, provide minimal feedback and operate on the assumption that individuals will, under the unconditional positive regard and assurance of the therapist, eventually develop a consistent view of themselves without much directive feedback from the therapist.

As already noted, after sharing personal information about themselves with a stranger through the psychological assessment, patients need and expect to have their self-disclosure acknowledged by the therapist. They usually appreciate that the therapist has taken the time and effort to discuss and try to understand their problems.

An Objective Means of Providing Feedback

Most psychologists and many psychiatrists are trained in techniques of psychological assessment and methods of providing feedback required in therapy. Beginning with a person's responses to personality-based information is an excellent way to provide feedback. The symptoms, attitudes, feelings, attitudes toward personal change, and other test responses are the patient's own self-perceptions, and the therapist organizes them into a standard format (profile or computer-based report) that compares the individual's responses with those of other people.

An interesting and valuable side effect of the appropriate use of psychological tests in psychotherapy is that it communicates to the patient that the therapist has available an objective mean of—a technology for—evaluating the client. Most patients will voluntarily participate in self-study, and many will recognize and appreciate the effort at accountability that the therapist is addressing in using objective assessment methods. One patient, a certified public accountant, was intrigued when the therapist used an "accounting procedure" to evaluate his problems and then summarized them on a chart! He was very cooperative with the posttreatment evaluation because he wanted to see what the "bottom line" was in terms of treatment gains at the completion of therapy. Most important, his Depression score on the MMPI-2 had dropped well into the normal range after he had experienced both behavioral and mood improvements.

Role of the MMPI-2 and BTPI in a Test Battery

In using psychological evaluation for treatment planning, many clinicians incorporate information from a broad base of techniques—clinical interview, projective testing, behavioral data, personal history—and do not rely on data from a single source. This book is about the use of two instruments, the MMPI-2 and BTPI, in treatment planning, but not to the exclusion of other measures. Because of space limitations, other procedures, such as the Rorschach, are not covered in any detail. The reader needs to keep in mind the importance of incorporating information from other sources into the test battery and assigning relative importance to information from various sources available to the clinician.

Importance of Demographic and Status Characteristics

The interpretation of any psychological test proceeds best in the context of a personal history. Important aspects of the case—for example, ethnic group membership, education level, marital status, and the presence of a precipitating stressor or trauma—are important variables to consider when MMPI-2 profiles are interpreted. Errors of interpretation can occur if personality test profiles, or other psychological test protocols, are considered apart from nontest parameters. Blind interpretation of test profiles can provide general information about a client's symptoms and behavior. These impressions, however, need to be verified by direct patient contact. A good discussion of this topic can be found in Henrichs (1987). The clinician also should keep in mind how relevant "backdrop" variables affect psychological test scores and interpretations. Background variables are important to the appraisal of MMPI-2 scores, and readers should be familiar with a basic text on the MMPI-2, such as Graham's text (2006), and Butcher's description of the BTPI (Butcher, 2005).

Summary

The therapist and the patient generally come to the first therapeutic session with differing perceptions of the nature and extent of the problems, what needs to be done in therapy, and how long it will take for the problems to be resolved. Patients typically view their problems as requiring a briefer period of time than therapists do. Therapists often consider time as being on their side and think that if they listen attentively for a long enough time, they will discover the source of a person's problems and will be able to assist the patient in resolving them.

Clear assessment of the nature and extent of the patient's problem is a pressing concern for the competent, responsible therapist. It becomes imperative for the therapist to use effective means to bring understanding to the problem and to communicate to the patient a clear picture.

2

Introduction to the Minnesota Multiphasic
Personality Inventory (MMPI-2)

H athaway and McKinley (1940, 1943) originally developed the
Minnesota Multiphasic Personality Inventory (MMPI) as a diagnostic aid for use in medical and psychiatric screening. In their original work,
they used a method of scale construction referred to as the *empirical* scale development, or criterion-referenced strategy, to develop the MMPI clinical scales
(see Butcher, 2000b). The items making up the clinical scales were selected with
assurance that each item on a given scale actually predicted the criterion or
membership in a clinical group. For example, in the development of Scale 2, the
Depression scale, responses of patients who were clinically depressed were contrasted with those of a group of "normal" individuals. The items that empirically differentiated the groups became the Depression scale; and the individuals
who had received high scores on this scale displayed symptoms found in the reference group of depressed patients. The test authors provided a set of appropriate norms for the basic MMPI scales to enable test users to compare a particular
patient's scores with responses of a large group of "normal" individuals. Thus,
a high score on the Depression scale indicates that the patient has responded in
a manner similar to the criterion group of depressed patients and different from
the normal group. (For a videotaped interview with Starke Hathaway in 1973
describing his original work on the MMPI, see website www.umn.edu/mmpi.)

The MMPI can serve as an objective, reliable screening instrument for appraising a person's personality characteristics and symptomatic behavior. The
interpretive information available on the MMPI has been widely researched and
documented through almost 70 years of clinical use. More than 18,000 books
and articles on the MMPI and MMPI-2 have been published and it has become
the most frequently administered clinical psychological test in the United States
(Lees-Haley, Smith, Williams, & Dunn, 1996; Lubin, Larsen, & Matarazzo, 1984).

Furthermore, there were more than 150 translations of the original MMPI and 32 translations of the MMPI-2. The test is used in over 45 countries (Butcher, 1985, 1996; Butcher & Pancheri, 1976). A number of factors account for the MMPI's broad acceptance by researchers and practitioners:

1. The MMPI-2 has been validated for a number of clinical and personality applications. The information it provides is relevant in many settings where personality profiles are helpful. The profile provides the clinician with a visual presentation of important personality information, plotted on an easy-to-read graph for each case, and it supplies extensive normative and clinical data for profile interpretation. A wide range of descriptive information is available on numerous clinical groups in the published literature.

2. The MMPI-2 provides an *objective evaluation* of the client's personality characteristics, by numerous research studies (for an up-to-date literature review see www.umn.edu/mmpi).

3. The MMPI-2 is one of the easiest personality assessment instruments to use in a clinical practice, since it requires little professional time to administer and score; however, the interpretation requires the care, skill, and experience of a trained practitioner.

4. The MMPI-2 is cost-effective, since administration and scoring can be done by clerical staff. Usually the only professional time required involves the interpretation. (For example, in clinical settings, it usually takes a patient only about an hour and a half to answer the items; it takes a clerical assistant about 15 minutes to hand-score and draw a profile; and it takes an experienced interpreter about 30 minutes to prepare a profile interpretation.) If the test is computer-scored it takes only a few minutes to key in the client's responses.

5. MMPI-2 administration, scoring, profile plotting, and even some interpretation can be accomplished by computer (Atlis, Hahn, & Butcher, 2006; Butcher, Perry, & Hahn, 2004). Automated MMPI reports can provide a very detailed and accurate clinical evaluation of a profile.

6. The MMPI-2 is one of the easiest clinical personality tests for students and professionals to learn, since there is an abundance of published material on MMPI-2 interpretation for the beginning interpreter. Some suggested general MMPI-2 interpretation resources to consider are:

Butcher, J. N. (Ed.). (1997). *Personality assessment in managed care: Using the MMPI-2 in treatment planning.* New York: Oxford University Press.
Butcher, J. N. (Ed.). (2000). *Basic sources for the MMPI-2.* Minneapolis: University of Minnesota Press.
Butcher, J. N. (2005). *A beginner's guide to the MMPI-2 (2nd ed.).* Washington, DC: American Psychological Association.
Butcher, J. N. (Ed.). (2006). *MMPI-2: A practitioner's guide.* Washington, D. C.: American Psychological Association.

Graham, J. R. (2006). *MMPI: Assessing personality and psychopathology (3rd ed.)*. New York: Oxford University Press.

Greene, R. (2000). *The MMPI: An interpretive manual (2nd ed.)*. New York: Allyn & Bacon.

Development of the MMPI-2

In response to the problems that had been noted with use of the MMPI (Butcher, 1972; Butcher & Owen, 1978; Colligan et al., 1983), the test publisher, the University of Minnesota Press, initiated a program to revise the MMPI and establish new, nationally representative norms for the instrument. A revision team that included James Butcher, John R. Graham, and W. Grant Dahlstrom was appointed to modify the existing item pool, add new items, and collect new normative data on the instrument. Auke Tellegen was added later to aid in data analysis.

The revision of the MMPI involved several stages (see Butcher et al., 1989, 2001). The existing item pool was modified by rewriting obsolete and awkwardly worded items, deleting repetitive ones, and increasing the content coverage of the item pool by including new items that deal with contemporary problems and applications. Once the revision of the MMPI item pool was complete (14% of the original items were rewritten and 154 new items were included to measure additional personality dimensions or problems), Form AX, a 704-item experimental version of the MMPI, was produced for the MMPI Restandardization Project (see Butcher, 2000a, for a discussion of the MMPI revision).

MMPI 2 Norms

To make the MMPI-2 relevant for contemporary populations, a large, nationally representative sample of subjects was randomly solicited from several regions of the United States to serve as the normative population. New T-score transformations were developed based on the MMPI-2 normative sample, which contained 2,600 subjects (1,138 males and 1,462 females). The normative sample closely approximates the 1980 U.S. Census in terms of age, gender, minority status, social class, and education. The new MMPI-2 norms are comparable to the original MMPI norms, based on linear T scores (see Butcher et al., 2001). The high degree of similarity between the MMPI validity and clinical scores in the original MMPI and the new MMPI-2 allows for the use of previous empirical research in interpreting scores based on the new norms. The MMPI-2 normative approach also equates T-score ranges so that a given T score has the same meaning across the clinical scales. Clinical research with the MMPI-2 shows that interpretations of the clinical scales are significant at elevations to $T > 65$.

Revision of the MMPI Booklet

After the new normative data had been collected, Form AX was further revised to reduce the item pool by eliminating many objectionable, obsolete, and non-working items. New norms were then developed for the final version of the revised MMPI (MMPI-2), which contains 567 items, including most of the original items in the standard validity and clinical scales. These scales were kept relatively intact to preserve the substantial research that has been accumulated on the instrument. To broaden and strengthen the instrument, 108 new items were added to the booklet. A number of scales have been developed for the MMPI-2 to increase its research potential and clinical utility; these scales are described in more detail in Chapters 4 and 5. The remainder of this chapter provides a brief introduction to MMPI-2 interpretation.

MMPI-2 Validity Data: Couple's Behavior Ratings

In the MMPI restandardization study, a number of people were asked to invite their spouses to participate in the study. A total of 822 heterosexual couples were administered the MMPI-2. Each participant also completed a marital adjustment questionnaire (Spanier's Dyadic Adjustment Scale) and was asked to complete a behavior rating questionnaire on his or her spouse. The 110-item Couple's Rating Form contained a wide range of behaviors, attitudes, and impressions that people would be expected to know about their spouses. These ratings provided an important resource of validity data on the MMPI-2 scales. Validity information based on the couple's ratings is included in this chapter to show that the MMPI-2 clinical scales are applicable with a "normal" range of individuals as well as within patient groups. The data presented here include the items that have the highest correlations with the clinical scales. Also included are correlations with a set of factor scales developed to summarize the Couple's Rating Form data (Butcher et al., 1989).

Recent MMPI-2 Validity Research

Research on the utility, validity, and reliability of the MMPI-2 since its publication in 1989 has been both comprehensive and extensive (for a discussion of MMPI-2 research strategies and methods see Butcher, Graham, Kamphuis, and Rouse, 2006). A number of empirical studies have reaffirmed the validity of MMPI-2 clinical scales and code types (Archer, Griffin, & Aiduk, 1995; Butcher, Rouse, & Perry, 2000; Graham, Ben-Porath, & McNulty, 1999). Readers interested in a more thorough examination of the research literature for the MMPI-2 should consult Graham (2006) or the reference file available at www.umn.edu/mmpi.

Part 1: The Validity Scales

The validity scales of the MMPI-2 shown on the left side of the profile sheet are included in the inventory to provide the clinician with information about the client's approach to the test. (Recent reviews of the empirical literature on the MMPI-2 validity scales can be found in Arbisi, 2006, and Bagby, Marshall, Bury, Bacchiocci, and Miller, 2006.) Extensive listings of references for assessing malingering and defensiveness are available in Pope, Butcher, and Seelen (2006). The validity scales indicate the presence of invalidating attitudes and provide the interpreter with clues to the credibility of the client's test and can provide the clinician with information that reflects the accessibility and openness of the examinee. Research with the original MMPI has shown that the validity indicators also provide information about the personality of the client. There are well-established empirical correlates for each of the validity scales. For a more detailed discussion of the construction and operation of the MMPI-2 clinical and validity scales, consult John Graham's text (2006).

The "Cannot Say" (?) Score

The "Cannot Say" (?) score is not a scale in the strict sense of the word but is simply the total number of unanswered or doubly answered items on the record. How many items can be omitted without invalidating the record? Clinical practice has suggested that records with 20 or more omitted items within the first 370 should be interpreted with caution; records with 30 or more unanswered items within the first 370 attenuate and invalidate the test. The client needs to answer all items if the supplementary and content scales are to be scored. Consequently, it is good practice always to evaluate the Cannot Say score before proceeding to the interpretation. If a large number of items have been left unanswered, it makes sense to return the booklet and answer sheet to the client, if possible, and have the record completed. An empirical study of the effects of item omission upon MMPI-2 scales and indices provides research support for interpreting the Cannot Say scores in evaluating cooperation in testing and provides important cautions about interpreting profiles with extensive item omissions (Berry et al., 1997).

Reasons for Cannot Say score elevations include reading difficulties, guardedness on the part of the patient, confusion and distractibility resulting from the patient's clinical state (e.g., an organic disease, intoxication), severe psychomotor retardation accompanying depression, rebellion or antagonistic behavior (often found among uncooperative subjects such as prisoners and adolescents), obsessional or overly intellectualizing subjects who ruminate a great deal about the content, and people taking the MMPI-2 in personnel selection settings.

Item omissions for clients in treatment planning situations are very important to evaluate. Any omitted items can be indicative of possible problems such as poor cooperation with the assessment, defensiveness, inability to share personal information, or ruminative indecisiveness. All of these factors can bode ill for the treatment relationship, and thus the Cannot Say score is very important in assessment for treatment planning.

Response Inconsistency Scales

Two validity scales to evaluate consistent responding have been included in the MMPI-2. Both of these scales, True Response Inconsistency (TRIN) and Variable Response Inconsistency (VRIN), were developed to assess the possibility that a person is responding to the items in a psychologically inconsistent manner.

True Response Inconsistency Scale   The TRIN scale comprises 20 pairs of items for which a combination of two true or two false responses is semantically inconsistent. For example, responding to items such as "Most of the time I feel sad" and "I am almost always happy" as both true, or both false, is inconsistent. Eleven of the 20 item pairs are scored as inconsistent only if the client responds true to both items. Six of the item pairs are scored inconsistent only if the client responds false to both items. Three additional pairs are scored as inconsistent if the client responds either both true or both false. The TRIN scale is scored by subtracting the number of inconsistent false pairs from the number of inconsistent pairs, and then subtracting the number from nine (the total number of possible inconsistent false pairs). This procedure yields an index ranging from 0 to 20. Extreme scores on either end of this range reflect a tendency either to indiscriminately answer false ("nay-saying" at the low end of the range) or to indiscriminately answer true ("yea-saying" at the upper end of the distribution).

Variable Response Inconsistency Scale   The VRIN scale is made up of 49 pairs of items for which one or two of four possible configurations (true-false, false-true, true-true, false-false) represent semantically inconsistent responses. For example, answering true to items like "I do not become tired easily" and false to "I always feel tired these days," or vice versa, represents a semantically inconsistent response. The scale is scored by summing the number of inconsistent responses. Scores may range from 0 to 49. The VRIN scale may be used to help interpret a high F score. For example, a high F score, together with a low to moderate VRIN score, rules out the possibility that the F score reflects random responding or confusion.

The Infrequency Scale (F)

The F scale was devised as a measure of the tendency to admit to a wide range of psychological problems or to "fake bad." An individual who scores high on the

F scale is admitting to a wide range of complaints that are infrequently endorsed by the general population and reflect a tendency to exaggerate problems.

The F scale consists of 60 items that range in content and are related to physical problems, bizarre ideas, antisocial behavior, and deviant personal attitudes. The following examples are similar to items on the F scale (typical exaggerated responses are given parenthetically):

1. "I do not believe in laws." (T)
2. "Someone has been trying to rob me." (T)

The construction of the F scale was simple and empirical. The scale consists of items that were infrequently endorsed by the normative population (usually less than 10%). Although this is one of the longest MMPI-2 scales, normal subjects usually endorse only about four items. Thus, a high score on the F scale reflects a tendency to exaggerate problems. Excessive endorsement of the items on this scale suggests that a person is attempting to present the most unfavorable picture of himself or herself.

Many reasons can be found for high scores on the F scale, usually reflecting confusion, disorganization, or exaggeration. Some of the more frequent situations producing elevated F scores are these:

1. Random response to the items. Since there are 60 items on the F scale, haphazard or random responding would result in about half of the items (or 30) being endorsed.
2. Deviant response set due to faking or falsely claiming mental illness. People who attempt to feign mental illness typically do not know which items to endorse and tend to overrespond by endorsing too many items. Actual patients are more selective in their response pattern.
3. Poor reading level and the person's inability to understand the items may result in an elevated F score.
4. Adolescent subjects typically have higher F scores than adults. This results, in part, from adolescent identity problems and possibly from some exaggerated responding as well.
5. Acutely psychotic or organically impaired people who are confused or disorganized may produce elevated F scores. The F scale is often associated with severity and chronicity of problems.
6. Persons in stressful situations may produce elevated F scores.
7. Individuals who produce high F scores may be attempting to get the attention of the clinician. Thus, high F scores may represent a "plea for help."

What Range of F Score Invalidates an MMPI-2 Profile? Although a T score of 70 is typically taken as the critical elevation suggesting invalidity of the performance, this is not the case for the F scale. Clinicians do not typically begin to concern themselves with profile invalidity until the F score gets to about the

90 T-score level, depending on the setting. In some settings, particularly at admission into an inpatient psychiatry unit or at incarceration in a correctional institution, it is appropriate to interpret (with caution, of course) profiles with an F score at about 90—109 T-score points.

The Back Side F Scale [F(B)]

The F(B) scale or Back Side F scale was developed for the MMPI-2 to detect deviant responding to items located toward the end of the item pool. Some clients may modify their approach to the items partway through the item pool and answer in a random or otherwise invalid manner. The items on the F scale are presented in the first part of the inventory, before item number 370; therefore, the F scale or the F-K index may not detect dissimulation later in the booklet. The 40-item F(B) scale was developed in much the same way as the original F scale—by including items that had low endorsement percentages among the normal population. There are several ways the F(B) can be usefully interpreted.

If the F scale exceeds the previously mentioned criteria for validity, then no additional interpretation of F(B) is needed, because the MMPI-2 would be considered invalid by F-scale criteria. If the T score of the F scale is considered valid and the F(B) is below T = 89, then a valid response approach is indicated and the clinical profile can be interpreted. However, if the T score of the F scale is considered valid and the F(B) is above T = 90, then an interpretation of F(B) is needed. In this case, cautious interpretation of the clinical and validity scales is possible; however, interpretation of scales such as the MMPI-2 content scales, which require valid response to the later-appearing items, needs to be deferred.

The Psychiatric Infrequency Scale [F(p)]

Arbisi and Ben-Porath (1995, 1997) developed a somewhat different type of infrequency scale for the MMPI-2 that addresses possible malingering of psychological symptoms in a mental health treatment context. The F(p) scale compares the responses of clients to those of psychiatric patients rather than the normative population, as F and F(B) do. This scale thus provides an estimate of symptom exaggeration that allows the psychologist to estimate the relative extremity of responding to patients in a psychiatric setting. High scores on the F(p) scale indicate that the person claims more psychiatric symptoms than inpatients who are currently hospitalized for psychiatric disorders. Thus, the items on F(p) are extremely unlikely symptoms. The score provides an indication of extreme endorsement of symptoms as compared with patients with severe disturbances (see also Rothke et al., 2000).

The Lie Scale (L)

The Lie scale was originally developed as a means of assessing general frankness in responding to the test items. The scale consists of 15 items that were selected on the basis of "face validity." The item content is obvious. When a number of these items (usually about eight or nine) are answered falsely, the individual appears to be claiming a greater amount of virtue and presenting himself or herself more favorably than most others do. Profiles with elevations on this scale should be interpreted with caution because the individual's generalized response to claim excessive virtue, or deny socially undesirable faults, has likely distorted the profile. High scorers on L generally distort responses to items on the clinical scales as well, producing profiles that underestimate the number and extent of problems a client may have.

Several possible reasons can be found for high scores on the L scale. A person who is trying to present a favorable impression (i.e., someone taking the test in a personnel selection situation or a domestic court custody case) may claim a great deal of virtue to impress the evaluator. People with limited intelligence or who lack psychological sophistication may also produce high L scores in their attempt to look good to the evaluator. And some subcultural groups (such as ministers) as well as some ethnic minority groups, such as Hispanics (see Butcher, Cabiya, Lucio, and Garrido, 2007), may present a favorable image on psychological tests. Some clients with neurotic disorders, such as somatization disorders, try to present a favorable (defensive) self-image to others.

Several personality characteristics are associated with elevations on the L scale. Individuals who score high on L appear to be naïve and low in psychological mindedness; they tend to be defensive and are characterized by denial and "hysteroid" thinking. They are often rigid in their thinking and adjustment and have a strong need to "put up a good front."

As described later, a high L score for a person in psychotherapy is usually considered a negative indicator. The person is presenting an overly virtuous response pattern and indicates an unwillingness or inability to self-disclose.

The Subtle Defensiveness Scale (K)

Meehl and Hathaway (1946) wanted to develop a measure that would detect more subtle kinds of defensive responding than were detected by the obvious content of the L scale. They wanted to identify the "false-positive" test misses by taking into account different degrees of defensiveness. About 22 of the K items were obtained by comparing the responses of normal subjects with those of 50 psychiatric patients with elevated L scores whose clinical scales were in the normal range (i.e., patients who were excessively defensive). Eight other items were included to counteract the tendency of certain types of patients to score excessively low on the scale without psychological justification. Twenty-four of the

30 K items are highly correlated with the Edward's Social Desirability Scale, a measure of social favorability.

In interpreting the MMPI-2, the K scale serves both as an indicator of invalidity and as a means of correcting for test defensiveness. Elevations on the K scale (particularly above a T score of 70) reflect test defensiveness. For example, individuals who seek to present a highly favorable view of themselves, such as those attempting to indicate that they are not in need of psychological treatment or a parent seeking custody of children in court, try to make good impressions on the MMPI-2 by denying problems. The result is an elevated K score. The K scale is correlated with other psychological variables, such as social class and education level. It is important to take the subject's social class and education into account when interpreting the K scale. Individuals from higher social classes may produce higher K scores (between 55 and 60). Consequently, the interpretation of test defensiveness in higher social status groups should not be applied until the T scores reach 70.

It has also been noted that other personality factors, such as self-acceptance, independence, self-esteem, and nonauthoritarian values, have been associated with moderate elevations on the K scale.

Defensive profiles (K over T = 70) in situations that call for frankness and openness, such as in a treatment planning context, might reflect the following characteristics: aloofness, rigidity, unwillingness to cooperate with the evaluation, denial of problems, and the presence of an unrealistic self-image.

Extremely low scores on K in cases where a moderate score is expected (e.g., in keeping with an individual's high social status) may be indicative of dissatisfaction, cynicism, "masochistic confessing," and poor response to treatment.

The Superlative Self-Presentation Scale (S)

The defensiveness scale, the Superlative Self-Presentation Scale (S), was developed by Butcher and Han (1995) as a means of improving the discrimination of defensive responding that might prove more effective than the K scale. Butcher and Han (1995) used a highly defensive group of test-takers (airline pilot job applicants who are characteristically defensive on the test) compared with the MMPI-2 normative sample. The 50-item defensiveness scale assesses the tendency of some test-takers to claim extremely positive attributes, high moral values, and high responsibility and to deny having any adjustment problems. Test-takers who score high on the S scale acknowledge fewer minor faults and problems than most people do taking the test. The S scale has been found to be associated with lower levels of psychological and health symptoms and the admission of fewer negative personality characteristics than people in the normative sample report. High scores are also associated with extreme claims of great "self-control" in test-takers by people who know them. High S responders are typically viewed by their spouses as emotionally well controlled and generally free of pathological behavioral features.

One way in which the S scale improves on the K scale as a measure of test defensiveness is that it possesses a greater number of items (50), which allowed for the development of a set of subscales with a homogeneous content that was not possible with the K scale, largely because of the smaller number of items. Five distinct subscales were identified with the S-scale items. These homogeneous item component scales enable the interpreter to determine particular ways in which the client is being defensive. For example, the test-taker may have endorsed relatively more items dealing with "Denial of moral flaws" or "Denial of irritability" (as is common among parents in child custody disputes) than with other items on S. The five S subscale groupings are as follows, along with sample items that are similar to MMPI-2 contents on each component scale:

- *Beliefs in human goodness:* Items such as "Most people will use somewhat unfair means to get ahead in life" (F) or "Most people are honest because they are afraid of being caught" (F)
- *Serenity:* Items such as "My hardest struggles are with myself" (F)
- *Contentment with life:* Items such as "If I had a chance to live my life over again, I would not change much" (T) or "I am very happy with the amount of money I make" (T)
- *Patience and denial of irritability and anger:* Items such as "I typically get mad easily and then get over it soon" (F) or "I often become impatient with people" (F)
- *Denial of moral flaws:* Items such as "I have enjoyed smoking dope" (F) or "I have used alcohol extremely at times" (F)

High scores on the S scale (T > 65) suggest that the client may not be open to behavioral change in therapy. An examination of the S subscale can help the practitioner gain a better understanding as to what underlying factors might be involved in the client's defensive stance.

Part 2: Correlates of the Clinical Scales

Scale 1: Hypochondriasis (Hs)

Scale 1 was designed to measure hypochondriasis—a pattern of "neurotic" concern over physical health. This was one of the first scales developed for the MMPI in 1940. In the construction of the Hs scale, items were selected that differentiated 50 cases of "relatively pure, uncomplicated hypochondriacal patients" from members of the Minnesota normative sample. Great care was taken by Hathaway and McKinley to exclude psychotics from the clinical criterion group.

After initial empirical item selection, the scale was revised in an attempt to correct for the excessive number of psychiatric cases who obtained high scores on the scale without having clear hypochondriacal features in their clinical picture. The Hs scale contains 32 items whose content ranges over a variety of bodily complaints (items similar to, "I have a great deal of stomach pain"; "I feel weak and tired most of the time"; and "I am troubled by nausea and stomach distress"). Persons endorsing a large number of these items are presenting concerns that cannot be attributed to a specific physical disorder. The complaining picture is vague and nonspecific and is usually suggestive of psychological factors in the clinical profile. Some elevation on scale 1 can accompany actual physical disorders, but a score of 65 or higher is believed to reflect a psychological or "character" problem.

The Hs scale is usually interpreted in conjunction with other clinical scales, particularly the scales in the "neurotic triad"—scales 2 and 3 (Depression and Hysteria). Correlates for the Hs scale include excessive bodily concern, fatigue, and experience of pain, a pessimistic outlook on life, complaining behavior, and reduced efficacy in life.

The interpretation of elevations on the Hs scale as indicating somatic concern among physically healthy clients was borne out in the couple's rating study for the MMPI Restandardization Project (Butcher et al., 1989). The correlates for Hs in the normative sample of males and females centered on worries over health (i.e., reporting headaches, stomach trouble, and other ailments, and appearing generally worn out to their spouses).

Scale 2: Depression (D)

The Depression scale was developed to measure symptomatic depression as reflected in a general frame of mind characterized by poor morale, lack of hope in the future, dissatisfaction with one's status in life, and the presence of psychic and somatic symptoms of depression. The D scale contains 57 items that were selected in two ways. Most of the items were obtained through their power to differentiate the criterion group of depressed patients (50 manic-depressive patients in the depressive phase) from a group of normal subjects. A number of items were included to minimize the D-scale elevations of psychiatric patients whose diagnoses were not depression. The item content of scale 2 reflects much of the behavior that is suggestive of clinical depression (items such as "I have great difficulty sleeping" [T]; "I have lost my appetite" [T]; "I am so sad that I cry easily" [T]). The items deal with a lack of interest in things, denial of happiness, a low degree of esteem or personal worth, and an inability to function.

It should be noted that scale 2 is the most frequent peak score found among clients in psychiatric settings. It was designed as a symptom measure that is sensitive to "current" mood. Among its other uses, the D scale is valuable as an indicator of change in the clinical picture. Clinicians using the MMPI have long been aware of the need to understand the D scale in terms of the configural relationships with other scales. The same level of elevation on the scale can have a different clinical meaning depending upon other scale elevations. Correlates for the D scale include such behaviors as feeling depressed, feeling pessimistic, having low self-esteem, feeling dysphoric, having a negative attitude toward the future, being guilt-prone, and being indecisive.

Interpretations of elevated Depression scores for normal subjects received substantial empirical support from the couple's rating study in the MMPI Restandardization Project (Butcher et al., 1989). High-D males and females were viewed by their spouses as generally maladjusted, lacking energy, and lacking in self-confidence, and as persons who get sad or blue easily, give up easily, are concerned that something bad is going to happen, lack interest in things, and act bored and restless.

Scale 3: Hysteria (Hy)

Scale 3 was developed as an aid in the diagnosis of conversion disorder and as a possible measure of the predisposition to develop this disorder. Conversion disorder or somatization disorder (i.e., development of physical symptoms such as loss of voice or psychogenic seizures) typically occurs only under stressful conditions. The criterion group used in the development of this scale comprised 50 patients who had been diagnosed with psychoneurosis or hysteria, or who had been observed to have hysterical features in their clinical pattern. This was a rather difficult criterion group to obtain in the early period of MMPI scale development. The final Hy scale consists of 60 items whose content falls broadly into two general areas—*physical problems* and *social facility* items (such as "My sleep is troubled" [T]; "I feel weak much of the time" [T]; "It is best to place trust in no one" [F]). The empirical correlates for elevations on this scale include such behaviors as being prone to develop physical symptoms under stress, presenting vague physical complaints, being repressed and lacking in anxiety, and being socially outgoing and coquettish in relation to others.

Scale 4: Psychopathic Deviate (Pd)

The Pd scale was designed to measure personality characteristics suggestive of antisocial or psychopathic personality disorders. The characteristics to be measured in this scale included general social maladjustment, disregard for rules or mores, difficulties with the law or authority, absence of strongly pleasant experience, superficiality in interpersonal relations, inability to learn from punishing experiences, and the presence of an impulsive and uncontrolled behavioral history. The clinical criterion group used in the development of scale 4 comprised patients who were being evaluated in a psychiatric setting and who had been diagnosed as having a psychopathic personality of the asocial or amoral type, analogous to antisocial personality disorder in the *Diagnostic and Statistical Manual* (DSM-IV). Patients with psychotic or neurotic features were not included in the clinical group. Most of the patients were between the ages of 17 and 22 years, and the majority were female. Each patient had manifested a long history of offenses, including stealing, lying, truancy, sexual promiscuity, forgery, and alcohol problems.

In contrasting this criterion group with the Minnesota normative sample, which was made up of older and more rural adults, some biases were obvious. A group of college subjects was also used in further refinement of the scale, because they more closely approximated the criterion group in terms of age and marital status. Use was made of two other groups: additional psychiatric patients who fit the criterion and 100 male inmates at a federal prison.

The Pd scale consists of 50 items that sample a wide range of content dealing with alienation from the family, school difficulties, and broader authority problems: poor morale; sexual problems as well as other personal shortcomings; assertion of social confidence and poise; and denial of social shyness or anxiety. The last two types of items, as in the Hy scale, appear somewhat incongruous and contradictory to the first four and appear to reflect social extraversion. The empirical correlates for the Pd scale include antisocial behavior, impulsivity, poor judgment, a tendency to externalize blame, socially outgoing behavior, a manipulative personality in relationships, and an aggressive stance in interpersonal situations.

The person with a high Pd score is usually considered unable to profit from experience, lacks definite goals, is likely to have a personality disorder diagnosis (antisocial or passive-aggressive), is dissatisfied, shows absence of deep emotional response, feels bored and empty, has a poor prognosis for change in therapy, blames others for problems, intellectualizes, and may agree to treatment to avoid jail or some other unpleasant experience but is likely to terminate therapy before change is effected.

Interpretation of elevated Pd scale scores for normal subjects received substantial empirical support from the couple's rating study in the MMPI Restandardization Project (Butcher et al., 1989). Normal-range subjects from the MMPI-2 normative sample who score high on Pd are viewed by their spouses as antisocial, impulsive, moody, and resentful. They were reported to take drugs other than those prescribed by a doctor, have sexual conflicts, and swear a lot.

Scale 5: Masculinity-Femininity (Mf)

The Mf scale was added to the MMPI item pool a few years after the clinical scales were developed. It was added for the purpose of identifying the personality features of sex role identification problems. This scale is *not* a pure measure of masculinity–femininity and is factorially complex because it contains two item groups—one measuring masculine interests and the other measuring feminine interests (Johnson et al., 1984). This scale is the least well defined and understood of the MMPI clinical scales. Problems with the Mf scale result from several factors. Empirical item selection was not strictly followed (see Terman and Miles, 1936), and the criterion group of male inverts consisted of only 13 cases (although the group was very homogeneous and included neither neurotics nor psychotics) (Hathaway, 1980). Scale derivation consisted of borrowing items from the Terman and Miles Inventory that showed promise of differentiating the criterion group. Since the Minnesota normative population had not responded to these items, another normative population was used (54 male soldiers and 67 female airline employees).

Items were further screened to determine how well they differentiated males from females. This was followed by a third set of comparisons to differentiate feminine men from "normal" men. A further attempt to develop a corresponding scale for female inverts by contrasting normal females with female patients was not successful.

The original Mf scale consisted of 60 items that deal with interests, vocational choices, aesthetic preferences, and activity–passivity. The same scale is used for both sexes, but it is scored in the opposite direction for females. In the MMPI-2 revision, four controversial and objectionable items were deleted, leaving the present Mf scale with 56 items.

The Mf scale is highly correlated with education, intelligence, and social class; consequently, any interpretations based on Mf-scale elevations must take these factors into account. Correlates for high Mf scores in males include sensitivity in an interpersonal situation, insecurity in male roles, broad cultural interests, and passivity in interpersonal relationships. Low-Mf males, on the other hand, are viewed as presenting an overly masculine image, somewhat narrow in interests, insensitive in interpersonal relationships, and more interested in action than reflection.

The Mf scale can provide very useful information in treatment planning assessments for men. For example, a very low Mf score for a man suggests that he tends to be oriented toward more "macho" activities and would not be very open to discussing personal problems in an interpersonal context. On the other hand, some elevation on the Mf scale (60 to 80 T-score range) suggests more openness to dealing with problems in therapy.

Fewer data exist on Mf scores for females; however, Graham (1990) showed that education level should also be kept in mind when interpreting Mf scores for females. Correlates of high Mf scores for females suggest rejection of traditional female roles, preference for male-oriented activities, and interpersonal insensitivity. Low-Mf women tend to be viewed as more traditional in interests and somewhat passive and dependent in relationships.

Scale 6: Paranoia (Pa)

The Pa scale was originally designed to assess the presence of attitudes and beliefs that would reflect paranoid thinking and behavior or would measure suspicious, mistrusting tendencies that often accompany other personality disorders, affective disorder, and schizophrenia. The criterion group of patients for developing the Pa scale comprised persons who had developed fairly well-defined delusional systems (although the diagnostic label *paranoia* was rarely applied to them). More often they were diagnosed as paranoid state, paranoid condition, or paranoid schizophrenia. In most cases, the symptoms manifested by the criterion group patients involved the presence of ideas of reference, delusions of grandiosity, feelings of persecution or suspiciousness, rigidity, and excessive interpersonal sensitivity.

Although the Pa scale provides useful information when evaluated in configuration with other clinical scales, it does not fulfill its original purpose of differentially diagnosing paranoid disorders. The Pa scale does not always detect the presence of paranoid or delusional thinking. Although persons who score high on scale 6 usually show paranoid ideation and delusions, persons who score low on scale 6 may be viewed as being *too* cautious in their interpretations and do not endorse the more blatant items on the scale.

The Pa scale consists of 40 items with both blatantly psychotic items such as "I believe that other people are plotting against me" and very subtle items such as "I believe that I am more sensitive than most people I know." This scale measures psychological processes such as interpersonal sensitivity, proclamation of high moral virtue, having feelings that are easily hurt, denial of suspiciousness, complaints about the shortcomings of others (cynicism), and excessive rationality.

The Meaning of Elevations of the Pa Scale   It should be kept in mind that elevated Pa scores in the normal population are quite different from elevated scores obtained by psychiatric patients. The correlates of scale 6 change markedly in character as the elevation goes from moderate (T = 60–65) to high (T = 66 and above). In clinic populations, moderate elevations on scale 6 suggest an individual who expresses hostility through "righteous indignation." Clinic patients with elevated Pa scores tend to be rigid, argumentative, and suspicious of others, with unusual thinking, hypersensitivity, and guarded relationships.

Scale 7: Psychasthenia (Pt)

The Pt scale was devised as an aid in diagnosing the neurotic syndrome *psychasthenia*, or the obsessive–compulsive syndrome. The syndrome psychasthenia is not at present a part of psychiatric nomenclature, but the personality features measured by this scale—obsessions, compulsions, anxiety or worrying, unreasonable fears, guilt feelings, etc.—appear in many other psychiatric disorders (e.g., depression, neurotic reactions, and psychoses). There is a great deal of evidence to indicate that the Pt scale is a good indicator of general maladjustment, tension, anxiety, and ruminative self-doubt.

The construction of this scale involved two steps. First, items were selected through empirical separation of a criterion group of 20 patients from the normative group. Next, this preliminary scale was refined through a statistical analysis of its internal consistency in which items were accepted that correlated highly with the total score on the empirically derived item set.

The scale consists of 48 items that deal with symptoms relating to anxiety, irrational fears, indecisiveness, low self-esteem, and self-devaluation. The utility of this scale in profile interpretation comes primarily from its configural relationship with other scales and a measure of "acuteness" of disturbance. For example, the higher the Pt scale elevation in relation to the Schizophrenia (Sc) scale, the more likely it is that the individual's problems are acute rather than chronic.

A peak score on scale 7 is not particularly common, even among psychiatric groups. When it occurs as the highest point, it tends to measure neurotic anxiety. Correlates for the Pt scale include anxiety, tension, feelings of inadequacy, difficulties in concentration, indecision, and rumination.

Interpretation of elevated Pt scores for normal subjects received substantial empirical support from the couple's rating study in the MMPI Restandardization Project (Butcher et al., 2001). Normal-range men and women with high Pt scores were viewed by their spouses as having many fears, being nervous and jittery, being indecisive, lacking in self-confidence, and having sleeping problems.

Scale 8: Schizophrenia (Sc)

Scale 8 was constructed to assess the disorders categorized under the broad grouping of schizophrenia. Several subtypes present a wide range of behavioral manifestations. This was one of the most difficult MMPI scales for Hathaway and McKinley to construct, in part because of the behavioral heterogeneity in the schizophrenia syndromes, but mainly because of the inclusion of such behavioral features as depression and hypochondriasis on earlier groups of items that separated the criterion group. The criterion patients for scale 8 were 50 persons who had been diagnosed as schizophrenic with various subclassifications. The Sc scale (which consists of 78 items) is composed of a number of preliminary subscales derived from the four subclassifications of schizophrenia: catatonic, paranoid, simple, and hebephrenic.

The item content on the Sc scale deals with social alienation, isolation, complaints of family alienation, bizarre feelings and sensations, thoughts of external influence, peculiar bodily dysfunction, general inadequacy, and dissatisfaction.

One should be cautioned against a narrow interpretation of scale 8 in any group and avoid diagnosing all persons with high scores on scale 8 as schizophrenic. Depending on configural relationships with other scales, elevations on scale 8 provide a great deal of information if one gets away from a narrow "diagnostic" or labeling frame of reference.

People in a normal population who score high on scale 8 reveal characteristics that can be informative. While a high score (T > 65) is somewhat rare in the normal population, it reflects unconventionality and alienation. High scorers feel a great deal of social distance and tend to doubt their own work and identity. Persons who have T scores that exceed 70 usually have schizoid mentation, although they are not necessarily psychiatrically disturbed. Correlates for the Sc scale include confusion, disorganization, unusual thinking, alienation, preoccupation, isolation, and withdrawal. Individuals with high-ranging scores are often reported to be psychotic.

Scale 9: Mania (Ma)

The Ma scale was developed as an aid in the assessment of the personality pattern of hypomania. This condition refers to a milder degree of manic excitement than that which typically occurs in the bipolar manic–depressive or manic disorders. The features that characterize this syndrome are overactivity and expansiveness, emotional excitement, flight of ideas, elation and euphoria, overoptimism, and overextension of activities.

Patients characterized by this pattern often manifest behavior that can be seen as psychopathic, and both psychopathic behavior and manic features are common. Elevated profiles on scale 9 are frequently obtained along with elevations on scale 4. Hypomanic behavior as reflected by elevation on scale 9 resembles the symptoms found in manic conditions, but it is usually less blatant and less extreme. In the development of this scale, the criterion group comprised patients who were less acutely disturbed than those with major affective disorders. Patients with the delirium and confusion of a manic state would not have been able to complete the test. The criterion group consisted of 24 patients who were not psychotic or manifesting agitated depressions, but who were classified as hypomanic. The 46 items on the Ma scale deal with expansiveness, egotism, irritability, lack of inhibition and control, amorality, and excitement.

People in the normal range who score high on scale 9 (T = 60–65) tend to be warm, enthusiastic, expansive, outgoing, and uninhibited; they are active and possess an unusually high drive level. Individuals who obtain low scores on the Ma scale often show low energy—listlessness, apathy, and low self-confidence. It should be noted that scale 9 is one of the most frequent peak scores in a normal population. Approximately 10% to 15% of subjects in normal-range groups obtain scores above T = 65, though usually below a T score of 70.

In psychiatric populations, scale 9 is frequently found to be the lowest score, reflecting low morale and lack of energy. The behavioral correlates associated with elevations on the Ma scale include overactivity, expansiveness, energetic behavior, unrealistic views about personal abilities, disorganization, excessive speech, failure to complete projects, and a tendency to act out in impulsive ways.

Interpretation of elevated Ma scale scores for normal-range individuals received substantial empirical support from the couple's rating study in the MMPI Restandardization Project (Butcher et al., 2001). High-Ma wives were rated by their husbands as follows: wears strange or unusual clothes, talks too much, makes big plans, gets very excited or happy for little reason, stirs up excitement, takes many risks, and tells people off about their faults. High-Ma husbands, as viewed by their wives, act bossy, talk back to others without thinking, talk too much, whine and demand attention, and take drugs other than those prescribed by a doctor.

Scale 0: Social Introversion (Si)

The concept of social introversion–extroversion (I-E) has had a long history—dating back to Jung (1922)—and a number of inventories have been devised to measure this personality dimension. The Si scale was not one of the original MMPI scales, but it is now included on the profile as a measure of I-E. This scale was originally developed by Drake (1946) and published as the Social I-E scale. The items were selected by contrasting college students' scores on the subscale for social introversion–extroversion in the Minnesota T-S-E Inventory (which measures social extroversion). The preliminary items were those that differentiated 50 high- from 50 low-scoring females, and the scale was cross-validated on males. The development of this scale differed from that of other MMPI scales in that the criterion groups were *not* from a psychiatric population.

The Si scale included in the MMPI contains 69 items and is designed to measure uneasiness in social situations, social insecurity and self-depreciation, denial of impulses and temptations, and withdrawal from interpersonal contacts.

Hostetler, Ben-Porath, Butcher, and Graham (1989) developed three homogeneous content subscales for the Si scale through an item factor analysis approach. The subscales for Si—Si1 (Shyness), Si2 (Social Avoidance), and Si3 (Self–Other Alienation)—are discussed in detail in Chapter 5.

This scale is a very useful measure of an individual's ease or comfort in social situations. In addition, it serves as an effective measure of the inhibition or expression of aggressive impulses. The scale operates as a suppressor scale in studies of delinquency; that is, elevations on Si are associated with low rates of delinquency. The configural relationships involving the Si scales are very important. Elevations on Si enable the interpreter to evaluate the meaning of various other scales on the profile.

The Si scale is also one of the most stable measures on the MMPI-2, with a long-term reliability of 0.736 over a 30-year time span (Leon et al., 1979). Correlates for high scores include the following: socially withdrawn, shy, reserved in social situations, unassertive, overcontrolled, and submissive in relationships. Individuals with low scores on the Si scale tend to be extroverted, outgoing, manipulative in social relationships, gregarious, and talkative.

Interpretation of elevated Si scale scores for normal subjects received substantial empirical support from the couple's rating study in the MMPI Restandardization Project (Butcher et al., 2001). High-scoring subjects were viewed by their spouses as follows: acts very shy, lacks self-confidence, avoids contact with people, is unwilling to try new things, and often puts himself or herself down.

Cautions to Keep in Mind when Interpreting MMPI-2 Clinical Scale Profiles

Several general considerations should be followed when interpreting MMPI-2 profiles.

1. *Be aware of the population base rate.* The population from which the profile was obtained should be taken into consideration when interpreting the profile (see Kamphuis & Finn, 2002, for a clear presentation of using base rates in clinical assessment). Specific populations tend to draw similar profile groups. Consequently, the interpreter should be aware of the types of profiles typically obtained in a given setting. For example, in alcohol treatment programs, profiles with significant elevations on scales 2 and 4 are common, while profiles with high-ranging 4, 9, and 8 scores are frequently obtained in correctional settings. Knowing the types of cases that typically occur in a given setting enables the clinician to moderate and focus interpretations appropriately.

2. *Refer to scale "numbers" (e.g., scale 4) when discussing an MMPI-2 scale rather than referring to the original scale names (e.g., Psychopathic Deviate scale).* The use of the original scale names is confusing to many people since some scale names have become archaic (e.g., the Psychasthenic scale). The actual scale has taken on considerably more detail and more explicit meaning as empirical research has accumulated. It is therefore more exact to discuss the scales in terms of their number.

3. *Interpret the pattern or "configuration" of scales rather than a scale-by-scale analysis of individual MMPI-2 scores.* It was originally thought that the MMPI scores would reflect the specific pathology measured by each scale and that an elevated score could be "read" as reflecting a particular scale's problems of depression. Early MMPI researchers soon realized, however, that more than one scale was frequently elevated with some

clinical problems. The pattern of scores or the profile configuration then came to be the important focus in MMPI-2 interpretation. An experienced MMPI-2 interpreter usually takes into account the shape of the profile as much as the elevation of the scores in interpreting the profile.

4. *Clinical scales in the MMPI-2 should be considered as having interpretive significance above a T-score level of T = 65 and having some suggestive correlates between a T-score of 60 and 64.*

The Restructured Clinical Scales (RC Scales) of the MMPI-2

Since its original publication in 1940 there have been hundreds of MMPI scales developed to measure a broad range of personality attributes and problems. For example, with the original MMPI there were scales published that addressed constructs such as "Success in Baseball," or "Worried Breadwinner and Tired Housewife," or "Pharasiac Virtue" (see Dahlstrom, Welsh, and Dahlstrom, 1975, for a description of a numerous MMPI-based measures). Most of the scales that have been published on the MMPI or MMPI-2 have not gained broad acceptance for use with clients even though some such as LB (Low Back Pain) or Ca (Caudality), both addressing medical problems, have been widely researched. Personality scales are usually not recommended or incorporated in standard clinical practice until they have been established as valid, reliable, and useful measures of personality characteristics or symptoms through extensive research.

A new set of MMPI-2 measures, the Restructured Clinical Scales (Tellegen et al., 2003), has been published and has been incorporated into computer scoring programs and thus have become widely available even though they have been insufficiently researched to ensure confidence for use in making clinical decisions. These scales are not being recommended in this book for use with patients in treatment planning because they have not been researched for this purpose. However, because they are available and may appear on computer-scored protocols, we provide a brief introduction to these scales and some of the controversy surrounding them. We encourage practitioners to gain a full understanding of them before using them for clinical decisions.

The Restructured Clinical Scales (RC Scales) were developed as supplemental measures to the original MMPI clinical scales. As noted in the test manual, the RC scales were considered to be of use in clarifying scale elevations on the clinical scales (Ben-Porath, 2003; Tellegen et al., 2003). The scales were developed in an effort to improve the traditional clinical scales by reducing item overlap, lowering scale intercorrelation, eliminating the so-called subtle items (i.e., items without content validity), and improving convergent and discriminant validity. In addition, the scale developers removed items that were correlated with a construct referred to as "demoralization," which was thought to be a property inherent in the MMPI-2 symptom scales that resulted in unnecessary overlap of constructs.

According to Tellegen et al. (2003), the RC scales were developed through the following steps. Initially, the authors developed a "Demoralization Scale" to isolate items from the eight clinical scales that tended to be influenced by a set of general maladjustment items. The "demoralization" was viewed as common to most clinical scales, resulting in construct overlap. Next, they developed a set of "seed" scales for the eight clinical scales composed of the items remaining after removing the demoralization component from the original scale. Then, the RC core constructs were expanded by including other MMPI-2 items from the item pool that were correlated with the core construct. Finally, the authors conducted both internal and external validity analyses to further explicate the operation of the scales. They provided analyses of the RC scales' internal validity and predictive validity with mental health patients from the Portage Path Outpatient Sample (Graham, Ben-Porath, & McNulty, 1999) and two inpatient samples (Arbisi, Ben-Porath, & McNulty, 2003), reporting that the RC scales have an equal or greater degree of association to external behavioral correlates to the traditional clinical scales.

The RC scales have been come under considerable criticism for several areas of weakness. The scales have seemingly drifted in meaning so far from the original clinical scales that they cannot perform as measures to refine the interpretation of the clinical scales (Butcher, Hamilton, Rouse, & Cumella, 2006; Nichols, 2006; Rogers, Sewall, Harrison, & Jordan, 2006). The RC scales are more closely associated with other MMPI-2 measures than they are with the clinical scales they were designed to refine (Rouse et al., in press). The RC scales appear to be low in sensitivity to clinical problems and thus scores are not elevated in populations in which they should be (Megargee, 2006; Rogers et al., 2006; Wallace & Liljequist, 2005). These points will be further described.

Construct Drift

The scale construction method employed ensured that the resulting scales would be unidimensional in scope and homogeneous in content; thus, they are likely to function in a manner similar to the MMPI-2 content scales. The scale authors limited their analyses to the traditional clinical scales and did not report relationships with other widely used supplemental scales such as the content scales, PSY-5 scales, and others. Although some of the RC scales contain items from the original clinical scales, a number of the scales bear little content relationship to the parent scale. For example, RC3 contains only five items on the original Hy scale, and those items are scored in the opposite direction to those on Hy. The most dramatic example of the lack of relationship to the original scales is the RC3 scale derived from Hy. This scale was substantially reshaped and the resulting measure (referred to as Cynicism) bears a stronger resemblance to the MMPI-2 content scale Cynicism (80% of the items overlap) than it does to the original Hy scale (see the article by Butcher, Hamilton, Rouse, and Cumella, 2006, detailing the true makeup and relationships with the Hy scale). Moreover, RC9 bears little resemblance to the Ma scale of the original MMPI and MMPI-2 (Nichols, 2006).

Redundancy with Other MMPI-2 Scales

Interestingly, virtually all of the RC scales bear a stronger relationship to some of the MMPI-2 content scales or PSY-5 than they do to the clinical scale they were designed to restructure. (Examples of the modest relationship between the RC scale and the parent scale can be found in Tellegen et al., 2003; Wallace & Liljequist, 2005; and Nichols, 2006.)

Both Nichols (2006) and Caldwell (2006) pointed out the high degree of redundancy between the RC scales and existing measures in MMPI-2 content and PSY-5 scales. In a recent study by Megargee (2006) using MMPI-2 scores of incarcerated felons, high positive correlations were found between the RC scales and content or PSY-5 scales: RC1 was highly correlated in the 0.90s with HEA, RC2 was correlated in the 0.80s with Scale INTR, RC3 was correlated in the 0.90s with CYN; RC4 was correlated in the 0.80s with Scale AAS, RC6 was correlated in the 0.80s with Scales BIZ, RC7 was correlated in the 0.90s with Scales A and NEGE, RC8 was correlated in the 0.90s with Scale BIZ, and RC9 was correlated in the 0.70s with ANG, ASP, Ho, and TPA.

In a recent reliability generalization study comparing the relationship of the RC scales to extant MMPI-2 measures, Rouse et al. (in press) conducted an analysis of 49 samples containing 78,159 individuals. They found that each RC scale was substantially correlated with standard MMPI-2 supplementary, content, and PSY-5 scales, and a reliability generalization analysis showed that the RC scale scores were generally less reliable than scores on comparable extant scales. This study supports previous conclusions that the RC scales do not meaningfully contribute to the range of constructs measured by the MMPI-2, and that they do not possess psychometric strength equal to that of existing scales.

Insensitivity to Clinical Symptoms
and Problems

A recent study by Megargee (2006) also raises questions about the sensitivity of the RC scales at detecting adjustment problems in correctional settings. Megargee found that in a large sample of incarcerated men and women (2,619 adult male prisoners, 797 female prisoners) half of the RC scale mean scores fell *below* the scores of the MMPI-2 normative sample and none of the scores were elevated in the clinically interpretable range, despite the fact that a large percentage of felons have been found to have mental health problems and/or personality disorders. For example, in the correctional sample, 35% of men had T-score elevations greater than or equal to 65 on the Pd scale; however, only 28% had RC4 scores greater than or equal to 65 T. For women, 24% of offenders had Pd T scores greater than or equal to 65, and 21% had RC4 scores in this elevated range.

Similar questions have been raised about the sensitivity of the RC scales in clinical settings. Rogers et al. (2006) reported that almost half of clinical cases studied had no elevations above the T score of 65, and Wallace and Liljequist (2005) found that the majority of client profiles (56%) had fewer scale elevations when plotted using the restructured scales versus the original clinical scales.

The RC scale authors (Tellegen et al., 2003) have recommended that the RC scales be used to refine the interpretation of traditional MMPI-2 clinical scales. However, this approach to interpretation appears to be immature given the problems noted above. Very little information is available that demonstrates the utility of the RC scales. The extent to which these scales contribute to MMPI-2 interpretation will depend upon future research. The authors have provided insufficient information on the use of the RC scales in diverse applications—for example, medical settings where the Hy is quite prominent, or personnel settings where the applicant is not presenting a pattern of severe psychopathology. No research has been published on the use of these measures in assessing clients for psychological treatment. Consequently, their use in treatment planning is not recommended at this time.

Abbreviated Forms of the MMPI-2

Past efforts to obtain effective abbreviated versions of the MMPI and MMPI-2 have not produced the desired results—shortened but valid measures. Virtually all of the 567 MMPI-2 items are currently contained in one of the widely used validity, clinical, content, or supplemental scales. Yet some researchers have attempted to reduce the number of items administered in an effort to obtain the same information with a reduced effort for patients. For example, Dahlstrom and Archer (2000) published a shortened form of the MMPI-2 (simply the first 180 items). This approach to shortening the MMPI-2 failed to produce an effective measure of the existing scales (Gass & Gonazalez, 2003; Gass & Luis, 2001). Gass and Luis, for example, reported that the short form of the MMPI-2 is unreliable for predicting clinical code types, identifying the high-point scale, or predicting the scores on most of the basic scales. The ineffectiveness of the 180-item short form was consistent with the results of a number of earlier efforts to develop short forms of the test in which the abbreviated test failed to capture the original MMPI scale performance (Butcher & Hostetler, 1990; Dahlstrom, 1980) and was not widely used in clinical assessment.

A recent approach to abbreviating test administration of the MMPI-2, based upon the newly derived RC scales as the core measures, has been announced (Ben-Porath and Tellegen, in press) with the goal of shortening test administration time while providing a useful personality assessment. However, less is not more. The goal of psychological assessment in treatment planning is to obtain an extensive amount of personality and symptomatic information on the client in order to enter the treatment process with a reliable and comprehensive picture of the client's personality. The idea of administering an inventory that requires about an hour and a half of the client's time is not unrealistic given the importance of the task. When it comes to the complex task of therapeutic assessment, it is important to administer the full form of the MMPI-2 and not simply have as a goal saving a few minutes of the patient's time using an unproven set of scales.

Summary

This chapter provides an overview of the MMPI-2, beginning with a discussion of the early work on the original MMPI and a brief introduction to the MMPI Restandardization Project and the MMPI-2. The chapter also includes a summary of the MMPI-2 validity and clinical scales for readers who need to review the development and correlates of the basic MMPI-2 scales. The new RC scales were described and cautions in their use in treatment planning provided. Chapter 3 directly addresses the use of these scales in treatment planning.

3

Hypotheses About Treatment from MMPI-2 Scales and Indexes

The focus of this chapter is on the correlates pertaining to psychological treatment that can be culled from the MMPI-2 validity scales, clinical scales, and selected MMPI-2 code types. The general descriptions were drawn from both the empirical and the clinical literature on the MMPI-2 and from the authors' clinical experience with the MMPI-2 in treatment planning. The major goal is to present the MMPI-2 scale profile classification system as a lens through which the clinician can view clients' problems. In the first part of this chapter the client's response attitudes and orientation toward therapy through the validity scales and patterns are discussed; the second section surveys the treatment implications for the MMPI-2 clinical scales; and the final part summarizes information related to a number of frequently obtained MMPI-2 profile code types.

Hypotheses About Patient Characteristics from the MMPI-2 Validity Scales

The MMPI-2 validity scales provide some of the most useful interpretive hypotheses about patients being evaluated in treatment. In using the MMPI-2 as a pretreatment measure, the clinician makes several assumptions about the patient, about people in the patient's support network, and about the treatment program itself. The manner in which a person being tested approaches the MMPI-2 items can provide valuable clues about that person's test-taking attitudes in comparison with those of other people seeking psychological treatment. Two basic questions need to be asked by the clinician about each candidate for testing: (1) *Is this person cooperating with the treatment program by responding to the MMPI-2 items in a frank and self-disclosing manner?* and (2) *Does this person need to be in therapy?* The first question can be directly assessed from the range and pattern of scores on the MMPI-2 validity indicators. The second question is more clearly addressed by clinical scale score and profile information.

In the summary of treatment information obtainable from the MMPI-2, some of the hypotheses may appear in tone to be negative, uncomplimentary, and pessimistic. These examples are not, however, meant to suggest bases for a decision either to refuse to initiate therapy or to terminate it. Our purpose in presenting the test correlates (sometimes extreme) is to encourage therapists to be aware of possible problems and pitfalls. Certain behaviors represent challenges, and the MMPI-2 can assist the clinician in recognizing and perhaps circumventing them.

Interpreting Patient Attitudes
Toward Treatment

The MMPI-2 validity scales—namely, the Cannot Say (?), True Response Inconsistency (TRIN) and Variable Response Inconsistency (VRIN), Infrequency (F), Back Side F [F(B)], Psychiatric Infrequency [F(p)], Lie (L), Subtle Defensiveness (K), and Superlative Self-Presentation (S) scales—serve as indicators of how patients view their own clinical situation, how well they have cooperated with the assessment, and how accessible they are to the therapist. Specific indications of treatment readiness can be obtained directly from elevations on the MMPI-2 response attitude scales and from the *configurations* or relative elevations on the validity scales. First, we will examine possible treatment hypotheses indicated by the individual validity indicators. Afterward, we will discuss the context of the validity scales by looking at the entire configuration of a profile.

Cannot Say (?) Score   The "Cannot Say" scale is useful in treatment planning because it reflects the patient's level of cooperation. The clinician assumes that the person is interested in being understood and is being cooperative in taking the test. People taking the test are asked to answer relevant to their particular case. Those who omit more than 8 to 10 items within the first 370 (the MMPI-2 validity and clinical scales are scorable from the first 370 items) are being more cautious and evasive than is expected under the conditions of pretreatment evaluation. If the number of omissions is between 11 and 19, then it is likely that the person would have considerable difficulty participating in a discussion of personal problems. Records with 20 or more omitted items among the first 370 suggest that a treatment-ready attitude is very unlikely. In some cases the therapist is probably going to need to deal with the client's reticence very early. Treatment termination before benefits can accrue is likely.

As noted earlier, item omissions among clients in psychological treatment are particularly troublesome in that they signal uncooperativeness or inability to disclose personal information. This scale score is a clear warning sign to the therapist that the client may not be sufficiently forthcoming in sharing problems fully.

VRIN and TRIN Scales   Inconsistent self-description can be an important signal of possible problems in therapy. If a client chooses to respond in an inconsistent manner, then his or her low credibility in self-observation and/or straightforward problem reporting could be a deterrent to progress. Even moderate elevations on TRIN or VRIN (T > 65) can be signals that the client may not be cooperative with the treatment plan.

The Family of F Scale [F, F(B), F(p)]   In addition to its role as a validity indicator, the F scale operates as a barometer of psychological distress. The lower the scale elevation (e.g., T < 50), the less likely it is that the individual is experiencing, or at least reporting, problems. Without recognized symptoms, there is little intrinsic motivation for seeking help, so it is unlikely that a person with an F score in this range would seek counseling.

If the F scale is between 51 and 59 T-score points, then the individual may be reporting symptoms of distress that could require psychological treatment. The level of distress, however, is considerably below that of most people who seek help. As we shall see in a later section, the configuration of validity scale scores is often more important in evaluating treatment readiness than the elevation of the validity scale scores. Consequently, for our present discussion a slight elevation on the F scale can be viewed as a problem-oriented self-review only if the F scale is higher than both the L and K scales.

When the F-scale range is between 60 and 79 the individual is engaging in appropriate symptom expression, particularly if F is greater than L and K.

When the F-scale range is between 80 and 90 the person is expressing a high degree of distress, confusion, and a broad range of psychological symptoms. Prompt attention to such a complaint pattern is suggested. This range also indicates that the patient is reporting a multiproblem situation and a lack of resources with which to deal with the problems. Such patients may be under a great deal of stress and may have lost perspective on their problems. This is the fairly common "plea for help" pattern seen in emergency settings or crisis contacts.

MMPI-2 records with an F score above T = 91 are technically invalid. A person with such a score has grossly exaggerated the symptom picture to the point that little differential information is available. Several hypotheses are available for protocols with such extensive distress or symptom presentations:

1. High F-scale records are frequently obtained in inpatient settings (psychiatric), particularly at admission, when a person is confused, disoriented,

or frankly psychotic. In such cases the clinical scale profile may still yield interpretable and useful information. The F(p) scale would be helpful in evaluating this possibility. The F(p) scale contrasts a client's extreme response pattern with inpatients as opposed to the normative sample as used with F and F(B). Thus, a T score of 80 or more indicates that the client is reporting more rare symptoms than even psychiatric inpatients do.

2. The high F-scale pattern is found when a person is seeking to be viewed as "disturbed" so that his or her needs will be given attention. This type of record is seen, for example, with incarcerated felons, who may seek to be viewed as having symptoms but who do not know how to present an internally consistent pattern suggestive of psychological problems.

The Back Side F or F(B) Scale   As noted in Chapter 2, the F(B) scale is important in the interpretation of the MMPI-2 scales with items toward the end of the test booklet. Because clinical and validity scales can be scored from the first 370 items, the F(B) scale has little relevance for their interpretation. For the scales described in Chapters 4 and 5, however, the F(B) scale has a great deal of importance.

The L Scale   People with a T score of 55 to 64 on the L scale are engaging in overly virtuous self-descriptions that could be counterproductive in therapy. A self-description that is highly principled, virtuous, and above fault should be a signal to the therapist that frank, direct, and open communication is going to be difficult. This difficulty in frank expression may derive from a number of factors, including membership in special population subgroups such as ministers or job applicants, who have a strong need to project responsibility and uprightness; individuals who are somewhat indignant about being assessed; or "neurotic" individuals who have unrealistic views of their motives and values. Some ethnic groups tend to have a higher range of L scores than the U.S. normative population. Hispanics as a group tend to endorse more L items than the general population; see the interpretive manual by Butcher, Cabiya, Lucio, and Garrido (2007) for further information on Hispanic clients' performance on the MMPI-2 or MMPI-A.

If the L scale is elevated at a T-score of 65 or more in a treatment evaluation context, then therapy is unlikely to proceed well, progress will be slight, and premature termination is likely. People with unrealistically high claims to virtue are much too rigid and "perfect" to change their self-perceptions much. They typically see little need to discuss their problems or to change their behavior.

K Scale   The K scale, if interpreted properly, can be a useful indicator of treatment readiness or, in some cases, hesitance to become involved in treatment. In general, in its lower ranges—usually below T = 40 to 45—the K scale reflects an openness to emotional expression; in its upper ranges—usually above

T = 70—it suggests an aloofness toward problem expression and discussion of emotions. The K scale is somewhat more complicated than this, however, and must usually be interpreted in conjunction with information about social class and educational level. Several interpretive hypotheses for level of K score are given in Table 3.1.

The Superlative Self-Presentation Scale (S)   This defensiveness measure was developed by Butcher and Han (1995) to improve on K as a measure of under-reporting symptoms. The developers used the responses of a sample of highly defensive job applicants (airline pilots) contrasted with the MMPI-2 normative sample to develop this 50-item defensiveness scale (S) that assesses the tendency of some test-takers to claim overly positive attributes, unrealistically high moral values, and very high responsibility and to deny having adjustment problems. People who score high on the S scale tend to endorse fewer minor faults and

Table 3.1.   Interpretations of K as a Function of Social Class in Treatment Planning

T-Score Range of K: *Low Social Class*

30–44	Some problem admission and symptom expression
	Problem-oriented responding
45–55	Expected level of K for this socioeconomic class
56–63	Somewhat reluctant to express problems
	Somewhat defensive
64–69	Moderate defensiveness
	Unwilling to discuss feelings
	Uses denial as a defense
70+	Highly defensive
	Outright distortion of self-presentation
	Attempting to manipulate others through symptoms characterized by extreme symptom denial

T-Score Range of K: *Middle to High Social Class*

30–44	Overly complaining
	Symptom exaggeration
	Lack of defenses
	Attempting to gain attention through symptom expression
45–55	Some admission of symptoms
	Apparent willingness to discuss problems
56–63	Expected range of scores for this socioeconomic class with no problems
64–69	Somewhat reluctant to discuss personal problems
70+	Defensive
	Evasive
	Unwilling to express feelings
	Disinclined to express symptoms
	Some denial of symptoms

problems than people from the MMPI-2 Restandardization sample. S has been found to be associated with considerably lower levels of symptoms and the admission of fewer negative personality characteristics than most people. High scores on the scale are also associated with an extreme presentation of high "self-control" that is unlikely. High S responders tend to be viewed by people close to them as emotionally well controlled and generally free of pathological behavioral features.

One important way in which the S scale can improve understanding of clients is through an evaluation of the set of five homogeneous subscales. These homogeneous item component scales focus the client's attention on which of the items in S the client has endorsed. For example, the test-taker may have endorsed (as many parents in custody evaluations do) relatively more items dealing with "Denial of moral flaws" or "Denial of irritability" than with other items on S. The subscales of S allow the interpreter to examine content he or she considers important. These subscale groupings are:

- *Beliefs in human goodness:* The client answers false to items with contents such as "Most people do unfair things to get ahead in life" or "Most people are only honest because they are afraid they will be caught."
- *Serenity:* Contains items similar to "My most difficult tasks in life are with myself" (F) and "I often find myself worrying about small things" (F)
- *Contentment with life:* Contains items similar to "I would not change anything that I have done in life if I could live my life over again" (T) and "I am very happy with the amount of money I make" (T)
- *Patience and denial of irritability and anger:* Contains items similar to "I tend to get angry easily and then get over it soon" (F) and "I often become impatient with others" (F)
- *Denial of moral flaws:* Contains items similar to "I have enjoyed using drugs such as marijuana" (F) and "I have used alcohol to extreme at times" (F)

Patterns of Response Attitudes: Treatment Implications

The MMPI-2 validity scales provide much information concerning attitudes toward treatment if their relative elevations are considered. In the paragraphs that follow several validity configurations are presented and illustrated with their treatment implications.

1. *The highly virtuous, "proper," and unwilling participant.* This validity configuration includes relatively high elevations on L, K, and S. All of these scales are elevated above scale F, but the elevation is less important than the shape of the configuration. For this pattern of "naïve" defensiveness, L and K will be higher than T = 60, with F lower than T = 60. In this pattern L is greater than K and S (Fig. 3.1).

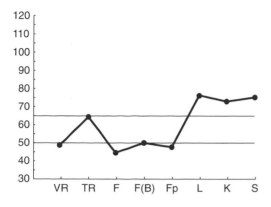

Figure 3.1. Validity pattern of a person presenting an overly virtuous self-view.

This configuration reveals attitudes that are contrary to easy engagement in therapy. Overly virtuous self-appraisal and test defensiveness suggest that the client rigidly maintains attitudes of perfectionistic thinking and a reluctance or refusal to engage in self-criticism. Such respondents view their psychological adjustment as "good" and feel little need for discussing problems. In fact, they feel a need to keep up a good front and to preserve their social image. Rigid beliefs, perfectionistic mental sets, and moralistic attitudes may be prominent in treatment interactions. In early treatment sessions such patients tend to stand off or remain aloof. They thus appear to be distant, unrealistic, and uninvolved in their own problem. Their S-subscale elevations may suggest a mindset to view the world in an unrealistic way and their own "moral views" as impeccable.

A similar test configuration results when respondents attempt to use the test to manipulate other people's view of them. For example, a parent seeking custody of a child will often present such a favorable self-image. Individuals in treatment programs for psychogenic pain may take a similar self-protective stance. Thus, this validity profile is accompanied by an unrealistic self-appraisal and reflects an inflexible mindset, a combination that suggests considerable difficulty in treatment engagement. It may be difficult for a therapist to pass beyond the "barrier of superficial smiles."

2. *The reluctant, defended, and unwilling participant.* Unlike the pattern of resistance just described, prospective patients with this pattern are less moralistic and defiantly virtuous in their self-presentation, but they are nonetheless reluctant to disclose their problem in therapy. The pattern of behavior marked by the K- and S-dominated validity configuration is one of denial, assertion of a positive social image, and presentation of positive mental health. This configuration is illustrated in Figure 3.2.

The behavior reflected in this profile suggests a subtle defensive attitude that denies any psychological need. Individuals with this pattern view (or at least describe) themselves quite positively. They are reluctant to disclose personal weakness and appear resistant in therapy. Two types of patients are commonly found with this validity pattern:

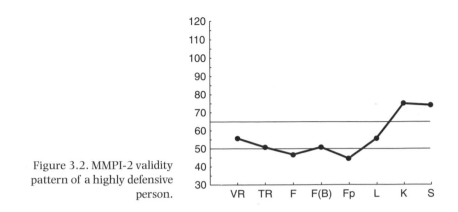

Figure 3.2. MMPI-2 validity pattern of a highly defensive person.

    a. Patients who are in the later stages of successful therapy. The K score usually increases in elevation once a person has regained—or gained—effectiveness in functioning.

    b. Patients who are reluctantly entering treatment at the insistence of another individual, such as a spouse or a court official.

3. *Exaggerated symptom expression—the need for attention to problems.* This exaggerated response pattern is frequently found among individuals seeking psychological help. They appear to be presenting a great number of problems and drawing attention to their need for help. In such cases there is an urgency in the complaint pattern and an indication that the patients feel vulnerable to the demands of their environment and that they do not have strength to cope with their problems. This validity configuration has been referred to a "plea for help" pattern, as depicted in Figure 3.3.

    One feature of this clinical picture that has implications for treatment is its amorphous quality. The problems being presented are nonspecific and the difficulties involve several life areas. As a consequence, the pa-

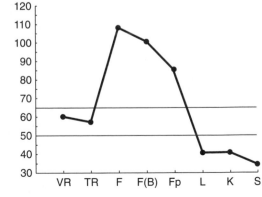

Figure 3.3. MMPI-2 validity configuration of a person presenting a "plea for help."

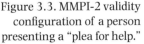

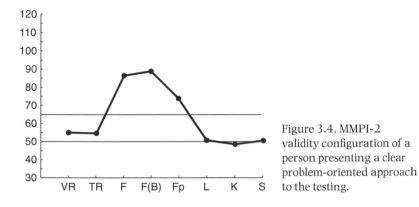

Figure 3.4. MMPI-2 validity configuration of a person presenting a clear problem-oriented approach to the testing.

tient may be unable to focus on specific issues in the treatment sessions. People with this MMPI-2 validity pattern appear prone to develop "crises" that seem, at times, to consume all of their energies and adaptive resources.

4. *Open, frank problem expression.* Moderate elevation on the context of lower L and K scores reflects a problem-oriented approach to self-appraisal and a relatively easier engagement in psychological treatment than the first two configurations discussed. In addition, such patients can focus on symptoms more effectively than the previously described high F scorers, and they are relatively more inclined to discuss their problems. This pattern clearly describes the willing, appropriate pretreatment MMPI-2 validity configuration presented in Figure 3.4.

The Need for Treatment as Reflected by the MMPI-2 Clinical Scales

Scale 1: Hypochondriasis (Hs)

People whose highest clinical scale elevation is on the Hypochondriasis (Hs) scale are reporting a great deal of somatic distress and are attempting to get the therapist to pay attention to their perceived physical ailments. They typically consider themselves not to have psychological adjustment problems but rather primarily physical problems.

Their poor response to verbal psychotherapy may be due to several factors, such as a desire to seek physical (medical) solutions, low motivation for behavioral change, or a cynical attitude toward life. They are usually found to be willing to tolerate psychological strain before change is considered. These people often are expert "doctor shoppers" who have great experience with many therapies and are quite critical of treatment staff. They may show hostility toward a therapist whom they perceive as not giving enough support. Be aware, too, that some clients enter into treatment to establish a "record" for their claims of personal injury or compensation.

Such patients may respond to behavioral treatment for chronic pain, but noncompliance and early termination of treatment are frequent problems. The therapist should be aware that medication use or abuse is common and that there may be a strong element of secondary gain from the symptom pattern. Thus, a reduction in symptoms may actually be deflating to the patient.

Scale 2: Depression (D)

High elevations on the Depression (D) scale reflect considerable expression of poor morale, low mood, and lack of energy to approach daily activities. People with this peak score usually have taken the test with a clear problem-oriented approach and are open—indeed receptive—to discussing their problems with a therapist. The MMPI-2 profile pattern reflects the following possible hypotheses:

1. The patient is expressing a need for help.
2. Distress and the motivation for relief are high.
3. He or she needs to resolve immediate, situational stress.
4. A supportive treatment setting is an important part in the early stages of therapy.
5. An activity-oriented approach to treatment may be effective at improving mood and rekindling the patient's interest in life.

Good response to verbal psychotherapy has been well documented in research studies involving the D scale. People whose D score is their highest scale tend to become engaged in therapy, remain in treatment, and show improvement at follow-up. Consequently, a good treatment prognosis in people with suitable verbal skills is expected for high scorers on the D scale.

Antidepressant medication may aid symptom relief among high-D patients. Behavioral or cognitive–behavioral therapy may help alter life attitudes and unrealistic evaluations of life. Patients with high-ranging, persistent depression scores may respond to electroconvulsive shock therapy if less drastic approaches prove ineffective.

Scale 3: Hysteria (Hy)

People with the Hysteria (Hy) scale as the peak score present themselves as socially facile, moral, inhibited, and defensive. Most important, they appear to be subject to developing physical health problems under stress. High-Hy individuals do not usually seek psychological treatment for their problems. Instead, they view themselves as physically ill or vaguely prone to illness and will frequently go to physicians for reassurance or "treatment," even though the actual organic findings are minimal. This MMPI-2 pattern suggests the following hypotheses:

1. The defensive attitudes held by high-Hy patients may thwart psychological treatment.
2. Patients tend to resist psychological interpretation and seek medical or physical solutions to their problems.
3. They may be naïve and have low psychological mindedness.
4. They tend to gloss over personal weaknesses.
5. Since they are well defended, they do not appear to "feel" much stress; thus, they may be unmotivated for change.
6. They seemingly enjoy receiving attention for their symptoms; thus, the role of secondary gain factors in their symptom picture should be evaluated.
7. They seek reassurance.
8. People with this clinical pattern may gain some symptom relief with mild, directive suggestion; these patients often respond well to placebo.
9. Individuals with this profile code may be interested in medical solutions, at times drastic ones such as elective surgery, and may actually become disabled through extensive, repeated surgery (e.g., for back pain).
10. Significant change may come only through long-term treatment; however, people with prominent elevation tend to drop out of therapy prematurely.

Scale 4: Psychopathic Deviate (Pd)

People with prominent elevations on the Pd scale are typically uninterested in seeking treatment or changing their behavior. They seldom choose treatment for themselves and seek therapy in response to the demands of others—for example, a spouse, family, or the court. They generally see no need for changes in their behavior and are inclined to see others as having the problems. They tend to feel little anxiety about their current situation.

They typically have many problems and pressures resulting from previous impulsive behavior. Very high elevations on Pd are associated with acting-out and impulsive behaviors; thus, they may also have legal difficulties, interpersonal relationship problems, and other problems resulting from poor judgment.

Substance abuse is likely to be a factor, and treatment may need to include alcohol or drug abuse assessment and referral. Addiction problems may continue during treatment and may be kept from the therapist.

In therapy, as in other relationships, patients with high Pd scores tend to be manipulative, aggressive, deceptive, exhibitionistic, and self-oriented. They are inclined to act out conflicts and may engage in therapeutically destructive behavior. They may leave therapy prematurely and without significant improvement.

Scale 5: Masculinity–Femininity (Mf)

The Mf scale, though not originally developed as a clinical scale, provides useful information for treatment planning. The scale assesses a person's level of cultural awareness and openness to new ideas. The Mf scale has different interpretive significance depending upon the level of elevation and the gender of the client. The following hypotheses should be considered.

In Males

1. *The man with a score below T = 45* may be viewed as a poor candidate for individual, insight-oriented psychotherapy. Individuals with this pattern tend to show low verbal skills, interpersonal insensitivity, or a lack of interest in discussing their problems with others. They are more "action-oriented" than reflective in their general approach to life. They show low psychological mindedness, have a narrow range of interests, and are noninsightful, and so are usually not interested in psychological matters or therapy.

2. *The man with a score of T = 67 to 70* demonstrates sensitivity, introspection, and insightfulness, characteristics that suggest openness to experience and amenability to individual psychotherapy. He may show some passivity and dependency and wish to be taken care of. He may also show some dependency in long-term therapy.

3. *The man with a score above T = 75* has a strong possibility of passivity and heterosexual adjustment issues that may severely affect his interrelationships. He might show a severe narcissism that could interfere with some types of therapy (e.g., directive, short-term treatment). There is some suggestion that he has problems dealing with anger, which could prove difficult in therapy. Passivity and an impractical approach to life may prevent him from trying new roles and alternative behaviors that might emerge out of therapy.

In Females

1. *The woman with a score below T = 40* may have an ultrapassive lifestyle suggestive of low treatment potential. There may be a need to approach relationships as "weak, dependent, and passive." She may show masochistic and self-deprecating, self-defeating behavior in relationships that could be difficult to alter. Patients with high 4–6 profiles with low Mf are thought to be passive-aggressive in interaction style and may strive to control others through procrastination and nagging. Seemingly overly compliant and partially compliant behavior may interfere with implementing treatment plans. Dependency and lack of assertiveness may be a central problem for low-Mf women. They might respond to assertiveness training if appropriate.

2. *The woman with a score above T = 70* may be overly aggressive and maladaptively dominant, behaviors that may contraindicate verbal psychotherapy. She may not be very introspective or value self-insights. She generally has difficulty expressing emotions and articulating problems. She may be rebellious, brusque, and cynical in dealing with others.

Scale 6: Paranoia (Pa)

The Pa scale is a very important scale for use in treatment planning because it assesses the client's trust in interpersonal relationships, flexibility toward personal change, and attitudes toward authority figures. High-Pa clients are generally not viewed as good candidates for psychotherapy because they tend to see others as responsible for their problems. They are often argumentative, resentful, and cynical. They may enjoy interpersonal encounters and verbal combat, and may even challenge the therapist. They tend to be aloof and defensive and do not confide in the therapist, which could prevent the therapeutic relationship from proceeding to one of mutual respect, warmth, and empathic feeling. The patient may have inaccurate beliefs that are rigidly maintained even against contrary evidence.

High-Pa patients tend to terminate therapy early; many do not return after the first visit because they believe that the therapist does not understand them.

Scale 7: Psychasthenia (Pt)

The Pt scale assesses a person's level of felt discomfort, tension, and cognitive efficiency. People with peak scores on this scale generally express a great need for help for their physical problems, which are probably associated with intense anxiety. They appear to be quite motivated for symptom relief. Their anxiety may be debilitating, causing them to be grossly inefficient and indecisive. They may need antianxiety medication to enable them to function and fall asleep at night.

Psychotherapy and a supportive, structured environment may be effective in allaying the anxiety and intense guilt of such patients. Cognitive restructuring therapy may facilitate dramatic behavior changes if the sources of anxiety or panic states are known. Directive, action-oriented treatment may assist them in redirecting their maladaptive cognitive behavior. Systematic desensitization therapy may serve to reduce tension. In some cases, patients (especially if Si is T > 60) may benefit from assertiveness straining. These patients have a strong tendency to intellectualize and ruminate. Insight-oriented treatment may be unproductive if it serves only to encourage discussion about their problems without implementation of newly learned adaptive behavior.

Patients with extremely high elevations on this scale (T > 90) may show considerable interpersonal rigidity and unproductive rumination. Consequently, the therapist may experience some frustration over their seeming unwillingness or inability to implement "well-worked-through insights" into actual behavioral change. The high-Pt individual is often so self-critical that he or she engages in perfectionistic behavior that impedes progress in treatment.

Scale 8: Schizophrenia (Sc)

Peak scale elevations on Sc generally suggest a problem-oriented focus in initial treatment sessions. The level of elevation, however, needs to be considered in terms of other scales. Increasing elevation of this scale suggests relative differences in the amount of unusual thinking, unconventional behavior, and problem severity and chronicity. It is useful for the therapist to evaluate the severity of potentially relevant information in this scale as shown in the following:

1. *A score of T = 70 to 79* indicates a chaotic lifestyle. Disorganized life circumstances may produce a multiproblem situation that is difficult to pinpoint in therapy. The patient may be experiencing extensive anxiety and emotional disarray while seeking relief for symptoms. Interpersonal difficulties may interfere with establishing rapport in treatment. Preoccupation with the occult or superstitious beliefs may undermine psychological treatment, and the patient may show immature, self-destructive behavior and act out conflict rather than deal with it in therapy sessions. Such patients may avoid emotional commitments and not respond well to therapy. They may feel that no one understands them. Their problems tend to be chronic and long-term; thus, lengthy treatment is anticipated.
2. *Scores of T = 80 and above* suggest severe confusion and disorganization in high-Sc patients, who may require antipsychotic medication. Hospitalization is sometimes required if the patient is unable to handle his or her affairs. Withdrawal and bizarre thought processes may deter psychotherapy. As outpatients, such patients may benefit from structured treatment programs such as halfway house contacts, outpatient follow-up, or day-treatment programs to provide some structure to their lives.

Scale 9: Mania (Ma)

It is useful to consider the relative elevation on the Ma scale to appraise an individual's motivation for and accessibility to treatment. The range of scores is explored in the paragraphs that follow.

1. *Scores below T = 45* indicate difficulty in psychological treatment because the patients may feel unmotivated, inadequate, depressed, hopeless, and pessimistic about the future. They may be experiencing multiproblem situations and have difficulty getting mobilized to work on these various

problems. An activity-oriented therapy program may provide the appropriate structure for treatment if it is not overly demanding.

2. *Scores of T = 46—69 reflect self-assurance.* If the Ma score is the highest peak in the profile, then the respondent is presenting a statement of self-assurance, self-confidence, and denial of problems. People with this pattern typically do not seek treatment. For all practical purposes, this should be considered a normal-range profile. Treatment recommendations may not be acceptable to the client.

3. *Scores above T = 70* indicate distractibility and overactivity, which may make individuals with this profile difficult, uncooperative patients. They may not be able to focus on problems and they tend to overuse denial to avoid self-examination. They are inclined to be narcissistic and they make unrealistic, grandiose plans. They frequently make shallow promises and set goals in treatment that are never met. They are manipulative and may disregard scheduled therapy times with ease—they are frequently "too busy" to make the session. They avoid self-examination by generating projects and ideas to occupy their time. Their low frustration tolerance may produce stormy therapy sessions punctuated by irritable and angry outbursts. Their problems with self-control lead them to act out their impulses. They may have problems with alcohol abuse that require evaluation and treatment.

Social Introversion–Extroversion (Si) Scale

The Si scale is one of the most useful scales in pretreatment planning because it addresses several aspects of interpersonal adjustment. The Si scale reflects problems of social anxiety and maladjustment, inhibition and overcontrol, and comfort in relationships. The level of elevation in the Si scale provides valuable clues to an individual's capacity to form social relationships as well as readiness to become engaged in a process of self-disclosure.

1. *Si scores below T = 45* identify patients who may not see the need for treatment. They tend to feel little or no anxiety and do not feel uncomfortable enough to change. They usually are rather superficial in their social relations and may be too glib to form deep emotional relationships. They are exhibitionistic and dominant and not reflective or interested in inward scrutiny. They may act out and experience problems of poor control.

2. *Si scores of T = 60 to 69* reflect difficulty in forming personal relationships. Treatment sessions often have a slow tempo. Patients are shy and inhibited and may have great difficulty expressing themselves. They are quite insecure and conforming; thus, they may expect the therapist to be directive and dominate the sessions. Group treatment methods or social skills training may be useful in teaching them to relate more effectively with others.

3. *Si scores of T = 70 or greater* suggest probable difficulty in developing an effective therapeutic relationship. These clients are quite inhibited and

may be unable to articulate their feelings; they are very slow to trust the therapist. Treatment sessions are typically slow-paced, with long silences. Patients may appear unmotivated and passive, yet quite tense and high-strung. Such people are overcontrolled and can have great difficulty making changes in their social behavior or in putting into practice new modes of responding outside the treatment setting.

MMPI-2 Code Types and Treatment-Related Hypotheses

The literature on MMPI-2 code types provides additional hypotheses for treatment planning. The following brief summaries of descriptive hypotheses associated with MMPI-2 code types may be useful for understanding patient behaviors in the early stages of treatment. The code type information provided here is for those types in which all relevant scales are greater than $T = 65$.

12/21

Individuals with the 12/21 profile type are typically not good candidates for traditional insight-oriented therapy. They send to somatize problems; they tolerate high levels of stress without motivation to change; they resist psychological interpretation of their problems; and they seek medical solutions to their problems.

1234

Alcohol or drug abuse problems are characteristic of people with the 1234 profile. Chemical dependency treatment may be required, and medical attention for ulcers or related gastrointestinal problems may also be necessary. Sometimes tranquilizers are prescribed for such patients because they show tension in addition to other psychological problems. Use of tranquilizers should be minimized or discouraged, however, because such patients have addictive tendencies. Psychotherapy, when attempted, is often a long and difficult process since these clients tend to resist psychological interpretations, blame others for their problems, and see no need for personal change. Acting-out problems commonly occur. The long-range prognosis for behavior change is usually considered poor for clients with this highly elevated profile configuration.

13/31

Individuals with the 13/31 profile are resistant to psychological treatment. They seek medical explanations for their difficulties, deny the validity of psychological explanations, are defensive, avoid introspection, show lack of concern for their physical symptoms, and show little motivation to alter their behavior. They may respond to mild direct suggestion and placebo in a medical setting. Brief stress-inoculation training may be successful if resistance is overcome. Long-term commitment to therapy is usually required for treatment of personality problems, but treatment resistance and lack of motivation for change may result in early termination of therapy.

14/41

Individuals with the 14/41 profile code tend to have longstanding personality problems and are inclined to have relationship difficulties, excessive somatic complaints, and patterns of aggressive behavior. Their symptomatic behavior can often be viewed as manipulative and controlling. They are likely to be resistant to psychological treatment and may fail to comply with treatment plans.

Insight-oriented treatment is likely to be somewhat stormy. Treatment sessions may become tense because of the patient's high level of hostility and aggressiveness, which may at times be directed toward the therapist.

23/32

The 23/32 pattern reveals considerable tension and stress, but affected patients may have difficulty articulating the sources of their problems. They tend to maintain their social "image," and they may have some problems in early stages of insight-oriented treatment. They often describe vague somatic problems such as weakness or dizziness. They generally view these complaints as their main problem and have difficulty going beyond the felt symptom itself. They tend to seek medical treatment such as pain medications or tranquilizers as the solution to problems caused by conflictive relationships. They may "energize" themselves through self-medication.

The degree of depression in people with this profile is usually high, and some symptomatic relief is considered necessary. Sometimes antidepressant medication is required to reduce tension and distress. Supportive psychological treatment might be successfully applied.

24/42

The treatment setting and referral problems are extremely important factors in interpreting the 24/42 MMPI-2 profile code. Since this is the mean configuration and one of the most frequent code types appearing in alcohol and drug treatment programs, an assessment for substance abuse is important. Acceptance and admission by the individual of such a problem is crucial in making positive life changes. People with this profile are often viewed as having longstanding personality problems that make them resistant to treatment. Therapy on an outpatient basis often ends in termination before behavior changes result. Some outpatients with this profile type fail to recognize or acknowledge their alcohol or drug abuse problems. Consequently, the therapist should be aware of possible substance abuse.

Some people with this pattern may respond to treatment in a controlled context that reduces acting out. Group treatment may be more successful than individual therapy.

27/72

People with either a 27 or a 72 code type are usually in such psychological distress that they seek help and are amenable to psychotherapy. Initial therapy sessions may be oriented toward problem expression and help-seeking behaviors. Reassurance and advice may be sought directly by such clients because they often feel that they do not have the personal resources to deal with their life circumstances.

Low self-esteem and self-defeating behavior may prevent such patients from taking action to remedy their problem circumstances. They usually seek considerable support, are introspective, and can be ruminative and overly self-critical in sessions. They generally establish interpersonal relationships easily, although this is apparently easier for 27s than for 72s, who are more anxious. People with the 72 code are quite prone to guilt and are overly perfectionistic. Their obsessive ruminations can be very unproductive in verbal psychotherapy. They tend to be obsessive about the need for change but have considerable difficulty actually trying out new behaviors.

Both 27s and 72s tend to experience acute disabling symptoms. Psychotropic medication might be required to reduce the acute symptoms: antianxiety medication for 72s (where anxiety is problematic) and antidepressants for 27s (where depression is primary). Of course, both anxiety and depression could occur with a 27 or a 72.

274/427/724

The 274 MMPI-2 code is rather different from the 27/72 code, largely due to the presence of personality problems reflected in the Pd (scale 4) configuration. Acute distress, possibly of a transitory and situational nature, is usually present. The presence of Pd indicates an antisocial lifestyle, which might have produced the depression by an injudicious pattern of self-indulgence. This profile code is commonly found among people who have alcohol or drug abuse problems. This possibility should be verified in early therapy sessions because a longstanding problem could suggest a poor prognosis.

Persons with this profile code are generally not very responsive to individual insight-oriented treatment. In outpatient settings they tend to leave treatment prematurely, cannot tolerate anxiety in treatment, and act out (e.g., by engaging in drinking bouts between sessions). They often show a "honeymoon effect"; that is, they have gains early in treatment but slip as their frustration mounts. They may respond best to environmentally focused changes and directive goal-oriented treatment. Group treatment methods in a controlled setting (e.g., alcohol treatment programs) may produce therapeutic gains.

28/82

Individuals with the complex MMPI-2 profile code 28/82 require careful consideration in terms of treatment planning since several major diagnostic problems are possible, as discussed in the paragraphs that follow.

1. *Psychotic behavior.* Problems reflected in this group are bizarre ideation, delusional thinking, social withdrawal, extreme emotional lability, and anger. Social relationship problems are usually evident.
2. *Affective disorder.* Mood disorder and social withdrawal are characteristic problems of this disorder.
3. *Personality disorder.* Emotional instability reflected in acting-out behavior, social relationship problems, and lability is present. Borderline personality is a likely diagnostic summary for patients with these problems.

Regardless of clinical diagnosis and treatment setting, several factors are important for the potential therapist to consider:

1. *Relationship problems:* People with this profile tend to have difficulty dealing with interpersonal relationships. This is likely to be manifest in stormy therapeutic relationships as well.
2. *Anger expression problems:* The 82/28 profile type tends to experience marked emotional control problems, including loss of control and expression of anger. Unmodulated anger toward the therapist is common during periods of emotional intensity.
3. *Social withdrawal:* Persons with the 28/82 profile may experience considerable ambivalence toward relationships. It is often difficult for them to enact new relationship "tactics" learned in therapy.

Individuals with this profile code tend to have several problems in their life. It is often difficult for them to focus on a problem area for any time before other aspects of their lives begin to fall apart. A therapist can provide a point of stability for such patients, who often require long-term treatment to work through their extensive problems. Many people with this profile require psychotropic medications (i.e., antidepressant and antipsychotic compounds) to control their emotions and thoughts, particularly in periods of intense crisis.

34/43

Patients with the 34/43 code typically enter therapy with problems in which their own lack of emotional control, particularly anger, is the salient feature. Their impulsive lifestyle and stormy interpersonal style are as likely to characterize therapy sessions as the other aspects of their lives. Self-control issues and acceptance of responsibility for their problems are likely to be central issues in treatment.

Clients with this pattern are often found to be resistant to psychological treatment because they project blame. Their conflict-producing interpersonal dynamics result in a rather rocky therapeutic course. Early termination in anger and acting out in frustration are common for such patients.

People with this profile may not seek treatment on their own but enter therapy at the insistence of a spouse or the court. Outpatient psychotherapy may be problematic because of emotional immaturity and a tendency to blame others for their own shortcomings. A motivation to change is sometimes lacking.

Some people with this pattern get into legal problems and require treatment in a more controlled setting. Group treatment has been shown to be effective for some patients with this extensive behavioral problem.

46/64

People with the 46/64 MMPI-2 profile code are generally antagonistic toward psychological treatment. They tend not to seek help on their own but are usually evaluated in mental health settings at the request or insistence of someone else. As a consequence, they are often hostile, uncooperative, suspicious, and mistrustful of the motives of others. Treatment relationships are usually rocky and initially very difficult to form. These people usually view their problems as being caused by someone else, and they project the blame for their circumstances on others.

Patients with this pattern are usually hostile and aggressive, and they commonly have a number of environmental difficulties as well. Treatment plans should be realistic. Because they are typically argumentative and they tend to defend and justify their actions to a considerable degree, therapy sessions with such patients are often marked by extreme resistance and lack of cooperation. Treatment often ends abruptly when the client becomes angry and frustrated. The therapist should be aware of the possibility of angry acting out by clients with the 46/64 profile code.

47/74

The 47/74 MMPI-2 profile code suggests some characteristic behaviors that are very pertinent for treatment planning, particularly the individual's tendency toward cyclic acting out followed by superficial remorse. Individuals with this pattern are generally found to show longstanding personality problems that center on an impulsive–compulsive pattern of self-gratification and consequent guilt. In the early stages of treatment, such strong behavioral trends may find the patient seemingly cooperative, remorseful, and goal-directed. Over time, however, the guilt appears to diminish and the desire for pleasure again appears to dominate. Thus, the "early gains" and sincere attitude toward change melt away, leaving the unswerving acting-out component in the character pattern to disrupt treatment.

Many 47/74 persons are found in alcohol and drug treatment programs or in other treatment settings (e.g., programs for those with eating disorders such as bulimia or pathological gambling) where the impulsive–compulsive lifestyle appears with some frequency. Therapists should be cautious about early and "easy" gains and should be aware of personality factors that may lie in wait for their turn at ascendancy.

48/84

Longstanding problems of unconventional, unusual, or antisocial behavior are likely to characterize early treatment sessions with the 48/84 profile type. Patients usually have substantial environmental and relationship problems, as well as intrapsychic difficulties. Individual psychological treatment planning with the 48/84 may be confounded by other problems—for example, drug or alcohol abuse, which needs to be addressed if treatment is to proceed effectively.

If the treatment approach is verbal psychotherapy, the early treatment sessions are likely to be chaotic, with numerous complicated involvements and little productive focusing. The treatment relationship, like other interpersonal involvements the person has, is likely to be stormy and difficult. Verbal psychotherapy, because of the 48/84's aloofness, unconventionality, and relationship-formation deficits, is likely to be unproductive at worst and difficult at best. Acting-out behavior is likely to complicate treatment planning as well as other aspects of life. The client's lack of trust may lead to early termination of therapy.

482

Patients with the 482 profile typically lack insight into their behavior and tend to have a low capacity for insight-oriented treatment. If depression is a strong component in the symptomatic picture, as is likely to be the case, they may respond to antidepressant medication. Underlying character disorder and addiction potential should be evaluated before medication is prescribed. Antipsychotic medications may be required to control possible thought disorder in 482s. Commitment to an inpatient facility may be necessary to protect such patients from injuring themselves or others.

Long-term change in the basic personality structure is unlikely to result from treatment. Symptomatic relief and emotional support may enable the individual to return to previous marginal adjustment.

49/94

Patients with the 49/94 code are usually less interested in treatment and the complex task of self-analysis and behavior change than they are in self-gratification and hedonistic pursuits. Persons with this profile code usually find their way into psychological treatment at the behest of another person, such as a spouse, employer, or the court. They are generally not motivated to discuss personal problems even though they are usually articulate and expressive. Their lack of anxiety usually proves to be a deficit that deters genuine change.

Individuals with this code are frequently found to be controlling and turn their "charm" and manipulative skill to the therapist in order to gain favor or attention. At times, the most effective treatment approach for 49/94s is difficult to determine, since manipulating and "conning" other people is an important adaptive strategy for 49s. It behooves the therapist to be forewarned of such tactics, whatever the proposed treatment approach. It is effective to confront this behavioral style when it becomes manifest. Individuals with this profile code usually do not respond well to punishment.

Outpatient treatment for the 49/94 often ends in premature termination when he or she becomes bored with the sessions. Since acting-out behavior is common among 49/94s, therapy can be disrupted by poor judgment and indiscreet behavior on the client's part. Individual insight-oriented treatment may be "enjoyed" briefly by 49s, but treatment may be terminated early, often abruptly. Group treatment methods (in controlled environments) have reportedly been effective; behavior modification procedures may be useful as well in helping the patient learn more adaptive behaviors.

68/86

Severe psychopathology characterizes the 68/86 profile type with both cognitive and emotional disturbances. Consequently, the therapist may have several important decisions to ponder in treatment planning.

Should the patient be treated on an inpatient or outpatient basis? Many people with this profile code require careful monitoring and external direction. When considering whether hospitalization is needed, the therapist should weigh the patient's potential for danger to self or others. Outpatient treatment can be complicated by regressed or disorganized behavior. Day treatment is often effective at helping these patients manage their daily activities.

Paralleling the question of an appropriate setting for treatment is the question of the need for psychotropic medication. The individual should be evaluated for medication needs if this has not been done. Major tranquilizers to control psychotic thinking are often helpful. Long-term, marginal adjustment is a problem; thus, frequent brief contacts for "management" therapy can be helpful. Insight-oriented therapy on an outpatient basis should proceed with caution since self-scrutiny may exacerbate problems and result in regression.

Regardless of the treatment setting and therapeutic approach, several factors influence treatment planning for the 68/86:

1. *Problems of relationship formation.* Individuals with this profile code are unskilled socially and may never have had a satisfactory interpersonal experience.
2. *Problems of mistrust* (projection). Suspicion and mistrust are characteristic of the way such people interact with others: they manage conflict and anxiety by projecting blame onto others.
3. *Cognitive distortion.* People with this profile show cognitive defects and may operate with a different form of logic than does the therapist. This poses a particular problem for cognitively based therapy. Delusions and hallucinations may be present.
4. *Impulsivity/poor judgment.* Patients may act impulsively and their behavior will at times be bizarre.
5. *Preoccupation with unnatural causation.* Many people with this pattern give as much credence to the occult (e.g., astrology, numerology) as they do to natural causes. Treatment suggestions or plans might be subverted as a result of an unusual belief system.
6. *Pan-anxiety.* Patients are usually extremely anxious, although their affect might be flat or blunted.
7. *Regression.* The individual's behavior might be extremely regressed and require careful management.

78/87

Since patients with the 78/87 profile code are usually experiencing intense anxiety and psychological deterioration, the therapist may need to begin therapy by providing a supportive atmosphere of reassurance to lower the client's level of distress. People with this profile are generally "crisis-prone" and appear to have little resiliency and few resources with which to manage their daily affairs. Structure and a directive crisis-management approach might be effective in helping the 78/87 manage intense stress. Many people who experience this level of tension and disorganization require psychotropic medication for relief of anxiety; referral for an evaluation of medication is indicated.

Insight-oriented psychological treatment may aggravate psychological problems and produce further deterioration in functioning. There is a tendency for this type of patient to over-intellectualize. A problem-focused treatment approach may be more effective in helping such patients deal with their problems. Social skills or assertiveness training may be appropriate if the patient is not psychotic. This approach may be productive since the 78/87 client is frequently lacking in social skills.

83/38

Patients with the 83/38 profile often report obscure, intractable somatic complaints. Relationship problems and lack of insight into psychological problems may contraindicate individual insight-oriented therapy. These patients may be responsive to pharmacological treatment and supportive/directive therapy.

96/69

Antipsychotic medication is likely to produce the most dramatic change in patients with the 96/69 profile codes. Traditional insight-oriented treatment is difficult because 69s show extensive relationship problems and lack of trust. Problem-focused treatment is most successful if the patient comes to trust the therapist.

89/98

Major tranquilizers are likely to be the most effective treatment for the 89/98 profile patient if the diagnosis is major affective disorder. Lithium may be useful in controlling affective disorder. Prolonged hospitalization may be necessary for patients who lack behavior control. Traditional psychotherapy is usually ineffective since these clients cannot focus on problems. Some 89s suffer from severe personality disorders that are entrenched and unresponsive to insight-oriented psychotherapy.

Summary

In this chapter we summarized the established correlates for the MMPI-2 validity and clinical scales and profile code types with respect to treatment planning. These MMPI-2 scales provide extensive treatment-related information that therapists can integrate into their treatment plans. In the next chapter, we turn to a description of several supplemental scales that have been developed for the assessment of specific clinical problems, a number of which provide valuable hypotheses for the psychological treatment context.

4

MMPI-2 Supplementary Scales in Treatment Evaluation

A number of supplementary or special-purpose scales have been developed for the MMPI-2 that may have relevance for treatment evaluation. These measures provide relevant personality information on symptomatic status or personality attributes that can aid the therapist in developing treatment plans with the client. Individuals interested in a more detailed discussion of these scales should consult recent MMPI-2 textbooks by Butcher (2005b) or Graham (2006).

Substance Abuse Indicators

Alcohol and other addictive substances are prominent in contemporary society, and abuse of them is common. Many individuals with psychological symptoms find temporary relief from the pressures of living through the use and abuse of these substances. Consequently, clinicians find that an assessment of the way in which their patients learn or fail to learn to deal with alcohol and other drugs is an important assessment question in a pretreatment diagnostic study. Many people who eventually develop alcohol or drug abuse disorders begin their abuse in an effort to deal with their psychological distress. The substance abuse pattern they develop comes to be viewed as an effort to manage their psychological distress. Rouse, Butcher, and Miller (1999), in an extensive study of the MMPI-2 with psychotherapy clients, found that all three substance abuse indicators to be discussed here (MAC-R, APS, and AAS) were more prominent in substance-abusing therapy clients than non-abusing clients. It becomes an important aspect in any pretreatment psychological assessment, then, to determine if alcohol or drug use is a pertinent or potentially confounding problem. Three scales to address substance abuse in clients will be described: the MacAndrew Scale

(MAC-R), the Addiction Proneness Scale (APS), and the Addiction Acknowledgment Scale (AAS).

MacAndrew Alcoholism Scale

MacAndrew (1965) was interested in developing a psychological assessment measure that would differentiate between alcohol-abusing and non-alcohol-abusing people who also had some psychological problems. He contrasted a group of 200 male alcoholics with a group of 200 male psychiatric patients from the same facility who did not have an alcohol abuse problem. The scale he developed, the MAC scale, contained 51 items. MacAndrew cross-validated the scale on a different sample and found comparable classification rates (82%). Since MacAndrew's original work, numerous other researchers (e.g., Apfeldorf & Huntley, 1975; Rhodes, 1969; Rich & Davis, 1969; Schwartz & Graham, 1979) have found high classification rates for the MAC scale, but these were not as high as MacAndrew's cross-validation.

Although MacAndrew initially found 51 items to discriminate significantly between alcoholics and nonalcoholics, he recommended the use of only 49 items, dropping two obvious alcohol items since he thought that alcoholics would deny these items. Most of the research on the MAC scale has employed the 49-item scale, and the norms now used are based on that set. Initially, MacAndrew recommended a cutoff score of 24 as indicative of alcohol abuse problems. This cutoff is probably too low because it is less than one standard deviation above the mean of the original Minnesota normals. A more conservative cutoff score is therefore recommended. A general rule of thumb for interpreting the MAC scale is as follows:

1. For males, a raw score of 26 to 28 suggests that alcohol or drug abuse problems are possible; a raw score of 29 to 31 suggests that alcohol or drug abuse problems are likely; and a raw score of 32 or more suggests that alcohol or drug abuse problems are highly probable.
2. For females, a raw score of 23 to 25 suggests that alcohol or drug abuse problems are possible; a raw score of 26 to 29 suggests that alcohol or drug abuse problems are likely; a raw score of 30 or more suggests that alcohol or drug abuse problems are highly probable.

In the MMPI restandardization the MAC scale was modified slightly because it contained four items that were eliminated as objectionable. To keep the same number of items on the scale (49 items), 4 new items were substituted for the eliminated items (see Butcher et al., 1989). These items were selected through procedures similar to those MacAndrew originally used in developing the scale—empirical discrimination between a group of alcoholics and a group of psychiatric patients.

The content of the MAC scale suggests that high-scoring individuals may have the following characteristics: they are socially extroverted, present themselves as self-confident, are assertive and exhibitionistic, enjoy taking risks, show concentration problems, and have a history of acting-out behavior such as school problems. An example of the utility of the MAC-R score can be seen in the following case (Figs. 4.1 and 4.2).

Case History: A Study of the Substance Abuse Indicators in Treatment Assessment

John W., a 48-year-old postal employee, was referred for a psychological evaluation by his physician, who suspected that he might be experiencing some psychological problems. He has been reportedly missing a great deal of work over the past year and has attempted to obtain medical permission for his numerous absences. He has been to see the physician on several occasions, in recent months for "medical problems," but a physical basis for his problems has been ruled out. Mr. W. was somewhat reluctant to make an appointment with the psychological staff since he viewed his problems as physical, not psychological. He was defensive on the MMPI-2, although he presented a general picture of somatic concern and physical weakness. His elevated MAC raw score (see Fig. 4.2) suggested the possibility that his problems could result, in part, from an underlying drug or alcohol abuse problem. In interview, when this possible problem was raised with him, he denied that he drank alcohol to excess and acknowledged only moderate use. Further discussion about his modes of "tension relief," however, did reveal that he had been taking Doriden (a highly addictive central nervous system depressant) for several years in order to sleep. His daily use of this medication suggested the likelihood of an addictive disorder, yet a referral to psychological treatment was refused.

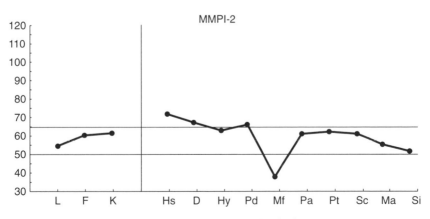

Figure 4.1. MMPI-2 validity and clinical scale profile of John W.

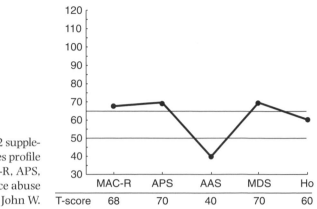

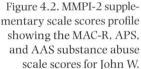

Figure 4.2. MMPI-2 supplementary scale scores profile showing the MAC-R, APS, and AAS substance abuse scale scores for John W.

	MAC-R	APS	AAS	MDS	Ho
T-score	68	70	40	70	60

Predictive Research on the MAC Scale

There is some disagreement over the extent to which MAC-R is useful in detecting substance abuse problems (see Gottesman & Prescott, 1989; Graham & Strenger, 1988). However, most textbooks recommend the use of the MAC-R in a conservative manner. There is a need to adjust the cutoff scores for both African Americans and women. For example, research has shown that African Americans typically score in the potential alcohol abuse range on the MAC scale and that classification rates are not as good as with white populations (Walters et al., 1983, 1984). In clinical practice, the ranges listed earlier should be set 2 points higher for minority Americans.

Research on the MAC-R shows strong support for its use in detecting substance abuse problems (Craig, 2005; Graham, 1989; Levenson et al., 1990; Smith & Hilsenroth, 2001). Craig (2005) reviewed the existing studies on the MAC/MAC-R across a number of studies totaling almost 32,000 clients, including adolescent and adult substance abusers, from studies published since the last MAC reviews (1989) through 2001. Results suggest that the MAC, and to some extent the MAC-R, significantly correlates with measures of alcohol and substance abuse in both male and female adolescents and adults across a diverse spectrum of the use–abuse continuum. They found that 100% of nonclinical groups scored below the clinical ranges on the MAC/MAC-R, while 79% of adolescent substance-abusing groups scored greater than 23, indicative of problems with substance abuse. Clients who abused alcohol, drugs, and polydrugs had mean MAC/MAC-R scores >23, which ranged from 77% to 100% of the cases. The MAC/MAC-R does well in discriminating persons who abuse substances compared to nonclinical, non-abusing groups. However, some diagnostic efficiency is lost with psychiatric patients and medical patients with seizure disorders. Increasing the cutoff score to greater than 25 improved diagnostic accuracy in these groups.

The assessment of substance abuse problems is clearly central to treatment planning. If a new patient has a high MAC-R score, the therapist should be aware of the complications that could occur during therapy when the individual becomes frustrated and acts out with excessive substance abuse.

Another valuable use of the MAC-R score in treatment planning involves application of the finding that a number of patients in treatment for substance abuse (about 15%) have low scores—less than a raw score of 24 for males and 21 for females—when it would be expected that their MAC-R scores would be high. The low MAC-R score typically indicates that a person is experiencing alcohol or drug abuse problems as secondary to other psychological problems, and treatment of the other problems may be necessary to clear up the substance abuse problems.

Addiction Potential Scale (APS)

After the revision of the original MMPI and expansion of the item pool, a broader range of substance abuse items became available in the instrument. Weed, Butcher, McKenna, & Ben-Porath (1992) were interested in developing an empirical scale that could improve upon earlier measures for the detection of substance abuse problems. The APS was developed as a measure of the personality factors underlying the development of addictive disorders. Items that differentiated alcohol and drug abusers were contrasted with psychiatric patients and nonclinical participants who were not substance abusers. For the development of the APS, larger samples of substance-abusing people, psychiatric patients, and normative population were tested in a cross-validated design than had been used in the original work on the MAC scale. The APS showed high reliability and predictive validity. This measure contains 39 items, only 9 of which overlap with the MAC-R scale. An elevated score on the APS is associated with the likely membership of the client in samples of substance-abusing patients. High elevations on APS suggest that the client shows a great potential for developing substance abuse problems. Low scores on APS are not interpreted because research has not been conducted on low-ranging scores at this time (see studies by Clements & Heintz, 2002; Rouse et al., 1999; Weed et al., 1992).

Addiction Acknowledgment Scale (AAS)

The MAC-R and APS were developed as empirical measures to detect the presence of personality or lifestyle characteristics associated with alcohol or drug abuse problems. These measures do not address acknowledging substance abuse on the part of the client but indirectly address the problem by finding how the client resembles substance abusers in general personality makeup.

In their research, Weed et al. (1992) took a somewhat different approach in an effort to address a patient's willingness or unwillingness to acknowledge having substance abuse problems. The AAS was developed as a measure of substance abuse problem denial.

The AAS evaluates a client's willingness to acknowledge problems with alcohol or drugs and provides a psychometric comparison of the client's actual admission of alcohol or drug problems with other known groups. The 13-item AAS scale, with fairly obvious item content, was developed using a combined rational and statistical scale development approach. The items were initially chosen because they contained clear substance abuse problems. These items were then correlated with the remaining MMPI-2 item set to determine if additional items were associated with the initial substance abuse indicators. The provisional scale was refined further by examining the alpha coefficients, keeping only those items that increased scale homogeneity. The AAS has been shown to be an effective assessment indicator of substance abuse problems in psychotherapy clients (Clements & Heintz, 2002; Rouse et al., 1999).

Given the obvious content structure, interpretation of the AAS is relatively straightforward. An elevated scale score, above a T score of 60, indicates that the client has acknowledged a large number of alcohol or drug use problems compared with people in general from the normative sample. The more items endorsed, the more problems the individual has acknowledged. A low score on the scale does not necessarily mean that the client does not have substance abuse problems, only that the person has not admitted to having problems or has denied problems. A particular client could have very significant substance abuse problems but choose to avoid acknowledging them.

The profile of the case example shown in Figure 4.2 illustrates the use of the three substance abuse detection scales (MAC-R, APS, and AAS) together because they provide different types of information about a client. The APS and MAC-R scales measure the potential for developing addictive disorders and provide information regarding the individual's lifestyle. The AAS scale provides a clear assessment of whether the client is aware of and willing to acknowledge these problems in the evaluation. In the case shown in Figure 4.2, both the APS and MAC-R indicated likely problems with substance abuse; however, the client acknowledged relatively few problems with drugs or alcohol, suggesting denial of problems.

Scales to Address Symptoms that Can Influence a Client's Progress in Treatment

Several scales that can be particularly helpful in unveiling treatment-related symptoms or issues will be discussed next. These include the Cook-Medley

Hostility Scale (1954) that was redeveloped for MMPI-2 by Han, Weed, Calhoun, and Butcher (1995), the Marital Distress Scale (MDS) published by Hjemboe and Butcher (1991), and the Post-Traumatic Stress Disorder Scale (PTSD) developed by Keane, Malloy, and Fairbank (1984).

The Ho Scale

The tendency of some clients to experience anger control problems can be an important factor in the therapy process. Therefore, gaining an indication of potential anger problems early in treatment can alert therapists to potential problems that could threaten progress. Cook and Medley (1954) developed the Ho scale as a measure of a person's ability to relate harmoniously to others, to establish interpersonal rapport, and to maintain morale in group situations. They developed the Ho empirically by contrasting groups of schoolteachers who had been judged to differ with respect to having the capability of getting along in the classroom with their students. High Ho scorers were teachers who were considered to be difficult to get along with interpersonally. In addition, high scorers were reportedly hostile and negative to their students and considered them to be dishonest, insincere, untrustworthy, and lazy.

Research on the Ho expanded its application with an entirely different population than the developmental sample—medical patients. The Ho became widely used as a measure of hostility in people with coronary disease (see Arbisi, 2006; Barefoot, Dahlstrom, & Williams, 1983), particularly as a measure of premorbid personality characteristics that were considered to be associated with later development of heart disease. People who have high levels of interpersonal hostility and cynical attitudes were thought to have a greater likelihood of developing hypertension than those having low hostility.

In the redevelopment of the Ho scale after the MMPI-2 was published, the scale required some modification since 9 of the 50 items on the scale were slightly reworded to make them more readable and contemporary. Thus, Han, Weed, Calhoun, and Butcher (1995) conducted a validation study of the revised items showing that the Ho scores were highly related to other MMPI-2 scales that measure cynicism and hostility (i.e., CYN, TPA, and ASP). In addition, high Ho scorers, based upon spousal ratings, were considered hotheaded, bossy, demanding, and argumentative. In interpretation, high-Ho clients are seen as possessing personality characteristics of cynicism and hostility. Low scores on the Ho are not interpreted as being low in hostility because only high point scores have been validated thus far.

Marital Distress Scale

The presence of relationship problems in patients entering therapy can be deterrents to progress. Relationship problems, especially those not disclosed in early treatment sessions, can be disruptive to the treatment process. Personality factors addressed by the MMPI-2 can provide valuable information as to potential problems or attitudes that might be coloring a client's relationships within his or her marriage.

Most of the research on using the original MMPI with couples in therapy involved exploring the personality profiles of husbands and wives using the traditional clinical scales. Studies of marital distress typically found that the Pd scale was the most frequently elevated scale among individuals experiencing marital problems (Hjemboe & Butcher, 1991). However, scale elevations on Pd are associated with many things other than just marital problems (e.g., anger control, impulsivity). With the publication of MMPI-2, research on couples in marital distress also found Pd to be the most prominent scale elevation, but one of the new content scales, Family Problems (FAM), was also found to be significantly related to marital distress. These scales were not originally developed to assess marital problems directly (Hjemboe & Butcher, 1991). Therefore, Hjemboe, Almagor, and Butcher (1992) developed an empirical MMPI-2 scale for assessing marital distress that focuses specifically on marital relationship problems.

The Marital Distress Scale (MDS) is a 14-item empirically derived scale designed to focus upon marital problems. Items were selected that were strongly associated with a measure of marital distress, the Spanier Dyadic Adjustment Scale. This item content for MDS relates to marital problems or relationship difficulties. As one would expect, the MDS shows a higher degree of relationship to measured marital distress than either the Pd or the FAM (Hjemboe et al., 1992).

Couples who are having marital problems typically describe these concerns openly to the clinician in an interview. It is therefore not surprising that they might also have a high MDS score. However, the MDS might be most valuable in the treatment context when it provides information that the clinician does not know—that is, when the MDS is elevated in a mental health treatment setting when the person is reporting other mental health problems or when marital problems were not the reason for referral. The MDS can signal problems of which the client is unaware or at least not reporting in interview.

The Assessment of Posttraumatic Stress Disorder (Keane PTSD Scale)

Many clients entering psychotherapy have recently experienced trauma of some sort such as failed relationships, an accident, military or terroristic trauma, and so forth. Moreover, a large number of people entering therapy have experienced traumas in the past that linger on as important and continuing sources of concern for the person. The evaluation of past trauma is usually an important step in the early stages of treatment.

One MMPI-2 scale, the Post-Traumatic Stress Disorder Scale (PTSD-Pk), was developed by Keane, Malloy, and Fairbank (1984) and has received a great deal of research attention in the past 20 years (Penk et al., 2006). In the development of the PTSD scale, the authors followed an empirical scale construction strategy. They used a group of 100 male veterans who had been diagnosed with PTSD in contrast with 100 male veterans having other psychiatric problems. They obtained 49 items that significantly discriminated the PTSD group from the general psychiatric sample. They found that this scale had an 82% "hit rate" in the classification of veterans with PTSD. The Pk shows a high degree of relationship to other anxiety measures on the MMPI-2 such as the Pt and is negatively correlated with the K. The Pk has been found to measure psychological distress, although not necessarily acute problems. The scale is also often elevated in samples of chronic psychiatric patients (Arbisi, 2006). (For a comprehensive review of the use of the MMPI-2 with PTSD clients see Penk et al., 2006.)

Personality-Based Measures and Stable Personality Features

Several personality measures have been developed for the MMPI-2 that assess long-term personality characteristics that would be important for a therapist to be aware of in assessing the client's capability of modifying his or her behavior in treatment.

The Personality Psychopathology Five (PSY-5) Scales

Harkness, McNulty, Ben-Porath, and Graham (1999, 2002) developed the Psychopathology Five (PSY-5) scales as a strategy for assessing the "Big Five" personality dimensions for psychopathology from the MMPI-2 item pool. In the development of these measures, Harkness and his colleagues studied how laypeople classified or described the personality of others. The PSY-5 concepts, as defined by Harkness (1992), serve as summary concepts of the psychological distance—a measurement of how similar or different two objects or concepts seem to individual people when viewing others. These scales can provide useful summary personality dimensions that describe personality functioning that would be manifest through the course of therapy since they address persistent personality characteristics of the client.

Aggressiveness (AGGR) This PSY-5 scale assesses behaviors and attitudes characterized as an aggressive personality style. This scale assesses offensive and instrumental aggression rather than aggression that is reactive to behavior of others. High AGGR scorers might intimidate others and use aggression as a way of accomplishing their goals. They apparently have characteristics of dominance and hate. Studies have shown that both men and women with high AGGR scores were more likely to have a history of being physically abusive toward others (Graham et al., 1999). In this research, the investigators found that therapists rated the high-AGGR patients as having both aggressive and antisocial features. For example, high-AGGR men were more likely to have histories of domestic violence and high-AGGR women were found to be more likely to have been arrested than low-AGGR women.

Psychoticism (PSYC)   The PSYC scale addresses whether the client experiences a mental disconnection from reality. The content on the scale contains items that address unusual sensory and perceptual experiences, delusional beliefs, and other peculiar behaviors or attitudes. Persons who score high also acknowledge experiencing alienation from others and unrealistic expectation of harm from other people. They tend to have a greater likelihood of experiencing psychotic behavior such as delusions of reference, disorganized thinking, bizarre behavior, and disoriented, circumstantial, or tangential thought processes. Those being seen on an inpatient basis are found to be more likely to manifest psychotic-like behavior such as paranoid suspiciousness, ideas of reference, loosening of associations, hallucination, or flight of ideas. Outpatients, as noted by Graham et al. (1999), had low rates of frank psychosis; however, those with elevated PSYC-scale scores were reported to have generally lower functioning and to have few or no friends. They were also found to be depressed on mental status examination. In this study, therapists rated high-PSYC patients as low in achievement orientation. High-PSYC men were described as being depressed by their therapists. High-PSYC women showed a tendency to report more hallucinations at intake in inpatient settings than women with low scores.

Disconstraint (DISC)   This scale was developed to provide an assessment of a client's potential to act impulsively. This pattern of impulsive behavior can involve three aspects: (a) accepting a higher level of physical risk-taking, (b) possessing a style characterized more by impulsivity than control, and (c) being less confined by traditional moral constraints. According to Harkness and colleagues, this dimension is closely related to Zuckerman's high-scoring "Sensation Seekers" (Zuckerman et al., 1972). People who score high on DISC have difficulty learning from past behavior or punishing experiences and tend to repeat their acting out over time.

High scorers on DISC tend to be high risk-takers; they are impulsive and nonconforming in their approach to life. They tend to become easily bored and do not like routine activities. In the Graham et al. outpatient sample (1999) outpatients who scored high on DISC had a history of being arrested and reported extensive alcohol, cocaine, and marijuana abuse. High DISC scorers were rated by therapists in the study by Graham et al. as both aggressive and antisocial. The outpatient high-DISC men had histories of perpetrating domestic violence.

Negative Emotionality/Neuroticism (NEGE)   The NEGE scale addresses the high degree of negative feeling and dysphoria that many people in mental health settings experience. High scorers tend to focus on problems rather than positive events in their lives. They tend to worry to excess over minor events and tend to be highly self-critical. They usually evaluate possible outcomes as negative when faced with uncertainty. Graham et al. (1999) reported that outpatients in their study were more likely to be given diagnoses with depression or dysthymic disorder. Therapists rated them as generally low functioning. High scorers also tended to complain a lot about physical problems.

Introversion/Low Positive Emotionality (INTR)   The PSY-5 INTR scale addresses the capacity of the client to experience feeling good and to work effectively with others. High scorers show little capacity to experience pleasure and are viewed as low in positive relations with others. They report a low ability to enjoy life, referred to as being low in "hedonic capacity." Both high-scoring men and women report being introverted and depressed. In the study by Graham et al. (1999), high INTR scorers were seen as depressed and sad in their interviews. They tended also to have low achievement motivation and were seen as overly anxious, depressed, introverted, and pessimistic by their therapists. They complained of numerous somatic symptoms.

Case 4.2 Case of an Uncooperative Marital Counseling Referral

Orville C., a 28-year-old long-distance truck driver, entered marital counseling at the insistence of his wife, Angela. Orville was reluctant to enter psychological treatment; he complained that his job kept him on the road much of the time and he couldn't take time away for therapy. They have been married for 3 years and have one child, age 1.5. Angela indicated to the therapist that Orville had been physically abusive toward her and that she was afraid he would hurt her or their child. During the initial treatment session, Orville was somewhat sullen and noncommunicative. He chose not to follow up for the scheduled second session.

In the MMPI-2 that was administered at the end of the initial session, Orville was somewhat defensive (K score of 64, L score of 60); his most prominent clinical scale elevation was on Pd (T at 70). His PSY-5 scores on AGGR and DISC showed a strong tendency for Orville to be angry and overly aggressive toward others. In addition, he showed an impulsive and nonconforming lifestyle (see the PSY-5 scale profile in Fig. 4.3).

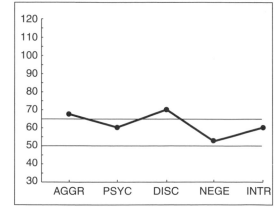

Figure 4.3. The MMPI-2 PSY-5 scale scores for Orville C.

No follow-up information is available because they did not return for additional sessions.

General Scales Providing Treatment-Related Information

Some MMPI-2 scales were developed with specific focus in the treatment context. Three measures—the Ego Strength Scale, the Responsibility Scale, and the College Maladjustment Scale—that have been widely used in providing the therapist with information about client functioning will be summarized.

The Ego Strength (Es) Scale

Rather early in MMPI history, clinical researchers saw promise in using the MMPI for predicting a client's response to psychological treatment and for determining which personality characteristics lead to treatment success or end in treatment failure. One interesting attempt to develop a specific scale to measure personality characteristics associated with a successful outcome in therapy resulted in the construction of the Ego Strength (Es) scale. The Es scale was developed by Barron (1953) to help predict whether an individual is likely to respond well to therapy.

The Es scale was developed by empirical scale construction procedures. Barron divided a sample of 33 patients into 17 patients who had been judged by their therapists to have clearly improved and 16 who were judged to be unimproved. The test responses of the patients were obtained before the therapy had begun. The scale was proposed as a pretreatment measure of prognosis for therapy. As the Es scale began to be used, and content analysis and intercorrelational studies followed, the meaning of the scale came to be viewed as a measure of adaptability and personal resourcefulness or the ability to manage stressful situations rather than as a predictor of treatment response.

In the revision of the MMPI, the MMPI Restandardization Committee deleted a number of items that were outmoded or objectionable. Sixteen items from the Es scale were among those deleted in the revision; consequently, the MMPI-2 version of Es contains 52 items.

An examination of the content of the Es scale suggests that no single unitary personality dimension is represented by the scale, but it is the sum of a number of complex adjustment factors. The Es scale contains items that can be grouped into the following categories by content: physical functioning and physiological stability; psychasthenia and seclusiveness; moral posture; sense of reality; personal adequacy and ability to cope; phobias; and miscellaneous other content.

In some respects, the Es scale is a measure of problem denial or whether a person is able to manage current stressors. Early correlational research related high scores on the Es scale to such factors as resourcefulness, vitality, self-direction, psychological stability, permissive morality, outgoingness, and spontaneity. High scorers on the Es scale typically show more positive changes in treatment than do low scorers, according to Graham (2006). Graham has summarized the correlates for the Es scale as follows.

A number of personality characteristics have been associated with high and low scores on the Es scale. People with high Es are thought *not* to be experiencing chronic psychopathology and are viewed as more stable, reliable, and responsible than others. They are thought to be alert, energetic, and adventuresome in their approach to life. They are considered to be tolerant in their views of others and to lack prejudice. They show a high degree of self-confidence and may be outspoken and sociable. Individuals with high scores on Es are thought to be resourceful, independent, and grounded in reality. Socially, they are thought to be effective in dealing with others and easily gain social acceptance. Individuals with high Es scores often seek help because of situational problems. They can usually manage verbal interchange and confrontation in psychotherapy without deteriorating psychologically. They can usually tolerate confrontations in therapy.

Individuals who score low on the Es scale are considered to have low self-esteem and a poor self-concept. They tend to feel worthless and helpless and have difficulty managing daily affairs. In an interview they may appear confused and disorganized and are likely to have a wide range of psychological symptoms, such as chronic physical complaints, chronic fatigue, fears, or phobias. They are likely to appear withdrawn, seclusive, overly inhibited, rigid, and moralistic. They are often seen by the therapist as maladaptive, unoriginal, and stereotyped in behavior. They are likely to demonstrate exaggerated problems or a "cry for help," have work problems, and show more susceptibility to experiencing day-to-day crises. Their problems are more likely to be viewed as characterological rather than situational in nature. They are likely to express a desire for psychotherapy and feel the need to resolve their many problems; however, it may be difficult for them to focus on problems.

Readers interested in a more extensive discussion of the Es scale should see Graham (2006).

Case History: The Value of Using the Es Scale in Treatment Planning

Sybil, the patient whose MMPI-2 profile is shown in Figure 4.4, is a 37-year-old single woman who lives with her parents. Her father is a semi-invalid but financially well-off retired businessman. Her mother, a successful attorney and partner in a large law firm, travels a great deal on business. Sybil was a rather reclusive woman with a substantial history of mental illness. She has been hospitalized on three occasions for depression and in each instance improved to the point that she could resume her limited activities. She did not finish college because of an early and seemingly poorly planned marriage. Her husband left town after 6 months without telling anyone where he was going. After several years, with her parents' prompting, she obtained an annulment of her marriage. She has not dated anyone since her husband left.

Her MMPI profile (an extremely elevated 28) shows severe psychopathology. She appears to be quite depressed at the present testing and has problems with her thinking and emotions. She is confused and disorganized and has been experiencing auditory hallucinations. She is also experiencing intense moods that are characterized by anger and despair. She shows some

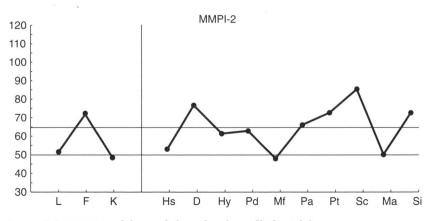

Figure 4.4. MMPI-2 validity and clinical scale profile for Sybil.

suicidal preoccupation. In the past, she has attempted to kill herself on two occasions.

Her poor prognosis for outpatient, insight-oriented psychological treatment is shown by her extremely low score on the Es scale (T = 35). Her Es score suggests that she has a very poor self-concept and low morale, is confused and fearful, and has chronic problems.

Problems in Interpreting the Es Scale in Treatment Planning   Although the Es scale provides the clinician with a measure of the patient's adjustment level and ability to cope with life stressors, it does not fulfill the original hope of being a predictor of treatment amenability that one could use in pretreatment evaluation to appraise potential treatment success. As an index of adjustment, it appears to be a redundant measure of general maladjustment measures, of which there are several in the MMPI-2, such as the Pt scale.

One difficulty in using the Es scale in clinical interpretation is that the scale contains a generally heterogeneous group of items, making substantive interpretation difficult. Several items on the Es scale have little content relevance to treatment prediction. These items were probably included on the scale as a result of chance, since the original scale construction used small sample sizes. For example, in the original MMPI the item "I like Lincoln better than Washington" has neither appropriate content nor empirical validity for the construct being assessed.

The most useful interpretations for the Es scale in treatment prediction were noted by Graham (2006). Graham pointed out, for example, that those who score high on the Es scale typically are better adjusted psychologically and are more able to cope with problems and stresses in their lives. Moreover, he pointed out that high scores on the Es scale indicate persons who have fewer and less severe symptoms and tend to lack chronic psychopathology. They usually are stable, reliable, and responsible; are tolerant and lack prejudice; and are alert, energetic, and adventuresome. They tend to be sensation seekers who are determined and persistent and may be opportunistic and manipulative. They usually are self-confident, outspoken, and sociable, deal effectively with others, and tend to create favorable initial impressions. Graham also noted that high-Es clients tend to seek help because of situational problems and can usually tolerate confrontations in psychotherapy. (For further discussion see Graham, 2006, pp. 182–185.)

In summary, people with low Es scores do not seem to be very well put together. Such individuals are likely to be seriously maladjusted psychologically. Problems are likely to be longstanding in nature; personal resources for coping with problems are extremely limited; and the progress for positive change in psychotherapy is poor. Graham (2006) also noted that low Es responders do not seem to have many psychological resources for coping with stress, and the prognosis for change in treatment for these persons is not very positive.

Responsibility Scale (Re)

In many pretreatment evaluations it is desirable to assess whether the person entering therapy assumes responsibility for himself or herself and whether he or she approaches social relationships in a responsible manner. People tend to respond to treatment and are more willing to alter their negative behaviors if they care about themselves and others. One possible measure that reflects whether a person possesses social responsibility is the Re scale developed by Gough, McClosky, and Meehl (1952). They developed the Re scale empirically by employing groups of people who had been rated (by peers or by teachers) as "most" or "least" responsible in their group. Responsible individuals were viewed as those who were willing to accept the consequences of their own behavior, were viewed as dependable and trustworthy, were thought to have high integrity, and were believed to possess a sense of obligation to others. Four groups of subjects were employed in the study (50 college men and 50 college women, 123 social science students from a high school, and 221 ninth-graders). The MMPI items that became the Re scale were those that empirically discriminated the most responsible from the least responsible people. The item content centered on espousing conventional behavior versus rebelliousness, social consciousness, emphasis upon duty and self-discipline, concern over moral issues, possession of personal security and poise, and disapproval of favoritism and privilege. The MMPI Restandardization Committee, in the final item selection for MMPI-2, eliminated two items from the Re scale as objectionable, bringing the total number of items on Re in the MMPI-2 to 32. The reduction in items did not result in a reduction in scale reliability: the test–retest correlations for Re reported for the MMPI-2 (Butcher et al., 1989) was 0.85 for males and 0.74 for females. This is consistent with the test–retest reliabilities (0.85 for males and 0.76 for females) reported by Moreland (1985) for the original MMPI.

Individuals who score high on Re, a T score above 65, are viewed as having a great deal of self-confidence and a generally optimistic, positive view toward the world. They are considered by others as conventional and conforming. They are seen as having a strong sense of justice and a deep concern over ethical and moral problems. They are thought to have a strong sense of fairness and justice, tend to set high standards for themselves, and manage their responsibilities well.

On the other hand, low scorers (below a T score of 40) are viewed as *not* accepting responsibilities well. They are considered undependable, untrustworthy, and lacking in integrity. The low-Re person is usually viewed as not having leadership potential because he or she lacks social concern and interest in others.

High scores on the Re scale in one's therapy patient can provide some reassurance that the client is likely to approach his or her relationships and daily activities with more self-confidence and social concern than people who make up the lower end of the distribution of Re scores. Low scorers, on the other hand, are likely to be more unconventional in their approach to others and too caught up in their own turmoil to concern themselves with "doing what is the right thing" with regard to others. Low-Re clients are often those who are likely to behave in selfish, nonsocially oriented ways. They may require more assistance from the therapist in defining the boundaries of reality and in seeing the social consequences of their behavior.

The College Maladjustment (Mt) Scale (Kleinmuntz)

Therapists or counselors working in a college counseling setting are often at a loss to evaluate the nature and extent of problems being experienced by college students seeking help. Not only are the prospective student-clients manifesting symptoms of psychological disorder or personality problems, but they may also be experiencing a great deal of situational turmoil that is sometimes difficult to separate from more longstanding pathology. For example, many college students experience transitional problems related to working through autonomy and independence issues with their parents, or becoming involved in peer relationships can cause them great, though perhaps temporary, discomfort. As a result of turbulent situational problems, it may be difficult for the clinician to gain an accurate assessment of the individual.

The use of a college-specific assessment measure within the MMPI-2 might aid the clinician in obtaining an appropriate appraisal of students' problems. One measure developed to assess college maladjustment, the Mt scale developed by Kleinmuntz, might be a valuable addition to the college counselor's initial assessment strategy because it provides a specific appraisal of college students.

Kleinmuntz (1961) developed the Mt scale as an aid in discriminating emotionally adjusted college students from those who are maladjusted. The items for the scale were derived by contrasting maladjusted male and female students (obtained from a student counseling clinic) who were seen in therapy for at least three sessions from 40 male and female well-adjusted students (students being evaluated in the context of a teacher certification program). In the original scale development 43 items were identified that separated the groups. Items were keyed so that endorsement increased the probability that the individual was in the maladjustment group. The MMPI revision process (see Butcher et al., 1989) eliminated 2 items on the Mt scale; consequently, the revised version of the scale on MMPI-2 contains 41 items.

The Mt scale has been shown to have high test–retest reliability. Kleinmuntz (1961) reported a test–retest reliability of 0.88; Moreland (1985) reported 6-week test–retest correlations ranging from 0.86 for females to 0.89 for males; and Butcher et al. (1989) reported 1-week test–retest correlations of 0.91 for males and 0.90 for females.

The Mt scale is thought to measure severe psychopathology in college students (Lauterbach, Garcia, & Gloster, 2002; Wilderman, 1984), and research has addressed the question of how effectively the scale predicts future emotional problems. Kleinmuntz (1961) concluded that the scale is more appropriate for detecting existing psychopathology than for predicting future emotional problems. Barthlow, Graham, Ben-Porath, and McNulty (2004) conducted a construct validity study of the Mt scale, reporting that a factor analysis of the scale revealed three main factors:

1. "Low Self Esteem," or the tendency to lack self-confidence and to make negative comparisons with others
2. "Lack of Energy," including such content as feeling tired and having difficulty starting to do things
3. "Cynicism/restlessness," including themes such as having ideas that are too bad to talk about, and restlessness

Students who score high on the Mt scale are viewed as being generally maladjusted, anxious, worried, and ineffective in dealing with current situations, tending to procrastinate rather than to complete tasks, and tending to have a pessimistic, negative outlook on life.

The college counselor whose counselee has high Mt scores needs to be aware that the student is reporting substantial psychological problems and probably requires a treatment program that addresses the significant personal problems and goes beyond simple academic counseling.

Summary

This chapter has presented information about several MMPI-2 supplementary scales that have relevance and potential utility in treatment-oriented assessment. The three widely used substance abuse indicators (MAC-R, APS, and AAS) were described and illustrated. The MAC-R and APS scales measure addiction potential, an important assessment concern in most pretherapy evaluations, while the AAS assesses the extent to which the client is willing to acknowledge substance abuse problems. Other measures that provide valuable symptomatic information were described, including the Ho scale, the MDS scale, and the PTSD scale. Three measures that address several problems common to many therapeutic settings were described. The Es scale, although developed to provide a measure of treatment potential, actually provides more information about a person's present ability to tolerate stress. Low scores on Es appear to reflect an inability to deal effectively with current problems. The Re scale can provide the clinician with information about how a client assumes responsibility and conforms to the values of society. Finally, for clinicians working in college counseling settings, the Mt scale might provide a perspective on the level of maladjustment experienced by college students who seek counseling.

In the next chapter, we turn to an interpretive approach that emphasizes the client's acknowledgment of problems through his or her response to the test item content—an approach that is very different from the traditional MMPI-2 test development strategies.

5

MMPI-2 Content Indicators in Evaluating Therapy Patients

The traditional interpretive approach for MMPI scales and profile codes involves the application of empirical correlates to scale scores and patterns. These empirically derived behaviors provide a solid basis for clinical description and prediction of behavior from the individual's self-report. The major strengths of this approach lie in the extensive external validation of the MMPI scales and profile codes; they provide valid and reliable test correlates that can confidently be applied to a broad range of treatment cases. One disadvantage to the MMPI empirical scale approach is that the heterogeneous item content of the scales makes face valid or intuitive interpretative statements difficult at times. In other words, items that empirically separate groups or prove themselves to be valid predictors may not "hang together" or be intuitively related to what the patient tells the therapist. The empirical correlates of the clinical scales, with rather heterogeneous content, may not be as intuitively understandable as are interpretations that are based on content-homogeneous scales.

There are a number of valuable content indicators for the MMPI-2 that can add immeasurably to the therapist's information about a client. By viewing the patient's responses to item content, the therapist can obtain valuable clues to the person's specific feelings, attitudes, problems, and resources.

Content interpretation is based on different assumptions from that of MMPI empirical scale elevations or code type analyses. One major assumption underlying content interpretation is that the subject *wishes* to reveal his or her ideas, attitudes, beliefs, and problems and *cooperates* with the testing. People taking the MMPI under clinical conditions usually provide accurate personality information. Subjects taking the MMPI under pressure or court order or in employment-selection situations, however, may distort their responses to create a particular impression. In these cases the content themes may not accurately portray the individual's problems.

This chapter addresses several approaches to summarizing important content themes in the patient's MMPI-2 and provides the therapist with clues to how this substantive information can be employed to shed light on the patient's view of his or her problems. Several ways of evaluating content themes in the MMPI-2 will be described and illustrated in this chapter: "critical" items, rationally derived content subscales, empirically developed subscales, and the MMPI-2 content scales.

The Critical Item Approach

The most direct approach to assessing content themes in the MMPI is to examine the patient's actual responses to individual items. The *critical item approach,* as this strategy has been called, involves using individual MMPI items as a means of detecting specific content themes or special problems the patient is reportedly experiencing. The critical item approach assumes that the patient responds to items as symptoms or problems, and reports his or her feelings accurately. The critical item or pathognomic indicator is one of the earliest approaches to personality test interpretation. In fact, Woodworth (1920), in his pioneering work on the Personal Data Sheet, included what he called "starred items," or pathognomic contents, that were believed to have a particular significance if answered in a pathological direction.

Of course, evaluation of specific items by reading through the record is a cumbersome and confusing way of attempting to understand the content, since there are too many bits of information to readily organize and integrate. Consequently, the clinician needs some ways of organizing or hierarchically arranging the items in order of importance before examining specific items. Early critical item approaches, such as the Grayson Critical Items (Grayson, 1951) or the Caldwell Critical Items, were largely developed by their authors by simply reading through the items and selecting those believed to reflect particular problems. Neither of these early sets of critical items was ever validated to determine if the specific items used were tapping uniquely important problems. The items were simply adapted for clinical or computerized psychological test use on the basis of the clinician's hunch that the item measured highly significant or "critical" problem areas.

There are two sets of MMPI-2 critical items that were empirically derived to aid the clinician in assessing specific problems of concern: the Koss–Butcher Critical Item List and the Lachar–Wroble Critical Item List.

The Koss–Butcher Critical Item List

Koss and Butcher (1973) were concerned that the existing sets of critical items were being used as indicators of specific pathology without an empirical data base for such predictions. In other words, the Grayson and Caldwell item groupings were initially developed by a rational examination of the item pool and were not actually empirically related to clinical problems in a valid way. Koss and Butcher (1973), Koss, Butcher, and Hoffman (1976), and Koss (1979) conducted empirical investigations of item responses and their relationships to psychiatric status for patients at admission to a psychiatric facility. They evaluated the effectiveness of the Grayson and Caldwell critical item lists for detecting crisis states and developed a new set of empirically based critical items that discriminated among presenting problems experienced by psychiatric patients at admission.

Koss and Butcher (1973) first defined several "crisis situations" that were frequently found among individuals seeking admission to a psychiatric facility. They interviewed several clinicians as to what were important crises that would require evaluation in clinical settings. Six crisis situations were thought to be particularly important because of their frequency or their significance:

1. Suicidal depression
2. Anxiety state
3. Threatened assault
4. Alcoholic crisis
5. Paranoia
6. Psychotic distortion

Koss and Butcher then reviewed presenting problems for more than 1,200 cases admitted to the Minneapolis Veterans Administration Hospital and grouped together individuals with similar problems. Then they performed an item analysis to detect MMPI items that discriminated the various crisis groups from each other and from a control group of general psychiatric patients. The resulting Koss–Butcher Critical Item List contains items that validly discriminated the crisis conditions.

The Koss–Butcher Critical Item List was expanded in the MMPI revision to incorporate new item contents of importance in the assessment of two major problem areas: substance abuse and suicidal threats. A number of new items have been added to the MMPI-2 for assessment of special problem areas, including four new items that empirically separate alcohol- and drug-abusing patients from other groups, which have been added to the Alcohol Crisis group, and four new items dealing with depression and suicide, which have been added to the Depressed–Suicidal Crisis group.

The Lachar–Wrobel Critical Item List

In a subsequent study, Lachar and Wrobel (1979) replicated about two thirds of the Koss–Butcher list and developed an expanded critical item list to include several other crisis categories.

Use of Critical Items

The most appropriate use of critical items is for detecting specific problems or attitudes the patient is reporting that might not be reflected in the clinical profile elevations. In this way significant themes are highlighted and can be used to illustrate inferences from the clinical scales or code type information. A case illustration highlights the effectiveness with which groups of similar items can reflect particularly pertinent problem areas.

Case History: Use of Critical Items in Evaluating Specific Problems

Charles D., a 48-year-old divorced post office employee, was referred for psychological evaluation by his physician, who had some concerns that he was clinically depressed. He was an introverted, shy man who had very little personal contact with other people. He had been working ineffectively for several months and had been absent from work a great deal. He had no close friends. When he was seen by the physician he reported extreme fatigue, lethargy, lack of energy, and a loss of interest in life.

After his referral to a psychotherapist, he was administered the MMPI-2 (see profile in Fig. 5.1). Although his clinical profile elevation was not marked, he nevertheless reported a number of significant problems, as noted in his endorsement of Koss–Butcher critical items (Table 5.1). He endorsed most of the items on the Depressed–Suicidal cluster, reflecting a considerably depressed mood and little interest in life. Given his highly dysphoric mood, suicidal ideation, and lack of a support network, outpatient treatment was not thought to be feasible. Instead, it was recommended that he be hospitalized in an inpatient program for treatment of his major affective disorder.

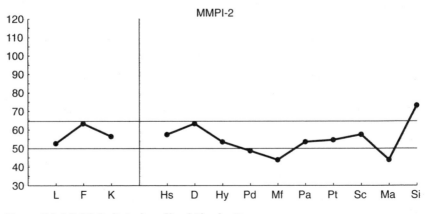

Figure 5.1. MMPI-2 clinical profile of Charles D.

Table 5.1.   Critical Item Content on the
Depressed Suicidal Group Endorsed by Charles D.

38.	(T)
65.	(T)
71.	(T)
95.	(F)
130.	(T)
146.	(T)
215.	(T)
233.	(T)
273.	(T)
303.	(T)
306.	(T)
388.	(F)
411.	(T)
454.	(T)
485.	(T)
506.	(T)
520.	(T)
524.	(T)

Limitations of the Critical Item Approach to Content Interpretation

The clinician needs to understand that although the critical item approach can provide important clues to specific problems the patient is experiencing, there are some clear limitations to this approach to MMPI interpretation.

1. *Limited range of problems.* The types of problems shown by the critical items are, of course, limited by the range of problems reflected in the categories employed. The critical item lists employed here address relatively few problem areas. Patients may be experiencing severe and debilitating problems that are not represented in published critical item lists.
2. *Unreliability of brief measures.* Responses to items can be very unreliable and should not be given the weight in interpretation that clinical scales and codes are given. Patients sometimes make mistakes or answer items incorrectly. The response to a particular item could be a mistake.

Critical item responses should be seen as possible hypotheses about specific problems that the patient might be experiencing. Clinicians should attempt to obtain more reliable information—for example, by the patient's response to scales—about suggested interpretations obtained from critical item responses.

MMPI-2 Content Subscales

The discussion in this section focuses on two sets of MMPI-2 content subscales or item groups containing similar content within an MMPI scale. The first group of subscales described is the Harris-Lingoes MMPI-2 subscales for D, Hy, Pd, Pa, Sc, and Ma. The second group of subscales is the MMPI-2 Si subscales developed by Hostetler, Ben-Porath, Butcher, and Graham (1989). The third group is the S scale (Butcher & Han, 1995) subscales described in Chapter 2.

Rationally Derived Content Subgroups: The Harris–Lingoes Subscales

The Harris–Lingoes subscales are item subsets that were developed for six of the MMPI empirical scales by rational analysis. Harris and Lingoes (1955) constructed their item subgroups by reading through the items on the D, Hy, Pd, Pa, Sc, and Ma scales and rationally grouping the items according to content themes. The authors did not provide subscales for scales 1 (Hs) and 7 (Pt) because these scales were believed to be "naturally" homogeneous in content and not subject to further reduction into subthemes. The Hs scale contains strictly somatic problems, and the Pt scale comprises anxiety indicators. A listing of the Harris–Lingoes subscales is given in Table 5.2.

Table 5.2   Description of the Harris–Lingoes Subscales for the MMPI-2

Scale 1   Hypochondriasis: None
Scale 2   Depression *D1—Subjective Depression   32 items* High scores suggest: feeling depressed, unhappy, nervous; lacks energy and interest; not coping well; problems in concentration and attention; feels inferior; lacks self-confidence; shy and uneasy in social situations feels inferior; lacks self-confidence *D2—Psychomotor Retardation   14 items* High scores suggest: immobilized, withdrawn; lacks energy; avoids people; denies hostility *D3—Physical Malfunctioning   11 items* High scores suggest: preoccupied with physical functioning; denies good health; wide variety of somatic complaints *D4—Mental Dullness   15 items* High scores suggest: lacks energy; feels tense; has problems in concentration and attention; lacks self-confidence; feels life is not worthwhile

(continued)

Table 5.2. *(continued)*

D5—*Brooding*   10 items
High scores suggest: broods, ruminates; lacks energy; feels inferior; feels life is
not worth living; easily hurt by criticism; feels like losing control of thought
process

Scale 3   Hysteria

Hy1—Denial of Social Anxiety   6 items
High scores suggest: socially extroverted and comfortable; not easily influenced
by social standards and customs
Hy2—Need for Affection   12 items
High scores suggest: strong needs for attention and affection; sensitive, optimistic,
trusting; avoids confrontations; denies negative feelings toward others
Hy3—Lassitude, Malaise   15 items
High scores suggest: uncomfortable and not in good health; tired, weak, fatigue;
problems in concentration; poor appetite; sleep disturbance; unhappy
Hy4—Somatic Complaints   17 items
High scores suggest: multiple somatic complaints; utilizes repression and
conversion of affect; little or no hostility expressed
Hy5—Inhibition of Aggression   7 items
High scores suggest: denies hostile and aggressive impulses; sensitive about
response of others

Scale 4   Psychopathic Deviate

Pd1—Familial Discord   9 items
High scores suggest: views home situation as unpleasant and lacking in love,
support, understanding; family critical and controlling
Pd2—Authority Problems   8 items
High scores suggest: resents authority; trouble in school and with law; definite
opinions about right and wrong; stands up for beliefs
Pd3—Social Imperturbability   6 items
High scores suggest: comfortable and confident in social situations; exhibitionistic;
defends opinions
Pd4—Social Alienation   13 items
High scores suggest: feels misunderstood, alienated, isolated, estranged; lonely,
unhappy, uninvolved; blames others; self-centered, inconsiderate; verbalizes
regret and remorse
Pd5—Self-Alienation   12 items
High scores suggest: uncomfortable, unhappy; problems in concentration;
life not interesting or rewarding; hard to settle down; excessive use of alcohol

Scale 6   Paranoia

Pa1—Persecutory Ideas   17 items
High scores suggest: views world as threatening; feels misunderstood, unfairly
blamed or punished; suspicious, untrusting; blames others; sometimes delusions
of persecution
Pa2—Poignancy   9 items
High scores suggest: sees self as high-strung, sensitive, feeling more intensely
than others; feels lonely, misunderstood; looks for risk and excitement

(continued)

Table 5.2. (*continued*)

Pa3—*Naïveté*   9 items
High scores suggest: extremely naïve and optimistic attitudes toward others; trusting; high moral standards; denies hostility

Scale 7   Psychasthenia: None

Scale 8   Schizophrenia
Sc1—*Social Alienation* 21 items
High scores suggest: feels misunderstood, mistreated; family situation lacking in love and support; lonely, empty; hostility, hatred toward family; never experienced love relation ship
Sc2—*Emotional Alienation*   11 items
High scores suggest: depression, despair; wishes he or she were dead; frightened, apathetic
Sc3—*Lack of Ego Mastery, Cognitive*   10 items
High scores suggest: fears losing mind; strange thought processes; feelings of unreality; problems with concentration, attention
Sc4—*Lack of Ego Mastery, Conative*   14 items
High scores suggest: fears losing mind; strange thought processes; feelings of unreality; problems with concentration, attention
Sc5—*Lack of Ego Mastery, Defective Inhibition*   11 items
High scores suggest: feels out of control of emotions, impulses; restless, hyperactive, irritable; laughing or crying episodes; may not remember previously performed activities
Sc6—*Bizarre Sensory Experiences*   20 items
High scores suggest: feels body changing in unusual ways; hallucinations, unusual thoughts, external reference, skin sensitivity, weakness, ringing in ears, etc.

Scale 9   Hypomania
Ma1—*Amorality*   6 items
High scores suggest: sees others as selfish, dishonest and feels justified in being this way; derives vicarious satisfaction from manipulative exploits of others
Ma2—*Psychomotor Acceleration*   11 items
High scores suggest: accelerated speech, thought processes, motor activity; tense, restless; feels excited, elated without cause; easily bored; seeks out excitement; impulse to do harmful or shocking things
Ma3—*Imperturbability*   8 items
High scores suggest: denies social anxiety; not especially sensitive about what others think; impatient, irritable toward others
Ma4—*Ego Inflation*   9 items
High scores suggest: unrealistic self-appraisal; resentful of demands made by others

The Harris–Lingoes content subscales are used to provide the interpreter with clues to the specific problem dimensions that contribute to the high elevations on the scale. For example, if the patient has a high score on scale 8, say a T score of 80, an inspection of the Harris–Lingoes subscales might show that the individual's score on Subjective Depression is contributing substantially to the overall score. The relative prominence of Subjective Depression in the individual's clinical picture suggests that themes related to low mood should be given priority in the test interpretation.

The Harris–Lingoes subscales are interpreted according to the content of the specific scale on which they are contained. Interpretation proceeds by examining the relative contribution of the subscales to the overall elevation found on the significantly elevated clinical scale. For example, if the D scale is elevated above a T score of 65, then the most prominent subscale elevations (those also above T = 65) would be considered salient for interpretation.

The value of clarifying the meanings of MMPI-2 scale elevations by evaluating subscale content can be seen in the case illustration that follows. The MMPI-2 Pd scale elevations are usually thought to be stable and unchanging over time. The case illustrated in Figure 5.2 provides some useful additional interpretive information about scale 4.

Case History: Understanding Clinical Scale Elevation Through Homogeneous Content Groups

Susan F., a 35-year-old office worker, was referred for marital therapy by her physician. After the first two sessions it became clear that her husband, an aggressive and self-centered man, was unwilling to come to therapy. Susan decided to continue therapy herself and remained in treatment (cognitive–behavioral therapy) for about 6 months, making substantial improvement in her mood and changes in her life. After divorcing her husband, she became romantically involved with another man who was apparently more mature,

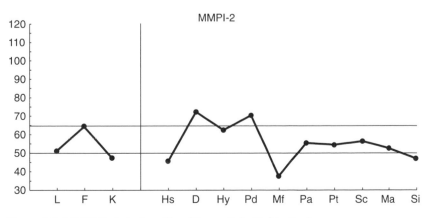

Figure 5.2. MMPI-2 clinical profile of Susan F. (initial testing).

better adjusted, and supportive than her ex-husband. Toward the end of treatment she was readministered the MMPI-2 prior to treatment termination. Her second MMPI-2 (Fig. 5.3) showed a marked change in two scales, Pd and D. Even the Pd scale, with its reputation for persistence over time, had diminished considerably at retest. The reasons for this reduction are evident when one views the Harris–Lingoes subscales for scale 4 (Table 5.3). The high elevations on the Pd and D scales at the initial testing were largely reflecting problems she was experiencing in her marital relationship; the problems were expressed through the content of the Family Problems and Subjective Depression subscales. When her relationships improved, her response to the second MMPI-2 showed diminished problems.

Clinicians using the MMPI-2 in evaluating clients in marital therapy might find that their clients' Pd-scale elevations (a frequent finding among marital therapy clients) can result from situationally based marital or family problems.

Limitations of Subscale Interpretation

There are some limitations to using the Harris–Lingoes content subgroups in MMPI-2 interpretation, particularly if the application involves comparing the T scores of subjects' subscales. Many of the Harris–Lingoes subfactors contain relatively few items, so the scale is likely to be relatively unreliable as a result of its brevity. Thus, the Harris–Lingoes scales are not as psychometrically reliable as longer scales and should be used clinically only as a guide to content interpretation, not as a psychometric predictor. For the most part, the Harris–Lingoes subscales are used to highlight or help the clinician focus on specific problems that are producing elevations on the clinical scales. The most prominent Harris–Lingoes elevation for a particular clinical scale can be used by the

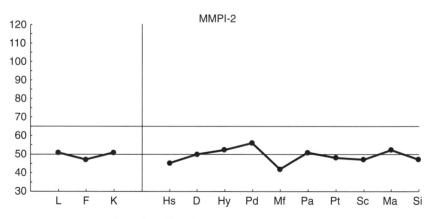

Figure 5.3. MMPI-2 clinical profile of Susan F. (second testing).

Table 5.3. Harris–Lingoes Pd Subscale Scores for Susan's Test and Retest on the MMPI-2

	T Scores First Testing	T Scores Second Testing
Pd1	80	57
Pd2	54	54
Pd3	58	54
Pd4	67	59
Pd5	55	67

clinician to determine which of the empirical correlates for that clinical scale elevation should be given the most prominence in the clinical report. The clinician should not interpret *all* subscale scores that appear to be elevated. Unless the clinical scale is elevated (greater than a T score of 65) and holds a prominent place in the profile code, the Harris–Lingoes subscales should not be interpreted. This strategy reduces the number of inconsistent or potentially contradictory statements in the diagnostic report.

The Si Subscales   Originally, the Mf and Si scales were not included in the Harris–Lingoes subclassification approach to the item content because these scales were not considered to be "clinical" scales and were less frequently included in clinical interpretation approaches. Recognizing the need for item on these scales, Serkownek (1975) developed a set of subscales for the original MMPI; however, these item groups were not considered sufficiently homogeneous by the MMPI Restandardization Committee (Butcher et al., 1989) to enable effective content interpretation and were not included in the MMPI-2 manual.

Hostetler, Ben-Porath, Butcher, and Graham (1989) developed a set of homogeneous subscales for the Si scale following a multistage approach involving both rational and empirical procedures. They initially conducted a series of factor analyses to identify homogeneous factors in the items making up the scale. The scales were refined by using item-scale correlations and rational analyses. The final set of three subscales (Table 5.4) was highly homogeneous (internal consistencies ranged from 0.75 to 0.82) and reliable (test–retest reliabilities ranged from 0.77 to 0.91).

Ben-Porath, Hostetler, Butcher, and Graham (1989) reported external correlates for the Si subscales. The correlates given in Table 5.5 were obtained from the MMPI-2 normative study (Butcher et al., 1989). The 822 normal marital couples from the MMPI-2 normative study rated each other on a number of personality variables. The most significant correlates for the Si subscales are informative. High scores on the Shyness subscale (Si1) are associated with such behaviors as acts very shy, avoids contact with people for no reason, does not

Table 5.4. Composition of the Si Subscales

Shyness/Self-Consciousness (Si1):	
True:	158, 161, 167, 185, 243, 265, 275, 289
False:	49, 262, 280, 321, 342, 360
Social Avoidance (Si2):	
True:	337, 367
False:	86, 340, 353, 359, 363, 370
Alienation (Self and Others) (Si3):	
True:	31, 56, 104, 110, 135, 284, 302, 308, 326, 328, 338, 347, 348, 358, 364, 368, 369

enjoy parties, is not talkative, and does not laugh and joke with other people. High scores on Social Avoidance (Si2) are viewed by spouses as follows: avoids contact with people, does not enjoy parties, and acts to keep people at a distance. High scorers on Self and Social Alienation (Si3) are viewed as having considerable psychological problems. They are seen as lacking in self-confidence, lacking an interest in things, being nervous and jittery, showing poor judgment, acting bored and restless, thinking others are talking about them, being suspicious of others, putting themselves down, lacking in creativity in solving problems, giving up too easily, blaming themselves for things that go wrong, and being unrealistic about their own abilities.

Interpretation of the Si subscales follows the same general strategies as that for the Harris–Lingoes subscales. Given significant elevations on the Si scale, an examination of the subscales could provide clues to the types of important content themes that contributed to the scale elevation. The relative prominence of these content themes gives the clinician interpretive descriptions to highlight in the diagnostic study.

The Si subscales (Ben-Porath et al., 1989; Hostetler et al., 1989) suggest the following personality characteristics to keep in mind for treatment planning.

Shyness (Si1)   High scorers feel shy around others, feel easily embarrassed, feel ill at ease in social situations, and feel uncomfortable as they enter new situations. Therapy is probably viewed by them as no different from other social contexts. High scorers on Si1 are likely to have initial problems feeling comfortable and relating to the therapist.

Social Avoidance (Si2)   High scores on this subscale reflect a great dislike of group activities, concerns about group participation, active efforts to avoid being in a crowd, dislike of parties and social events, and a strong aversion to interpersonal contacts. Individuals with high Si2 subscale scores are likely to report considerable difficulty with other people and with entering social or group situations. Some forms of behavior therapy in which the individual is encouraged to participate in social activities may be difficult to initiate since

Table 5.5. Correlation of Si Subscales with Spouse's Ratings

Item	Si1	Si2	Si3
Men (n = 822)			
Acts very shy	0.38	0.15	0.03
Avoids contact with people for no reason	0.23	0.20	0.08
Is friendly	−0.22	−0.15	−0.10
Talks too much	−0.19	−0.13	−0.05
Laughs and jokes with people	−0.19	−0.17	−0.01
Acts to keep people at a distance	0.18	0.17	0.11
Enjoys parties, entertainments, or having friends over	−0.18	−0.31	−0.04
Is self-confident	−0.18	−0.03	−0.15
Lacks an interest in things	−0.18	0.08	0.21
Gives up too easily	0.11	0.01	0.19
Is creative in solving problems and meeting challenges	−0.12	0.03	−0.19
Is unrealistic about own abilities	0.08	0.01	0.19
Is pleasant and relaxed	−0.10	0.01	−0.18
Women (n = 822)			
Acts very shy	0.33	0.18	0.13
Avoids contact with people for no reason	0.28	0.20	0.18
Enjoys parties, entertainments, or having friends over	−0.25	−0.32	−0.14
Acts to keep people at a distance	0.21	0.24	0.13
Is self-confident	−0.25	−0.11	−0.29
Gets nervous and jittery	0.13	0.03	0.25
Gives up too easily	0.14	0.06	0.24
Lacks an interest in things	0.15	0.07	0.24
Has many fears	0.11	0.05	0.23
Is creative in solving problems and meeting challenges	−0.18	0.01	−0.23
Shows sound judgment	−0.07	0.03	−0.22
Puts own self down	0.18	0.11	0.22
Acts bored and restless	0.08	0.03	0.22
Is unrealistic about own abilities	0.13	0.08	0.20
Worries and frets over little things	0.12	0.06	0.20
Has a very hard time making any decisions	0.12	0.01	0.20
Gets very sad or blue and is slow to come out of it	0.13	0.07	0.20
Thinks others are talking about her	0.13	0.02	0.20
Is suspicious of others	0.05	0.02	0.19
Blames self for things that go wrong	0.11	0.11	0.18
Lacks control over emotions	0.05	0.05	0.18
Is very concerned about death	0.10	0.08	0.18

the individual has a prominent, pathologic aversion to group settings. Various cognitive–behavioral approaches may be considered for these people.

Self–Other Alienation (Si3)   High scores on this subscale reflect personality traits that make the individual vulnerable to failure in social interactions. High scores reflect low self-esteem, low self-confidence, self-critical tendencies, self-doubt about personal judgment, and a feeling of being ineffective at determining one's own fate. High scores also reflect nervousness, fearfulness, and indecisiveness. In addition, high scores indicate that the person is suspicious of others, considers others to be malevolent, and thinks others are talking about him or her. High scores on Si3 show great self-doubt and concern about others. Such intense feelings of alienation are likely to be deterrents to treatment motivation and, if present, need to be preempted from producing a negative treatment outcome.

An attempt to develop similar subscales for the Mf scale was unsuccessful because of the lack of enough homogeneous subsets of Mf items to produce psychometrically sound scales.

The Superlative Self-Presentation Scale (S) Subscales

As noted in Chapter 3, the S subscales (Butcher & Han, 1995) can provide information about a client's defensiveness if his or her response approach has been to deny problems. People who score high on S endorse few minor faults and problems—considerably fewer than those who took the test in the MMPI-2 Restandardization Study. The S is associated with lower levels of symptoms and the admission of fewer negative personality characteristics than even the normative sample report. The S scale also provides a look into possible reasons why the individual was defensive. Five homogeneous content subscales on the S scale, if elevated, provide clues as to factors. These item component scales can focus the interpreter's attention on which of the items in S the test-taker has emphasized. For example, the test-taker may have endorsed (as many parents in custody evaluations do) relatively more items dealing with "Denial of moral flaws" or "Denial of irritability" than people in the general population endorse. High scores on a particular subscale grouping suggest extreme responding in asserting that they, for example, have the following:

- *Beliefs in human goodness* high scores reflect attitudes suggesting that the person's general view of the motivations of most people is unrealistic.
- *Serenity* high scores indicate that the person, unlike most people in mental health assessments, claims that he or she has no problems or difficulties that worry him or her, even minor problems.
- *Contentment with life* high scores suggest that the client claims that life, for him or her, is perfect and that he or she has no concerns.

- *Patience and denial of irritability and anger* high scores suggest that the client overly denies having anger or irritability.
- *Denial of moral flaws* high scorers, for example, emphatically assert that they have not engaged in behavior such as using marijuana or drinking alcohol to excess.

The MMPI-2 Content Scales

Wiggins (1966) developed a set of MMPI content scales that were representative of the major content dimensions in the MMPI item pool and that were psychometrically sound enough to operate as scales. Wiggins started with the 26 content categories defined by Hathaway and McKinley (1940) and later reduced the number of content groupings to 13 clusters of items. He applied internal consistency procedures to this revised set of items, producing 13 scales with homogeneous item content and with a large enough number of items to provide high scale reliability. The Wiggins content scales, which have been widely used and researched over the past 20 years, have provided valuable information for the MMPI interpreter. The scales are not available in the MMPI-2, however, since many items making up the scales were deleted from the inventory as outmoded or objectionable.

A new set of MMPI content scales was developed for the revised version of the MMPI by Butcher, Graham, Williams, and Ben-Porath (1990). These investigators developed 15 new content scales using the original items contained in the MMPI clinical and validity scales, some special scales, and many of the new items that were included in the revised version of the MMPI.

The MMPI-2 content scales were developed in stages. First, three raters independently sorted the 704 items in the experimental booklet of the revised MMPI (Form AX) and grouped similar items into related item groups. Next, provisional content scales were developed by including only items that all three raters agreed belonged to each of the content groupings. Next, using one of the normal samples collected for the MMPI restandardization study, the authors computed item-scale correlations for all of the 704 MMPI items with the total score for each of the provisional content scales. This procedure was implemented to eliminate items that had low item-scale correlations and to detect other possible items that were highly correlated with the provisional scale.

In the next step the homogeneity and internal consistency of the items on the working version of the content scales were computed. Items were kept on a scale if they correlated at a 0.50 level with the total score. One final step was undertaken to ensure discriminant validity among the content scales: items on a particular scale would be dropped if they correlated more highly with the total score of another scale.

The MMPI-2 normative sample of 1,138 males and 1,462 females was used in the development of the norms for the MMPI-2 content scales. An important feature of these new norms is that they were adjusted to fit the same uniform distributions as the clinical scales, making T scores on the two sets of scales highly comparable; this was not the case with the Wiggins scales. The final MMPI-2 content scales are described in Table 5.6.

Unlike the Harris–Lingoes subscales, the MMPI-2 content scales can safely be used psychometrically since they contain a sufficient number of items and substantial scale reliabilities. Interpretation of content scale scores typically proceeds by profiling the scores and inspecting the scale elevations for deviations. Content scale scores in the 65 T-score range and above are considered

Table 5.6   Description of the MMPI-2 Content Scales

1. *Anxiety* (ANX, 23 items): High scorers on ANX report general symptoms of anxiety, including tension, somatic problems (i.e., heart pounding and shortness of breath), sleep difficulties, worries, and poor concentration. They fear losing their minds, find life a strain, and have difficulties making decisions. They appear to be readily aware of these symptoms and problems and are willing to admit to them.
2. *Fears* (FRS, 23 items): A high score on FRS indicates an individual with many specific fears. These specific fears can include blood; high places; money; animals such as snakes, mice, or spiders; leaving home; fires, storms, and natural disasters; water; the dark; being indoors; and dirt.
3. *Obsessiveness* (OBS, 16 items): High scorers on OBS have tremendous difficulties making decisions and are likely to ruminate excessively about issues and problems, causing others to become impatient. Having to make changes distresses them, and they may report some compulsive behaviors like counting or saving unimportant things. They are excessive worriers who frequently become overwhelmed by their own thoughts.
4. *Depression* (DEP, 33 items): High scores on this scale characterize individuals with significant depressive thoughts. They report feeling blue, uncertain about their future, and uninterested in their lives. They are likely to brood, be unhappy, cry easily, and feel hopeless and empty. They may report thoughts of suicide or wishes that they were dead. They may believe that they are condemned or have committed unpardonable sins. Other people may not be viewed as a source of support.
5. *Health Concerns* (HEA, 36 items): Individuals with high scores on HEA report many physical symptoms across several body systems. Included are gastrointestinal symptoms (e.g., constipation, dizziness and fainting spells, paralysis), sensory problems (e.g., poor hearing or eyesight), cardiovascular symptoms (e.g., heart or chest pains), skin problems, pain (e.g., headaches, neck pains), or respiratory troubles (e.g., coughs, hay fever, or asthma). These individuals worry about their health and feel sicker than the average person.
6. *Bizarre Mentation* (BIZ, 24 items): Psychotic thought processes characterize individuals high on the BIZ scale. They may report auditory, visual, or olfactory hallucinations and may recognize that their thoughts are strange or peculiar. Paranoid ideation (e.g., the belief that they are being plotted against or that someone is trying to poison them) may be reported as well. These individuals may feel that they have a special mission or special powers.

(continued)

Table 5.5   (*continued*)

7. *Anger* (ANG, 16 items): High scores on the ANG scale suggest anger-control problems. These individuals report being irritable, grouchy, impatient, hot-headed, annoyed, and stubborn. They may lose self-control and report having been physically abusive toward people and objects.

8. *Cynicism* (CYN, 23 items): Misanthropic beliefs characterize high scorers on CYN. They expect hidden, negative motives behind the acts of others—for example, believing that most people are honest simply for fear of being caught. Other people are to be distrusted, for people use each other and are friendly only for selfish reasons. They likely hold negative attitudes about those close to them, including fellow workers, family, and friends.

9. *Antisocial Practices* (ASP, 22 items): In addition to holding similar misanthropic attitudes to high scorers on the CYN scale, high scorers on the ASP scale report problem behaviors during their school years and other antisocial practices like being in trouble with the law, stealing, or shoplifting. They report that they sometimes enjoy the antics of criminals and believe it is all right to get around the law, as long as it is not broken.

10. *Type A* (TPA, 19 items): High scorers on TPA are hard-driving, fast-moving, and work-oriented individuals who frequently become impatient, irritable, and annoyed. They do not like to wait or be interrupted. There is never enough time in a day for them to complete their tasks. They are direct and may be overbearing in their relationships with others.

11. *Low Self-Esteem* (LSE, 24 items): High scores on LSE characterize individuals with low opinions of themselves. They do not believe that they are liked by others or that they are important. They hold many negative attitudes about themselves, including beliefs that they are unattractive, awkward, clumsy, useless, and a burden to others. They certainly lack self-confidence and find it hard to accept compliments from others. They may be overwhelmed by all the faults they see in themselves.

12. *Social Discomfort* (SOD, 24 items): SOD high scorers are very uneasy around others, preferring to be by themselves. When in social situations, they are likely to sit alone rather than joining in the group. They see themselves as shy and dislike parties and other group events.

13. *Family Problems* (FAM, 25 items): Considerable family discord is reported by high scorers on FAM. Their families are described as lacking in love, quarrelsome, and unpleasant. They even may report hating members of their families. Their childhood may be portrayed as abusive, and marriages seen as unhappy and lacking in affection.

14. *Negative Work Attitudes* (WRK, 33 items): A high score on WRK is indicative of behaviors or attitudes likely to contribute to poor work performance. Some of the problems relate to low self-confidence, concentration difficulties, obsessiveness, tension and pressure, and decision-making problems. Others suggest lack of family support for the career choice, personal questioning of career choice, and negative attitudes toward coworkers.

15. *Negative Treatment Indicators* (TRT, 26 items): High scores on TRT indicate individuals with negative attitudes toward doctors and mental health treatment. High scorers do not believe that anyone can understand or help them. They have issues or problems that they are not comfortable discussing with anyone. They may not want to change anything in their lives, nor do they feel that change is possible. They prefer giving up rather than facing a crisis or difficulty.

clinically interpretable. Interpretation of the content scales typically involves applying content descriptions for high or low scores in the profile.

One caution regarding interpretation of content scale scores is in order. Some confusion could result from scale scores, such as Depression (DEP), being confused with the clinical scale with a similar name, the Depression (D) scale. It is possible to obtain an elevated score on D and a moderate or even low score on DEP. This could result in an internal inconsistency in interpretation unless the clinician is aware that the two scales actually measure different clinical attributes despite their common name. The reason for this potential inconsistency is that although the names are similar, the constructs and correlates of the scales are actually somewhat different.

An illustration of the use of content scales and the MMPI-2 clinical scales is provided in the following discussion. (See the MMPI-2 clinical profile in Fig. 5.4 and the content scale profile in Fig. 5.5.)

The content scale profile shown in Figure 5.5 was produced by a 43-year-old man who was reporting some acute family problems. He sought help from a psychologist when his wife threatened to report his past incestuous relations with his oldest daughter if he did not give up his current relationship with his 19-year-old secretary. His most highly elevated score was on the Family Problems scale, suggesting that he viewed his problems as largely resulting from his family situation. The high score on Antisocial Practices (ASP) suggests that he possesses attitudes that are antisocial in character; he tends to violate rules and to disregard societal norms. Finally, he obtained a high score on the Negative Treatment Indicators scale, suggesting that he possesses attitudes that are contrary to cooperating with a treatment effort. He shows a high resistance to change.

Two content scales—the Negative Treatment Indicators scale (TRT) and Negative Work Attitudes scale (WRK)—may have particular significance for

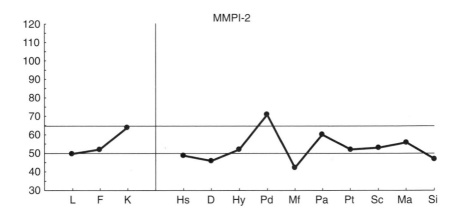

Figure 5.4. MMPI-2 clinical profile of an incest perpetrator.

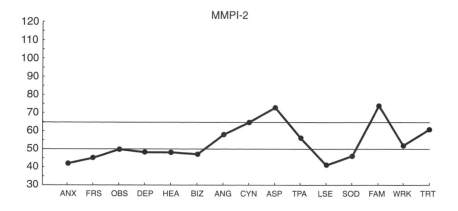

Figure 5.5. MMPI-2 content scale profile of an incest perpetrator.

treatment evaluation and the individual's potential for rehabilitation. A more detailed discussion of these scales follows.

Research on the MMPI-2 Content Scales

The MMPI content scales have been validated in a number of studies (Barthlow, Graham, Ben-Porath, & McNulty, 1999; Ben-Porath, Butcher, & Graham, 1991; Ben-Porath, McCully, & Almagor, 1993; Bosquet & Egeland, 2000; Lilienfeld, 1996). Studies have shown that the MMPI-2 content scales possess external validity that is equal to or greater than that of the original MMPI clinical scales (Ben-Porath et al., 1991; Butcher, Graham, Williams, & Ben-Porath, 1990). Other studies have reported strong behavioral correlates for the MMPI-2 content scales and personality characteristics:

- Lilienfeld (1991; 1996) found that the ASP scale was associated with *DSM-III-R* antisocial disorder diagnoses.
- Faull and Meyer (1993) found that the DEP content scale outperformed the MMPI-2 Depression scale in assessment of subjective depression in a sample of medical patients.
- Two studies established external correlates with the ANG content scale. Schill and Wang (1990) found the ANG scale to have concurrent validity for predicting anger control problems. Clark (1993, 1996) found that patients in a chronic pain program who had high scores on ANG showed frequent and intense anger, often felt unfairly treated by others, felt frustrated, were quick-tempered and overly sensitive to criticism, tended to externalize anger, were impulsive, and had anger-control problems.
- Brems and Lloyd (1995) reported that the Low Self-Esteem content scale accurately predicted clients who experienced self-esteem problems.

- Bagby, Marshall, Basso, Nicholson, Bacchiochi, and Miller (2005) found the DEP to be the most powerful predictor in distinguishing bipolar depression from schizophrenia.
- Clark (1996) reported that the TRT correlates for this patient sample were similar to those for normative sample men and that the external test correlates indicate that TRT, TRT1, and TRT2 scores reflected, at least in part, emotional distress. In addition, TRT and TRT1 were significant predictors of treatment-related change and posttreatment functioning.
- Gilmore, Lash, Foster, and Blosser (2001) found the TRT scale to predict clients who were more likely not to return to treatment sessions.

Treatment Planning with the MMPI-2 Content Scales

The MMPI-2 content scales provide a direct assessment of many of the individual's problems and personal attitudes that require attention in treatment sessions. Elevated scores on these scales provide important clues concerning the focus of therapy since they summarize problems the individual considers important in his or her case.

Negative Treatment Indicators Scale (TRT)   The TRT scale was developed as a means of assessing the individual's potential to cooperate with treatment and to detect the presence of personality factors or attitudes in the client reflecting an unwillingness or inability to change. The scale includes attitudes or beliefs that reflect a rigid and noncompliant orientation toward personal change, such as a lack of insight into one's own motives, an unwillingness to discuss problems with others, a dislike of healthcare providers, an inability to work out problems, and alienation from others.

High scorers on this scale are presenting the view that they are unwilling or unable to change their life situation at this time and that they are pessimistic about the future. A therapist armed with this information in the early stages of treatment might attempt to deal with the individual's negative treatment views before they result in early termination of therapy. Note the high TRT score obtained by the individual reported in Figure 5.5.

Negative Work Attitudes Scale (WRK)   Many individuals experiencing psychological problems find that their work deteriorates or that they are unable to maintain productive attitudes toward life. The WRK scale was developed to assess the possibility that the individual possesses attitudes or habits that would be counterproductive to rehabilitation efforts. The items on the scale center on the person's attitude toward work or his or her perceived inability to function in productive activities. The content themes include such beliefs or attitudes as inability to function or to make decisions, quick resignation when faced with difficulty, feelings of low success expectation, feeling weak and helpless, and possessing a dislike for work.

People who score high on this scale are presenting the view that they have many problems that prevent them from being successful at work. Therapists should be aware that work-related problems are or could become central problems in any person's life situation. Therefore, people with high scores on this scale may have a poor prognosis for achieving treatment success since their environmental pressures are likely to absorb much of their energies.

Summary

This chapter focused on content interpretation—a different interpretative strategy from the traditional approach to MMPI scale and code types. In content interpretation, the clinical interpreter assumes that the client has responded to the item content in an open, frank manner and has endorsed content relevant to his or her current symptoms and behavior. Content interpretation is based on the view that the client is able to report important symptoms or problems truthfully. Content interpretation requires no additional interpretive assumptions beyond the view that the client has endorsed problems central to his or her present situation. The content scales or indexes are interpreted on face value; that is, the content measure is viewed as a "summary statement" concerning the client's present symptoms, mood, personality characteristics, and behavior.

Three major approaches to MMPI-2 content interpretation were summarized and illustrated. The use of MMPI-2 critical items was presented, along with a discussion of the limitations of this approach. It is important to remember that critical items are best viewed as hypotheses for further evaluation, not as psychometrically sound measures of personality and behavior.

The use of MMPI-2 subscales (Harris–Lingoes) for six of the clinical scales (D, Hy, Pd, Pa, Sc, and Ma) was described and illustrated, along with three new subscales for Si. These subscales contain content-homogeneous item groups that can aid the clinician in understanding the scale elevation on the parent scale by determining the relative contribution of each content theme to the overall scale score. Care should be taken in the psychometric use of the content subscales because they are relatively short.

Finally, the interpretation of the MMPI-2 content scales was described and illustrated. These scales have the advantage over other content approaches in that they contain strong psychometric properties and can therefore be interpreted psychometrically. They also address important, clinically useful content dimensions for understanding patient symptoms and behavior. These dimensions were not previously tapped by the MMPI because they rely on new items written specifically for assessing previously neglected content areas. Most relevant to the topic of this book is the new Negative Treatment Indicators scale (TRT).

6

The Butcher Treatment Planning Inventory (BTPI)

The Butcher Treatment Planning Inventory or BTPI (Butcher, 2005) is an objective personality and symptom questionnaire that is considerably newer than the MMPI and MMPI-2. Another difference is that the BTPI was created specifically for use in psychological treatment planning, which sets it apart not only from the MMPI-2 but also from many of the assessment measures that are employed for this purpose. Its three sets of scales assess overall profile validity and degree of cooperation with the assessment process, interpersonal and related factors that affect treatment progress, and current psychological symptoms. It is intended to be used at several possible points during the course of therapy. At the outset of intervention, its data provide a means of assessing the therapy climate and gauging factors that are likely to facilitate and impede psychotherapy progress. For example, it can help therapists determine how motivated clients are to make behavioral changes as well as the degree to which clients believe that psychotherapy will help them to make those changes. It also assesses the general climate of therapy and how easily the therapeutic relationship is likely to be established. Its information about specific symptom issues affecting the client can highlight key treatment targets. As with any repeatable measure, clients' scores at treatment onset can serve as baseline measures against which to compare scores obtained further along in the therapeutic process, affording an objective gauge of progress and change (see Perry, 1999; Perry & Butcher, 1999).

A solid base of research supports the utility of the BTPI. Hatchett, Han, and Cooker (2002) demonstrated its usefulness in predicting premature termination from treatment among a large sample of university counseling center clients and identified that multiple BTPI scales were associated with ending a course of counseling early. Another college student sample (discussed in greater depth later in this chapter) also demonstrated links between elevated BTPI scores and receptivity to psychological intervention in the future (Butcher, Rouse, & Perry, 1998). Other research by Butcher, Rouse, and Perry (2000) also revealed connections between elevated scores on the BTPI and problematic behaviors such as terminating treatment prematurely and having difficulty in setting realistic treatment goals. Findings such as these support the BTPI's utility for describing clients in the treatment planning process.

Inventory Development

The construction of the BTPI was precipitated by two basic yet key observations of the author in his psychotherapy practice:

1. Obtaining treatment-related information about clients can benefit therapists considerably when it comes to designing treatment plans that best suit their needs, especially when it is done within the early phases of therapy formulation.
2. The simplest way to obtain such information about the client is to ask the client to provide it.

Bringing together the parallel traditions of intervention and objective personality assessment, Butcher created an instrument whose core function was to aid therapists in gauging the therapeutic climate by identifying potential impediments to progress in the forms of personality characteristics, behavioral tendencies, and psychological symptoms. The instrument was also informed by such concepts as the therapeutic model of assessment (e.g., Finn & Kamphuis, 2006; Finn & Tonsager, 1992, 1997) and "assessment therapy" (Finn & Martin, 1997). In these studies, the therapist uses a feedback model to discuss psychological assessment information with the client in a manner intended to encourage behavioral change. Research has demonstrated that the working alliance fostered by this type of interaction can carry over into subsequent psychotherapy (Hilsenroth, Peters, & Ackerman, 2004).

The scales in the inventory were both rationally and empirically developed by first identifying key constructs to assess. This determination was grounded in clinical practice and the extant literature on treatment process and outcome (e.g., Beutler, 1995; Butcher & Herzog, 1982; Garfield, 1978; Koss & Butcher, 1986). There was no intention of tying the BTPI scales or the items to a particular therapeutic orientation, as the instrument was intended to assess treatment-related variables transcending theory. Nevertheless, the clinical experience of its author resulted in a predominance of behavioral and cognitive–behavioral concepts.

Scale items were generated rationally, with an attempt to balance brevity of completion time with comprehensiveness in appraising the constructs of interest. After the initial item pool was administered to a sample of normal individuals, the early scales were refined. In addition, two empirically derived validity scales were developed. The result was a self-report measure focusing on client behavior and consisting of 210 true-or-false items. Under typical conditions, the instrument requires about 30 minutes to complete.

Scale and Composite Structure

As shown in Table 6.1, the BTPI items represent 14 scales. The scales themselves fall into three clusters: Validity scales (four scales), Treatment Issues scales (five scales), and Current Symptom scales (five scales). Similar to the MMPI-2, the BTPI Validity scales assess the overall manner in which the respondent approached the test and provide objective information about his or her self-report. The number of items left unanswered on the inventory is also considered with regard to profile validity. The maximum number allowed is eight for the full inventory, with two omissions permitted per scale. Raw scores should be prorated to account for any omissions falling below those cutoffs.

Table 6.1. Summary of BTPI Scales and Composites

Scale Name	Abbrev.	Implications of Elevated Score (T > 60)*
Cluster 1: Validity Indicators		
Inconsistent Responding	INC	Random item endorsement
Overly Virtuous Self-Views	VIR	Unrealistically positive self-portrayal
Exaggerated Problem Presentation	EXA	Amplification of symptoms
Closed-Mindedness	CLM	Reluctance to consider new ideas
Cluster 2: Treatment Issues Scales		
Problems in Relationship Formation	REL	Difficulty in creating relationships
Somatization of Conflict	SOM	Somatic experience of distress
Low Expectation of Therapeutic Benefit	EXP	Pessimism about treatment
Self-Oriented/Narcissism	NAR	Self-centeredness
Perceived Lack of Environmental Support	ENV	Feelings of being unsupported
Cluster 3: Current Symptom Scales		
Depression	DEP	Depressed mood
Anxiety	ANX	Tension, nervousness
Anger-Out	A-O	Externalized anger, hostility
Anger-In	A-I	Internalized anger, self-blame
Unusual Thinking	PSY	Unusual beliefs and behaviors

Composite Name	Abbreviation	Included Scales
General Pathology Composite	GPC	DEP, ANX, A-O, A-I
Treatment Difficulty Composite	TDC	PSY, REL, SOM, EXP, NAR, ENV

Validity Scales

One of the two empirically derived scales on the BTPI is Inconsistent Self-Description (INC), consisting of 21 item pairs. Each item pair should be endorsed in a semantically consistent fashion. For example, "I feel much better now than I have in months" and "I feel much better now than I have in a long time" should both be answered either *true* or *false*. If one is answered in each direction, that discrepancy would be reflected in the individual's INC raw score. The respondent's total raw score on this scale reflects the quantity of inconsistent response pairs in the profile.

The other empirically derived scale is Exaggerated Problem Presentation (EXA). At 61 items, it is the longest scale on the BTPI. Its purpose is to assess the likelihood of overreporting psychological problems or characteristics. Individuals who produce high scores on this scale usually have endorsed many more symptoms than the typical psychotherapy client. Respondents may produce elevated scores on this scale because they feel overwhelmed by their difficulties, and they may also produce elevations because of secondary gain factors. Sample items on this scale are "I never get irritated at other people even when they do something against me" (F) and "I feel very hopeless about other people I know" (T).

All of the other Validity scales were rationally derived (as were all of the Treatment Issues scales and Current Symptom scales). Overly Virtuous Self-Views (VIR) is a 15-item scale. Its items measure the tendency to present oneself in an unrealistically positive way and to claim better adjustment than is true for the average person. When clients produce an elevated score on this scale, it is due to their "putting their best foot forward" to an unrealistic degree. As a result, these are individuals whose self-reports are suspect and whose characterization of their current level of functioning is not regarded as credible. Typical VIR items include "I have never met anyone I didn't like" (T) and "I always give 10% of my income to charity" (T).

Closed-Mindedness (CLM) evaluates the degree to which respondents decline to disclose information about themselves and resist the idea of making cognitive and behavioral changes. An elevated score on this 19-item scale is associated with a preference not to talk about oneself or reveal personal information to others. In addition, high scores are associated with a dislike for hearing the views of others, feelings of being misunderstood, and a preference for keeping others at arm's length. Items on this scale include "It makes me uncomfortable to talk about myself" (T) and "I usually keep a good distance from others and do not express my feelings openly" (T).

Treatment Issues Scales

The second BTPI cluster consists of five scales that tap specific issues that bear on treatment. Problems in Relationship Formation (REL) contains 18 items that assess lack of interpersonal trust, difficulty in relating to others, and general vulnerability to relational problems. An elevated score on this scale is suggestive of someone who is apt to have few friends and may prefer solitude. "I think most people make friends just to use them for their own benefit" (T) and "I am very hard to get to know" (T) are included on this scale.

Somatization of Conflict (SOM) is 16 items long. This scale measures the tendency to produce or develop somatic complaints in the face of emotional conflict. Individuals whose scores are high on this scale have reported experiencing multiple specific physical problems, including headaches and stomach problems, as well as more generalized somatic distress. They have also indicated that their physical symptoms occur in conjunction with stressors and life difficulties. Sample items on this scale include "I have been in poor health for some time now" (T) and "My worries are not affecting my physical health" (F).

The 25-item Low Expectation of Therapeutic Benefit scale (EXP) assesses skepticism about the appropriateness and value of undertaking therapy and making substantive changes. High scorers on this scale report being cynical about the potential benefit of following others' advice, including that of healthcare professionals. They also indicate a dislike for trying out new activities. Their reluctance to accept others' feedback makes them unlikely to comply with treatment suggestions. Items on this scale include "I don't really feel the need to make any changes in my life now" (T) and "I really like to try out new and different things" (F).

Self-Oriented/Narcissism (NAR) provides information about the tendency to be self-centered and self-indulgent in relationships. Elevated scores on this 19-item scale are produced by those who view themselves very favorably. They tend to exhibit a sense of entitlement and to believe that others' needs should be subordinate to their own. They are inclined to demonstrate selfishness in relationships and may believe that they do not receive the amount of attention that they merit. Items from this scale include "I deserve much better treatment than I usually get from other people" (T) and "I usually get a lot of compliments about how I look" (T).

The last of the Treatment Issue scales is the 17-item Perceived Lack of Environmental Support. It assesses clients' impressions of their social environments, tapping into the extent to which they regard themselves as lonely and emotionally distant from those around them. High scores on this scale are produced when respondents regard their lives as unpleasant because those around them are not supportive. Such individuals may resent others for having let them down. "I don't feel that my problems are understood by anyone I know" (T) and "My home life is filled with arguing and bickering" (T) are included on this scale.

Current Symptom Scales

Cluster 3 is made up of five scales that assess for psychological symptoms. Depression (DEP) is an 18-item measure that was developed to assess low mood states. An elevated score is associated with depressed affect, limited energy for daily activities, problems sleeping, and the impression of life as unpleasant. Some high scorers are also experiencing suicidal ideation, which warrants additional assessment. Two items on the scale are "I frequently find myself feeling sad these days" (T) and "I no longer enjoy living as I used to" (T).

The Anxiety scale (ANX) is 15 items long. It assesses fearfulness, nervousness, tension, and worry. A high ANX scorer is likely to obsess over small matters, often to such a degree that daily functioning is impaired by an inability to make even minor decisions. Examples of ANX items include "I am so tense at times that I can't sit still" (T) and "I do not have any worries or problems that I cannot solve myself" (F).

The BTPI contains two anger-related scales, both of which are 16 items long. Anger-Out (A-O) assesses the tendency to externalize such feelings. High scorers on A-O express their anger in a hostile and aggressive fashion and generally behave irritably. They tend to view the world as filled with antagonism, and their resentment may cause them to strike out at others when they feel that they have been wronged. "I sometimes have thoughts of hitting or injuring someone else to get back at them" (T) and "At times I am so tense that I feel I am going to explode" (T) are both included on this scale.

Whereas A-O items measure overt hostility, Anger-In (A-I) items assess respondents' tendency to be intropunitive. Elevated scores are suggestive of passivity and self-condemnation, even for problems that are not of the individual's own doing. Low self-esteem and self-destructive behaviors are other correlates of a high A-I score. Sample items from the scale include "I have gotten so angry with myself in the past that I have attempted to end my own life" (T) and "I am usually the person to blame when things go wrong" (T).

Finally, the 15-item Unusual Thinking (PSY) scale evaluates the presence of atypical behaviors and beliefs. The PSY scale assesses difficulties in accurately perceiving and processing information. Those who produce elevated scores may be very mistrustful and suspicious of others. Their thinking may be superstitious or magical. Higher scores are suggestive of frank delusions and hallucinations. The items "I have proof that the government has spied on me in the past" (T) and "I sometimes hear voices or see visions that other people do not see" (T) are both included on PSY.

Composites

In addition to the 14 scale scores, the BTPI contains two composite measures. Each is composed of a different collection of individual scales. The first of these is known as the General Pathology Composite (GPC). Its raw score is calculated by combining the T scores from four of the Current Symptom scales: DEP, ANX, A-O, and A-I.

The fifth Cluster 3 scale, PSY, is included in the other composite, which is known as the Treatment Difficulty Composite (TDC). In addition, the TDC contains the scores from all of the Treatment Issues scales: REL, SOM, EXP, NAR, and ENV. The TDC raw score is calculated by summing the T scores for each of its component scales.

Administration and Scoring Guidelines

The BTPI is intended for individuals over the age of 18. It typically is administered using a traditional paper-and-pencil format. Based on the Dale–Chall formula for assessing readability (Chall & Dale, 1995; Dale & Chall, 1948), it requires the ability to read English at a fourth-grade level. For those who cannot read (due to literacy issues, eyesight problems, or other factors), it is permissible to read the instrument aloud. Regardless, it should be administered in the presence of a trained administrator.

There are two forms of the BTPI available for use. Figure 6.1 shows the BTPI Full Form, which contains all 210 items and requires approximately 40 minutes' completion time under optimal conditions. The Symptom Monitoring Form (Fig. 6.2) contains 80 items and requires around 20 minutes' completion time. Both of the forms use the MHS QuikScore™ form, which facilitates hand-scoring and eliminates the need for scoring templates. As with the MMPI-2, administration of the BTPI to individuals is recommended, but group administration is also possible, if needed.

Normative Information

The computer-based interpretive information for the BTPI includes empirical, externally validated data (based upon the concurrent validity, predictive validity, and therapist rating data obtained in the normative and clinical samples, to be discussed in the following pages) as well as theoretical hypotheses. The latter are based on the assumption that endorsement of the BTPI items represents a direct communication between the client and the therapist.

The 14 BTPI scales use T scores for comparing a client's performance with a comparison group. Three sets of norms are available: a representative normative sample, a young adult (college) sample, and a heterogeneous sample of therapy patients. T scores ranging from 35 to 60 are considered to fall in the "average" range. T scores of 61 to 70 are regarded as "above average," or moderately elevated. T scores above 70 are considered "very much above average." Table 6.1 provides a summary of the clusters and the implications of score elevations.

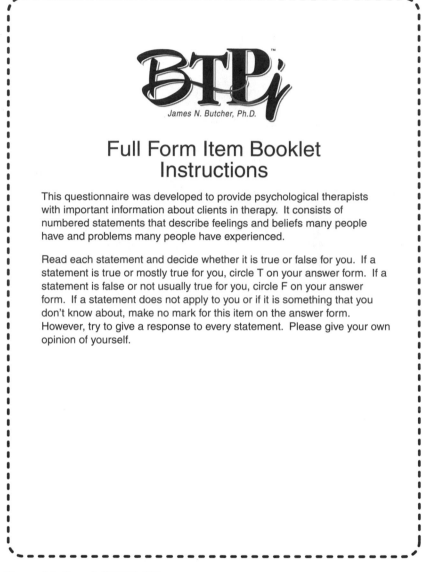

Figure 6.1. Sample BTPI Full Form.

Three sets of linear T scores were developed to simplify the interpretive process for the 14 BTPI scales: scores for men, scores for women, and scores for the combined male/female group. The normative groups are described below. Separate T scores were also developed for interpretation of both of the composite scores.

James N. Butcher, Ph.D.

Symptom Monitoring Form
Item Booklet

Instructions

This questionnaire was developed to provide psychological therapists with important information about clients in therapy. It consists of numbered statements that describe feelings and beliefs many people have and problems many people have experienced.

Read each statement and decide whether it is true or false for you. If a statement is true or mostly true for you, circle T on your answer form. If a statement is false or not usually true for you, circle F on your answer form. If a statement does not apply to you or if it is something that you don't know about, make no mark on the answer form for this item. However, try to give a response to every statement. Please give your own opinion of yourself.

Figure 6.2. Sample BTPI Symptom Monitoring Form.

The Normative Study

The BTPI was administered to a representative sample of 800 individuals (400 men and 400 women) from eight regions across the United States. The sample was chosen so as to be representative of the U.S. population on the bases of sex, age, education, and race/ethnicity. One quarter of the individuals in the normative sample were re-administered the BTPI a median of 7 days after the initial testing in order to establish test–retest reliability. Those coefficients ranged from 0.55 (for INC; because it is a measure of random responding, scores are expected not to be consistent over time) to 0.90. Most values fell at or above 0.80, suggesting acceptable test–retest reliability for the instrument. Internal consistency reliabilities were high range, except for INC, whose heterogeneous items would not be anticipated to be psychometrically related to one another, and EXP, which examines a theoretically complex construct and is not intended to be an internally consistent measure.

In addition to completing the BTPI, the participants in the normative study completed questionnaires assessing life history, life functioning, and physical health, and they also completed other measures, including the Inventory of Interpersonal Problems (IIP; Horowitz, Alden, Wiggins, & Pincus, 2000; Horowitz, Rosenberg, Baer, Ureño, & Villaseñor, 1988), the Beck Depression Inventory–II (Beck, Steer, & Brown, 1996), the Beck Anxiety Inventory (Beck & Steer, 1990), and the Symptom Checklist-90-R (Derogatis, 1994). Concurrent validity analyses demonstrated that the BTPI scales were largely positively correlated with each of these as well as with other measures of interpersonal relationships and psychological problems, given convergent and discriminative validity configurations.

The College Student Study

An additional study of the BTPI's psychometric properties used college student participants (Butcher et al., 1998) to examine psychotherapy attitudes within this population. College students were chosen for study as a representative segment of non-patient individuals. The sample was composed of 379 undergraduates at the University of Minnesota who participated as part of an introductory psychology course. Then, 100 of the students were re-administered the BTPI approximately 30 minutes after the initial administration. Once again, test–retest reliability coefficients were uniformly high, mostly near 0.90. Internal consistency values were in the range of 0.70 for all scales but INC and EXP (as anticipated, given the factors previously discussed with regard to these scales).

Two concurrent validity studies of the BTPI were conducted among 289 of the students. One hundred of them completed the IIP in addition to the BTPI, and another 150 completed the BTPI and the MMPI-2. As was the case within the normative sample, BTPI–IIP correlations were largely positive. There were several relationships of note with regard to the BTPI–MMPI-2 correlations: INC on the BTPI was positively and significantly correlated with MMPI-2 VRIN, both of which assess variability in responses. The BTPI's PSY scale was significantly correlated with F, F(B), and scale 8 (Sc) on the MMPI-2, consistent with the overlap in these scales' intended assessment of unusual thinking.

The 100 students from the test–retest study also completed a brief "Therapy Experience Survey." This was a seven-item measure created for the study, and students' responses were examined in conjunction with their BTPI scores. Among other things, the survey items addressed respondents' previous participation in psychological treatment, their previous consideration of psychological intervention, and their willingness to recommend psychotherapy to people whom they regarded as being in need of professional help. Students who had never previously been in counseling were found to have lower expectations about the potential helpfulness of therapy (i.e., higher scores on EXP) than those who had been in therapy before. Reported unwillingness to participate in therapy was associated with elevated scores on EXP, CLM, and REL. Consistent with previous findings related to gender disparities in openness to treatment, female students were more likely than male students to have considered undertaking psychotherapy, to have participated in it, to have considered recommending it to someone else, and actually to have recommended it to others.

The Clinical Study

The final normative group for BTPI was composed of outpatient psychotherapy clients. An extensive field study, the Minnesota Psychotherapy Assessment Project, assessed 460 psychotherapy clients and their 64 therapists. The sample was drawn from England and from 13 states across the United States. Most therapists either were independent practitioners or worked in a mental health outpatient setting, and the majority held a Ph.D. in clinical psychology. They most often endorsed "cognitive–behavioral" as their treatment orientation. The participating clients were mostly female, college-educated, Caucasian, and self-referred for treatment. The most common diagnoses were adjustment, affective, and anxiety disorders.

The majority of the internal consistency reliability estimates for the scales within the clinical sample ranged from 0.70 to 0.89. According to a multivariate analysis of variance examining score differences between the normative and clinical samples, the clinical sample had higher-ranging scores than the normative group, particularly on the Current Symptom scales and the GPC. On VIR and EXP, however, scores were significantly lower for the clinical sample, suggesting greater willingness to acknowledge faults and more hopefulness about treatment among the psychotherapy clients.

Each client also completed the MMPI-2, and his or her therapist additionally compiled a list of external behavior correlates to describe current functioning. Correlations between the BTPI and MMPI-2 scales were consistent with the college sample previously described. With regard to the relationships between therapist-rated behaviors and elevated BTPI scale scores, there were significant correlations between dissociative symptoms and REL; antisocial behavior and EXP; marital conflict and ENV; self-mutilation and A-I; anorexia and A-I; and defensiveness and A-O.

The BTPI scales were subjected to factor analysis using all three samples described previously. Four factors were extracted on the basis of a principal components analysis and normal Varimax rotation. Factor I, "Neuroticism," accounts for over 45% of the variance on the measure. It includes EXA, ENV, SOM, DEP, ANX, A-I, A-O, and PSY. Factor II, "Cynicism-Uncooperative," includes REL, INC, CLM, and EXP. Factor III, "Self-Orientation/Anger," includes NAR and A-O (which loads secondarily on it). The sole scale loading on factor IV, "Defensiveness," was VIR.

Table 6.2. Indications of Treatment Resistance on BTPI Scale Scores

Scale	Potential Treatment Implication of Elevated Score
INC	Uncooperativeness
VIR	Opposition to self-disclosure
EXA	Inability to focus on specific symptoms and associated interventions
CLM	Poor response to criticism and personal feedback
REL	Problems trusting others and establishing a therapeutic alliance
SOM	Inability to deal directly with psychological difficulties and material
EXP	Belief that change is not possible, low likelihood of compliance with suggestions
NAR	Unwillingness to modify behavior in order to suit others
ENV	Experience of limited emotional support to facilitate making changes
DEP	Depression too severe to enable treatment compliance
ANX	Anxiety too severe to enable treatment compliance
A-O	Anger directed toward others
A-I	Passivity in treatment, self-blame if treatment does not proceed as desired
PSY	Mistrust of the therapist, difficulty with accurately processing stimuli

Interpretative Strategies

With any profile, interpretation begins with the Validity scales. As was reviewed in previous chapters on the MMPI-2, it is critical to verify that the client has been cooperative with the assessment process before using any questionnaire report data to make important treatment decisions. Moreover, the manner in which clients respond to questionnaires such as the BTPI bears upon their potential motivational sets in entering treatment.

Before examining particular scale scores, it is critical to ensure that BTPI respondents have not omitted more than eight items on the entire inventory or more than two items on any one scale. Omissions exceeding these levels will invalidate the results of the instrument or scale. They also suggest a level of uncooperativeness that is likely to bear on treatment with the client, which should be discussed with him or her during a feedback session.

The Validity scales provide additional sources of information about possible lack of cooperation with treatment. Clients who produce elevated scores on INC have been inconsistent in their endorsement of items. This type of response style is apt to translate to their treatment, such that they may have problems in giving honest and accurate reports in a one-to-one interaction with their providers (or in therapy groups). Those who produce high scores on VIR have presented themselves as being unrealistically honorable and righteous, once again suggesting the possibility of inaccurate self-description in treatment. High scorers on EXA had endorsed more extreme symptoms than others.

Some clients may resist reporting any problem-related information on the instrument As noted, there are different levels of "elevation" associated with various T scores on the BTPI scales and composite. As such, the interpretation of elevated scores will vary, depending on how far above the "average" range a score falls. At moderate levels (T = 60–64), elevated PSY scores suggest unusual belief systems and ideas. When scores are higher (T > 65) delusional thinking may be present.

As composites, the GPC and TDC function as summary scores. In this way, they provide collective information about the respondent that is especially useful in progress monitoring. Individuals' scores on the two measures can be tracked and compared over time, as a means of evaluating whether there has been statistically significant change in the individual's report and to what degree.

Treatment Monitoring

It is also increasingly important, in the age of managed care, for clinicians to be able to document progress and assess whether additional treatment is warranted at any given point in the therapeutic process. To the extent that changes in scale scores are indicative of reported attitudinal and behavioral transformations, reductions in score levels can be viewed as evidence of therapeutic progress. Similarly, a lack of substantial change in scores may be indicative of a client's failure to benefit from intervention thus far in the relationship.

Therapeutic progress can readily be assessed in the course of treatment. Not only can persistence of high scores on the BTPI scales be used as an objective justification for extending the therapy, but an examination of the scores themselves can facilitate discussion between client and therapist about why therapy may not have been more beneficial to this point. Perhaps new scale elevations have replaced or accompanied those that were present at the initial testing, possibly indicating the presence of new life problems that are impairing the client's ability to achieve maximum benefit from the treatment as was previously formulated. The initial identified problem may be taking a backseat to formerly secondary issues that have moved to the forefront, resulting in the client's inability to engage fully in therapy as it is now progressing. In this scenario, comparison of the original and more recent BTPI profiles will provide a means by which to evaluate which necessary changes have been made and which are ongoing.

To facilitate re-administering the BTPI at various points throughout treatment, an abbreviated Symptom Monitoring Form has been created and validated (Butcher, 2005). This form reduces the number of items by focusing upon the symptom scales. The use of the Symptom Monitoring Form is based upon the confidence that the client is open and cooperative and that test validity measures are not needed at this point in the treatment.

The Symptom Monitoring Form consists of only 80 items and can typically be administered in around 15 minutes. This form provides therapists with their clients' scores on the Depression, Anxiety, Anger-Out, Anger-In, and Unusual Thinking scales. This abbreviated form should be used when there is very little or no threat that the client will provide invalid self-report test data and the therapist is confident that the treatment issues scales are not relevant. As its name implies, the Symptom Monitoring Form is most useful for tracking symptoms throughout the course of therapy, within the context of observing the changes that occur in clients' perceptions of their psychological problems as treatment progresses.

Outcomes Assessment with the BTPI

Assessment of the client's functioning after completion of therapy is important for gauging the degree to which the client has made progress in treatment. To this end, the BTPI can be re-administered at therapy termination and the scores from this assessment compared with those obtained in the initial testing. This comparison will allow both the therapist and the client to evaluate the efficacy of the therapy and can facilitate a discussion between both parties about the changes that have (or have not) occurred.

The BTPI can play an integral role in helping the therapist and client determine when to discontinue the intervention, as an examination of score differences can aid in the determination of when substantive therapeutic changes have been made by the client. As Ben-Porath (1997) has noted, the types of assessment data provided by measures like the BTPI can allow for therapy termination decisions to be made empirically and objectively rather than subjectively, as is the case when only the impressions of the therapist and client (or, increasingly more commonly, the managed care administrators) are available.

Research Applications

The serviceability and practicality of the information provided by the BTPI extend beyond the purely clinical domain and into the realm of research as well. Through an examination of pretreatment and posttreatment scores, the inventory can aid in the determination of which intervention strategies are beneficial within different groups of clients and diagnostic problems and, consequently, what therapeutic changes may be indicated for future clients with similar difficulties. The data collected through the Minnesota Psychotherapy Assessment Project on the 460-member clinical sample discussed previously (Butcher, 2005) are intended for this purpose, and the other normative data also lend themselves to further evaluation through research.

7

Use of Computer-Generated Reports in Treatment Planning

M any clinicians find that computer-based psychological test interpretations are valuable aids in pretreatment planning for several
reasons. First, psychological test results can be processed rapidly and the information from the MMPI-2 or BTPI can be immediately available to incorporate
in therapy planning early in the intervention, even in the initial session. Second,
a computer-based test result can provide extensive personality information in
a readily usable form without the need for the therapist to search through the
empirical research for each patient's profile. The automated MMPI-2 or BTPI
report summarizes the most valid test correlates in a readable format. Finally,
the automated personality test report is an informative, interesting format for
use in providing test feedback to clients, a process that is discussed in more detail
in Chapter 8.

The theoretical basis for computer-generated personality predictions was
provided by Meehl (1954), who showed the power of actuarial prediction and
personality description over intuitive test analysis procedures. Meehl's view of
actuarial prediction was that test interpreters, basing their decisions on empirical experience, would outperform clinicians making decisions following intuitively based decision procedures. One of Meehl's students, Halbower (1955),
demonstrated convincingly that empirically established MMPI test correlates
could be accurately applied to new cases meeting the test criteria. Meehl's com-
pelling argument on the strength of the actuarial procedure over clinically
based decisions influenced a number of investigators to develop "actuarial tables" for personality descriptions using MMPI scales and combinations of scales

(Altman, Gynther, Warbin, & Sletten, 1973; Archer, Griffin, & Aiduk, 1995; Arnold, 1970; Boerger, Graham, & Lilly, 1974; Butcher, Rouse, & Perry, 2000; Fowler & Athey, 1971; Gilberstadt & Duker, 1965; Graham, 1973; Gray, 2005; Green, Handel, & Archer, 2006; Greene et al., 2003; Gynther, 1972; Gynther, Altman, & Sletten, 1973; Gynther, Alman, & Warbin, 1972; Gynther, Altman, and Warbin, 1973a, 1973b; Gynther, Altman, Warbin, & Sletten, 1972, 1973; Halbower, 1955; Horan et al., 2005; Keller & Butcher, 1991; Kelly & King, 1978; Lewandowski & Graham, 1972; Liu et al., 2001; Livingston et al., 2006; Marks & Seeman, 1963; Marks, Seeman, & Haller, 1974; McNulty, Ben-Porath, & Graham, 1998; Meilkle & Gerritse, 1970; Persons & Marks, 1971; Sellbom, Graham, & Schenk, 2005; Sines, 1966; Slesinger, Archer, & Duane, 2002; Streit, Greene, Cogan, & Davis, 1993; Warbin, Altman, Gynther, & Sletten, 1972; Yu & Templer, 2004). Research on MMPI profile patterns has established a validated and extensive interpretive base for the instrument for a number of patient types. Correlates for the MMPI-2 clinical scales are robust and can be automatically applied, even by automated procedures such as a computer, to cases that meet test score criteria.

History of Computer-Based MMPI Interpretations

Computer-based MMPI interpretation has a long history (Atlis, Hahn, & Butcher, 2006). The first computer-based interpretation of the MMPI following the actuarial approach was initiated at the Mayo Clinic (Pearson & Swenson, 1967) in the early 1960s. In this system, more than 100 statements of pre-established test correlates were programmed to print out descriptions of the patient who produced specified profile types. The computer output included an MMPI profile, along with a listing of up to six of the relevant descriptors. This computer interpretation system, though limited in scope, was readily accepted by the psychology and medical staffs at the Mayo Clinic. In the 1970s several other more comprehensive and sophisticated MMPI interpretation programs were developed. Later computer-based MMPI programs typically provided information in a narrative report format, rather than a listing of correlates as the Mayo System provided, and incorporated more extensive information (Fowler, 1987).

Today, computer-based interpretation of psychological tests has become a widely accepted clinical tool (Butcher, Perry, & Hahn, 2004). The computer-based reports have become a central part of many clinicians' diagnostic appraisal of their clients' problems. Using the computer-based report as an "outside opinion" of the client's problems can be very valuable to the process of providing feedback to clients. We will now turn to a discussion of procedures and practices of computer-based interpretation with the MMPI-2 and BTPI.

Availability of Various Administrative Formats for Computer-Based MMPI-2 Reports

There are a number of options available for administering and processing MMPI-2 protocols to obtain a computer-based MMPI-2 report. For further information contact:

Pearson Assessments
  5601 Green Valley Drive, 4th Floor
  Bloomington, MN 55437
  Phone: 800-627-7271, Ext. 3313
  Fax: 800-632-9011 or 952-681-3299
  Email: pearsonassessments@pearson.com

Processing by Microcomputer

Most clinics or practitioners today have access to a microcomputer and can obtain immediate processing of the MMPI-2 in their own office without sending the MMPI-2 answer sheet by mail or fax to the scoring service. Patients respond to the inventory by marking their answers on an answer sheet. A clerical person enters the individual's responses into the computer following a simple procedure using software provided by the test scoring service. The test answers are then processed by microcomputer and a report is printed out immediately.

Optical Scanning of the MMPI-2 Answer Sheet

Clinics or practitioners with a relatively high volume of assessments (e.g., 10 to 15 cases a week) would find the use of an optical scanner for scoring MMPI-2s a valuable addition to their assessment program. The optical scanner reads the answer sheet and communicates the scores directly to the microcomputer. The scores are processed and a report is immediately produced.

The costs incurred in purchasing a table-top optical scanner from Pearson Assessments is about $3,000, but this can be quickly compensated for in savings of clerical time in processing. The scanner is relatively bug-free and operates with very low maintenance cost.

Computer Administration and Processing of Patient Responses

Another possible MMPI-2 administration format is the computer-administered test. The MMPI-2 items are presented on the video screen, and the subject is instructed to respond to them on the computer keyboard. Once the individual has completed the inventory, the microcomputer scores the test and generates a report, which is printed on an attached printer. This administration format is usually interesting to the client and easy to take. However, this is a somewhat inefficient use of the computer in that it usually requires the individual about an hour to an hour and a half to take the test in this manner. This ties up the computer for that period and only one person at a time can take the test.

Adaptive Computer Administration of the MMPI-2   As noted in Chapter 2, this test-administration format employs the flexibility of the computer in deciding which items on the inventory to administer. The full MMPI-2 would not be administered; only items that add to the information about the client are given. Each client would be administered a different form depending on his or her answers to previous items. This concept is analogous to the way a clinical interview is conducted. An interviewer does not usually ask the same questions of all clients; instead, the questions are contingent on answers the subject has previously given. For example, if the interviewee has responded "no" to the question "Are you married?" the interviewer would not ask any further questions about the client's being married. If the subject responded "yes" to the question, then he or she would "branch" into questions concerning the nature and quality of the marriage. Several studies have demonstrated that "branching" or adaptive strategies could be developed for MMPI-type items that reduce the testing time by about half (Ben-Porath, Slutsky, & Butcher, 1989; Ben-Porath, Waller, Slutsky, & Butcher, 1988; Butcher, Keller, & Bacon, 1985; Clavelle & Butcher, 1977), but the information lost in this adaptation may limit the effectiveness of the assessment As noted earlier, adaptive administration using less than the full form of the MMPI-2 is not recommended for clinical assessments in which client's problems need to be fully explored. Abbreviated test administrations do not provide a full or sufficient picture of the client's problems to serve as a treatment planning instrument.

Mail-In Service

For clinicians with a low volume of patients and ample time to process this MMPI-2 test results (e.g., if the therapist sees the patient on a weekly basis), mailing in the MMPI-2 to Pearson Assessments for processing is probably the easiest test-processing option. The test is administered to the client in a paper-and-pencil form, and the answer sheet is mailed to Pearson Assessments, where it is processed within 24 hours of receipt. The report is then sent back to the clinician by return mail. Express mail delivery or fax reporting of results is possible if needed.

How Computer-Based Interpretation Programs for the MMPI-2 Work

Computerized psychological test reporting programs are expert systems or forms of "artificial intelligence" in which computer programs simulate the cognitive processes of clinicians interpreting the MMPI-2 (Butcher, 2005c). The general procedure or model on which MMPI-2 interpretation systems operate is quite simple. The database for MMPI-2 interpretations comes from several sources, such as the established empirical literature for MMPI scales and indexes, correlates for specially constructed "supplementary" scales such as the Mf, MAC-R, Si, and Es, and predictive decisions or personality descriptions based on scale relationships or *indexes* (e.g., the Megargee Rules for correctional settings; Megargee, 2006; Megargee, Cook, & Mendelsohn, 1967). More comprehensive interpretation systems also attempt to integrate information from the content themes presented by the subject as reflected through the MMPI-2 content scales, the Harris–Lingoes content subscales, or the critical items. And the clinical experience of the system developer also becomes a part of the program interpretation.

The MMPI-2 computer programs usually allow for the following operations:

1. *Scoring and processing answer sheets.* Scoring of relevant scales and compilation of MMPI-2 indexes from raw scores is addressed first, and then profiles are drawn. (Only systems that have been licensed by the copyright holder—the University of Minnesota Press—can score the MMPI-2 by computer. Unlicensed interpretation systems can produce MMPI interpretations, but the raw scores need to be obtained by hand scoring of the answer sheet.) The appropriate test variables, such as code types, are obtained to serve as the indexing variables for the report. Finally, special aspects such as relevant critical item content are listed on the printout.
2. *Organizing relevant variables.* The index variables are used to search stored data bases (reference files, look-up tables, and classification or decision rules) to locate the relevant personality and symptom information for the client being assessed.

   a. Determining profile validity and elimination of invalid records
   b. Searching stored data files for prototypal information on the case
   c. Integrating test information into a unified report

3. *Communicating the results in a readable format.* This involves printing out a narrative report that addresses the believability of the report and provides a summary of the individual's symptomatic status, personality characteristics, and significant problems.
4. *Highlighting special problems or issues.* The computer system might also provide additional information about the client based on his or her responses to particular items or scale relationships that address specific problems.

5. *Indicating appropriate cautions.* The American Psychological Association has recommended guidelines for computerized psychological assessment, and appropriate qualifying statements concerning computer-based psychological reports need to be included in the report to prevent its misuse.

As you will see in a later section, MMPI computer interpretations vary in terms of their comprehensiveness and accuracy in describing and predicting individual behavior. Users need to be careful in deciding which available scoring and interpretation program to use.

Relative Accuracy of Computer Interpretation Systems for the MMPI-2

Research studies comparing the relative accuracy of computer-based reports with reports written by a trained clinician are not available. It is not known whether computer-based MMPI reports are more or less accurate than reports developed by a clinician. Most of the early computer-report evaluation research employed rather vague "satisfaction" ratings to determine whether a report was valid (Moreland, 1985). There have been several empirical validation studies involving the Minnesota Report. Moreland and Onstad (1985) found that reports produced on actual patients were judged significantly more accurate than randomly generated reports. Shores and Carstairs (1998) found Minnesota Reports to be highly accurate in detecting fake-good and fake-bad clients. Butcher, Berah, Ellertsen, Miach, Lim, Nezami, Pancheri, Derksen, and Almagor (1998) found that the Minnesota Reports generalized well across cultures and were highly accurate when rated by practitioners. (See also the review of MMPI-2 systems by Williams & Weed, 2004.)

The most comprehensive empirical validation studies of computer-based MMPI reports were conducted by Eyde, Kowal, and Fishburne (1987) and Fishburne, Eyde, and Kowal (1988). These investigators compared the relative accuracy of seven MMPI computerized reports: Applied Innovations, Behaviordyne, Caldwell Report, Psych Systems, Minnesota Report (NCS), Western Psychological Services, and Tomlinson Reports. The investigators submitted protocols on several patients to each computer-assessment firm. They disassembled the computer-generated statements, disguised their origin, and gave these statements to raters (familiar with the actual cases) to rate for accuracy. Once the accuracy ratings were complete, the investigators reassembled the reports and computed accuracy ratings. The Minnesota Reports were among those judged to be accurate enough for clinical use. The high degree of variability in accuracy level shown by this study provides a note of caution for clinicians selecting a computer-based assessment program.

We will now turn to a discussion of one MMPI system—the Minnesota Report distributed by Pearson Assessments.

Illustration of Computer-Based Assessment: The Minnesota Clinical Report

The Minnesota Report, a computerized interpretation for the MMPI-2, was originally developed as an aid in clinical assessment (see Butcher, 1987a, b, 1989a, b). The Minnesota Report was revised in 1989 to incorporate the new MMPI-2 norms and new clinical information and most recently in 2005 (Butcher, 2005c). Several goals have been kept in mind in developing the Minnesota Report interpretation systems:

1. The interpretive system was developed as a conservative evaluation of the client based as closely as possible on established research.
2. Several specific programs were developed to match needs according to setting or application. Reports were developed for a number of settings:

   a. Adult inpatient
   b. Adult outpatient
   c. College counseling
   d. Correctional
   e. Medical settings
   f. Chronic pain programs
   g. Substance abuse programs

1. Special demographic considerations were taken into account in the development of the system. Reports are tailored to certain demographic characteristics of a case, particularly age and marital status. New data on personality correlates for the scales from the MMPI-2 Restandardization Project were incorporated in the reports.
2. The interpretive reports were developed in a format that would be clinically useful, with information provided to meet the clinician's informational needs concerning symptom description, diagnostic hypotheses, and treatment conditions.
3. The interpretive system was written in a format that allows for easy modification as new research findings on the MMPI-2 emerge.

Illustration of the Minnesota Report

Computer-based MMPI-2 interpretation will be illustrated with an in-depth evaluation and exploration of two individuals who were being assessed for substance abuse treatment programs. The two people were a man, aged 23, who was being evaluated for admission into an inpatient substance abuse program, and his girlfriend, a 25-year-old woman, who was being evaluated for outpatient substance abuse treatment.

Case 135

Sam L., a 23-year-old man, was evaluated in conjunction with his entry into a substance abuse program. He has been using cocaine daily for at least 2 years and recently had an episode of disorientation that became very frightening to him and the woman with whom he lived. The episode lasted for several hours and, according to his girlfriend, he was alternately violent toward he (he struck her several times and threatened her with a knife) and suicidal (he apparently sat on a window ledge for about 45 minutes threatening to jump). She called his brother, who subdued him and took him to a hospital emergency room. He was admitted and sedated. The next morning, he signed himself out and returned home. His girlfriend was already packing to move out on his return. He pleaded with her to stay, and she agreed, provided he seeks help. She has also used cocaine during the past 8 months while they have lived together and has agreed to enter treatment with him (see Case 136).

He is the second of two sons (his brother, age 25, is a CPA). His mother, age 48, is a college graduate and has taught elementary school for 5 years (she did not finish her college studies until Sam entered college, although she had completed 2 years before her oldest son was born). There is no reported psychiatric history in the immediate family.

The patient graduated from college at age 21, having majored in business. His GPA was 2.9. Since graduation he has been employed as an industrial salesman for a chemical manufacturing firm (solvents). His work history is reported to be good, and he has received four salary increases during 27 months, as

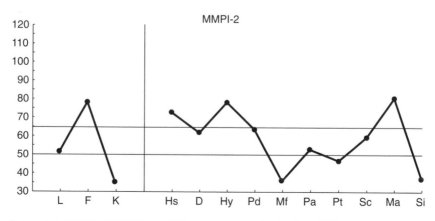

Figure 7.1. MMPI-2 Validity and Clinical scale profile for Case 135.

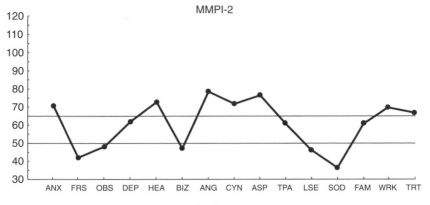

Figure 7.2. MMPI-2 Content scale profile for Case 135.

well as a bonus during the past year. He indicated that he enjoys his work and expects to become an assistant sales manager in the near future. He has asked for and received a 3-week leave of absence. He reported an unremarkable developmental history with no serious injuries or illnesses. He reported that he was close to both parents and especially close to his brother, with whom he shared a bedroom until age 9. He and his brother both played Little League baseball and were in Boy Scouts until he was 15. The patient claims many high school and college friends and was in a fraternity in college. He reportedly first had sex at age 15. He dated one girl regularly during his sophomore year in college, but she broke up with him. He met his current girlfriend about 18 months ago, and they began living together in his apartment about 9 months ago. They have discussed marriage, but he is reluctant until he feels more secure in his work. He admits that their sexual relationship is "not always good," but he now attributes this to his cocaine addiction (she reported that he has a high frequency of impotence or premature ejaculation; she also notes that he frequently asks her to dress in unusual ways to provoke him).

Sam reported that he became involved with cocaine casually during his senior year in college (he had been using marijuana since high school) and that he found it helpful to him in dealing with the pressures of his job. Ultimately, he began using it daily (he gets it through a coworker). Sam claims that he usually would not use it during the day, except during the past months, but he did use it each evening at home. He drinks wine daily (one or two glasses).

Sam is 5 feet 11 inches, 175 pounds, athletic-looking, blonde, quite attractive, and neatly dressed. During the interview he was often guarded and asked that questions be repeated, but in responding he seemed open and willing to be cooperative. He was especially cautious in describing his feelings for his girlfriend: "She's just great; I don't know how she's put up with me. She really deserves better. I hope everything works out for her; I owe her a lot."

The treatment program that he is entering requires 14 days (minimum) of inpatient routine followed by a minimum of 6 weeks of outpatient treatment (twice per week—once individual and once group). His girlfriend will not go through the inpatient routine but instead will begin an 8-week outpatient routine (individual and group). Drug screening prior to the evaluation was positive but not toxic. The neuropsychological screening was essentially negative.

Case 136

Susan, a 25-year-old woman, was evaluated because she applied for outpatient treatment in a substance abuse program. She admits to the frequent use of cocaine (in the evenings) with her boyfriend (see Case 135). He has become disabled because of cocaine addiction and is entering an inpatient program. She says that she wants to enter treatment (1) to help with his rehabilitation, and (2) because she feels unable to "say no" when drugs are offered to her. She does not want to go through the inpatient program for fear of losing her job. If accepted into the outpatient program, she will be seen twice a week—once individually and once in a group—for a minimum of 8 weeks.

She is the only child of a couple who divorced when she was 9. She lived with her mother, who is now 47, and an aunt, now age 51, until age 22. Her mother works as an assistant manager in a bookstore, and her aunt is a secretary. She has had no contact with her father, age 50, for 6 years except for occasional letters or cards. He remarried and moved to a distant state shortly after high school graduation. Prior to that time he visited five to eight times per year, usually on special occasions (Christmas, birthday, etc.). He was apparently treated for alcoholism when she was in junior high school, and to the best of her knowledge he has remained dry. He works for an oil company in a blue-collar position. She is vague about the reasons for her parents' divorce but suspects that her father was unfaithful to his wife and was alcoholic.

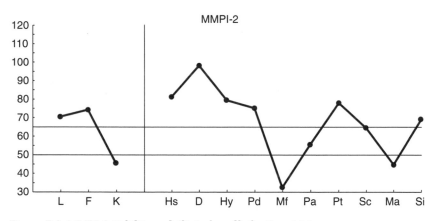

Figure 7.3. MMPI-2 Validity and Clinical profile for Case 136.

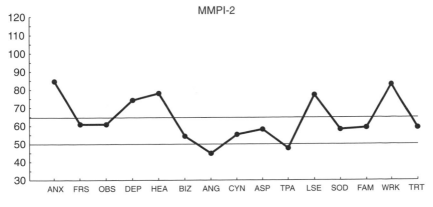

Figure 7.4. MMPI-2 Content scale profile for Case 136.

She reported that a series of urinary infections caused her to be bedridden quite often when she was between the ages of 3 and 6, and she entered school a year late. She had problems with skin rashes in grades 6 through 8 that were apparently caused by allergies, and for that reason she was exempt from gym classes. That problem cleared up by the time she entered high school, although she continued with allergy shots until age 16. She graduated from high school at age 19 (C+, B− average). She worked 1 year in the bookstore where her mother works and then began training as a dental technician. She completed that course, was certified at age 22, and obtained a position as dental assistant with a group practice, where she still works. She says that she likes her work and anticipates staying in her present position indefinitely.

She says that because she was "frail" she often did not join in the games of other children during elementary school, and because of her allergy problems she did not have many friends in junior high or in her first 2 years of high school. She began menstruation at age 13 and had serious cramping problems for the next 2 years. She went to her first school dance at age 16. Not long after, at another dance, a boy kissed and fondled her. She had her first experience of intercourse with him about 4 months later, which she says was not very pleasant for her. She abstained from future sex until she was in dental training. After completing her training she began sharing an apartment with two other girls (a secretary, age 27, and an airline agent, age 25). Since that time she has "slept with 8 or 10 guys," but did not experience orgasm until she met her current boyfriend at a party about 18 months ago. They have been living together for the past 9 months. She says, "I love him and he loves me. If we didn't do all the coke we'd get along a lot better, but when we get high, things just don't go right and he loses his temper a lot when that happens." She says that sex with him is "really good except when he has trouble and then he makes me do a lot of weird things." Apparently he buys exotic underwear for her and asks her to dance in it. He has also bought her a vibrator. If she is reluctant he loses his temper, although he has not been assaultive to her until his recent episode of disorientation. She is clearly concerned abut his treatment and implies that she is quite apprehensive about their future relationship.

She is 5 feet 5 inches, 126 pounds, with long brown hair, and though not striking, somewhat attractive. She was cooperative and smiled a great deal while talking about herself. The drug screening was negative although some trace activity was noted. Neuropsychological screening was negative.

(This case was provided by John Exner, a long-time contributor to the literature on the Rorschach and developer of the Rorschach Comprehensive System, who died in 2006. The Rorschach protocols were processed by Rorschach Workshops, Asheville, N.C.; the scoring summaries are reproduced in the book's appendix with the permission of John Exner, which he provided for the first edition of this book.)

Psychological Test Results: Minnesota Reports for the MMPI-2

The Minnesota Report narrative interpretations for Cases 135 and 136 are shown below.

Minnesota Report Narrative for Case 135

MMPI-2 The Minnesota Report: Adult Clinical System Interpretive Report

Profile Validity   This is a valid MMPI-2 profile. The client has cooperated in the evaluation, admitting to a number of psychological problems in a frank and open manner. Individuals with this profile tend to be blunt and may openly complain to others about their psychological problems. The client tends to be quite self-critical and may appear to have low self-esteem and inadequate psychological defense mechanisms. He may be seeking psychological help at this time since he feels that things are out of control and unmanageable.

Symptomatic Patterns   The client is exhibiting a pattern of physical problems which has reduced his level of psychological functioning. These symptoms may be vague and may have appeared suddenly after a period of stress or trauma. The pattern of pain, physical symptoms, irritability, low frustration tolerance, and anger outbursts suggests that the possibility of an organic brain dysfunction should be evaluated.

The client seems to have a rather limited range of interests and tends to prefer stereotyped masculine activities over literary and artistic pursuits or introspective experiences. He tends to be somewhat competitive and needs to see himself as masculine. He probably prefers to view women in subservient roles. Interpersonally, he is likely to be intolerant and insensitive, and others may find him rather crude, coarse, or narrow-minded.

In addition, the following description is suggested by the content of this client's responses. He complains about feeling quite uncomfortable and in poor health. The symptoms he reports reflect vague weakness, fatigue, and difficulties in concentration. In addition, he feels that others are unsympathetic toward his perceived health problems. He seems to be highly manipulative and self-indulgent. He seems to have had much past conflict with authority and is quite resentful of societal standards of conduct.

Interpersonal Relations   He is probably experiencing difficulty with interpersonal relationships. He may have an overly critical, perfectionistic, and rigid interpersonal style, and may be prone to losing his temper.

His social interests appear to be high and he seems to enjoy social participation. However, his interpersonal behavior may be problematic at times in the sense that he may lose his temper in frustrating situations.

The content of this client's MMPI-2 responses suggests the following additional information concerning his interpersonal relations. He appears to be an individual who holds rather cynical views about life. Any efforts to initiate new behaviors may be colored by his negativism. He may view relationships with others as threatening and harmful. He feels some family conflict at this time. However, this does not appear to him to be a major problem at this time. He feels like leaving home to escape a quarrelsome, critical situation, and to be free of family domination. He feels intensely angry, hostile, and resentful of others, and would like to get back at them. He is competitive and uncooperative, tending to be critical of others.

Behavioral Stability   Apparently rather unstable, he may behave in erratic, unpredictable, and possible aggressive ways. Social introversion-extraversion tends to be a very stable personality characteristic over time. The client's typically outgoing and sociable behavior is likely to remain similar if retested at a later time.

Diagnostic Considerations   The possibility of an organic illness should be evaluated. If organic problems are ruled out, the most characteristic diagnosis would be Conversion Disorder or Somatization Disorder. His behavioral characteristics can also be exhibited by individuals with a Post-Traumatic Stress Syndrome.

Treatment Considerations   If physical findings are negative, there is a strong possibility that the problems are based on psychological factors. Discussing the possible psychological basis to his disorder with him may be somewhat problematic since he tends to resist psychological interpretation.

Insight-oriented treatment approaches tend not to be very appropriate for individuals with this personality makeup. They are not very insightful and may resist actively entering into a therapeutic relationship. Individuals with this MMPI-2 profile tend to have problems establishing a psychotherapeutic alliance, since they view their problems as organically based.

The strong hostility component in this personality pattern may militate against his developing a positive therapeutic relationship. Behavior modification procedures may be valuable in reducing his agitation and anxiety. Cognitive–behavioral anger control procedures may be employed to reduce his aggressiveness and potential for loss of control. He harbors some negative work attitudes which could limit his adaptability in the work place. His low morale and disinterest in work could impair future adjustment to employment, a factor which should be taken into consideration in treatment.

Note: This MMPI-2 interpretation can serve as a useful source of hypotheses about clients. This report is based on objectively derived scale indexes and scale interpretations that have been developed in diverse groups of patients. The personality descriptions, inferences and recommendations contained herein need to be verified by other sources of clinical information since individual clients may not fully match this prototype. The information in this report should most appropriately be used by a trained, qualified test interpreter. The information contained in this report should be considered confidential.

Conclusions from the Minnesota Report
Narrative for Case 135

The client's approach to the MMPI-2 was oriented toward presenting himself as having considerable problems and low resources for dealing with them at this time. As noted in the narrative report, he perceived his problems as mostly centering on poor health. He attempted to convey that his present problems were largely somatic in origin. As described in the computer report, the symptom pattern he presented often follows a period of intense stress or trauma. In addition, the narrative report, attempting to account for the excitability, sense of frustration, and anger in his response pattern, suggests that these problems might reflect some organic impairment in his case.

The client seems to be viewing his physical problems as his most important treatment need at this time; however, this self-presentation (as viewed largely through the MMPI-2 clinical scales) is highly exaggerated. The content scales provide a somewhat different and perhaps a more pathological view of his personality functioning. His performance on the content scales suggests a severe personality disorder that requires careful consideration in any treatment plan. A number of statements in the narrative report address clear antisocial personality features and anger control problems that require consideration in his case. His psychological adjustment was considered to be unstable, and the possibility of erratic, unpredictable, and aggressive behavior was noted in the report.

The narrative report also addresses the client's somewhat negative view of women. He appears to be rather intolerant and insensitive in relationships with women and may easily become frustrated and lose his temper with them.

The computer report presents a somewhat cautious picture concerning his treatment amenability, noting that individuals with this pattern tend not be very insightful or reflective in viewing their problems and may resist psychological interpretation. Insight-oriented treatment may be inappropriate for him because of his cynical attitudes about life and his tendency to exaggerate physical problems in dealing with conflict. Since he apparently has a problem with anger control, treatment relationship difficulties may be encountered. The computer report suggests the possibility that a cognitive–behavioral treatment approach to anger control might result in a reduction of his aggressiveness and loss of control.

Another situation that needs to be considered in any rehabilitative effort with him is that he presents some negative work attitudes that could hamper future adjustment to life. These negative work attitudes should be addressed in treatment if he remains in therapy.

Minnesota Report Narrative for Case 136

MMPI-2 The Minnesota Report: Adult Clinical System Interpretive Report

Profile Validity   The client has responded to the MMPI-2 items by claiming to be unrealistically virtuous. This test-taking attitude weakens the validity of the test and shows an unwillingness or inability on the part of the client to disclose personal information. The resulting MMPI-2 profile is unlikely to provide much useful information about the client since she was too guarded to cooperate in the self-appraisal. Despite this extreme defensiveness, she has responded to items reflecting some unusual symptoms or beliefs. Many reasons may be found for this pattern of uncooperativeness: conscious distortion to present herself in a favorable light; limited intelligence or lack of psychological sophistication; or rigid neurotic adjustment.

The client's efforts to thwart the evaluation and project an overly positive self-image produced an MMPI-2 profile that substantially underestimates her psychological maladjustment. The test interpretation should proceed with the caution that the clinical picture reflected in the profile is probably an overly positive one and may not provide sufficient information for evaluation.

Symptomatic Patterns   This client's profile presents a broad and mixed picture in which physical complaints and depressed affect are salient elements. The client is exhibiting much somatic distress and may be experiencing a problem with her psychological adjustment. Her physical complaints are probably extreme, possibly reflecting a general lack of effectiveness in life. She is probably feeling quite tense and nervous, and may be feeling that she cannot get by without help for her physical problems. She is likely to be reporting a great deal of pain, and feels that others do not understand how sick she is feeling. She may be quite irritable and may become hostile if her symptoms are not given "proper" attention.

Many individuals with this profile have a history of psychophysiological disorders. They tend to overreact to minor problems with physical symptoms. Ulcers and gastrointestinal distress are common. The possibility of actual organic problems, therefore, should be carefully evaluated. Individuals with this profile report a great deal of tension and a depressed mood. They tend to be pessimistic and gloomy in their outlook toward life.

In addition, the following description is suggested by the content of this client's responses. She is preoccupied with feeling guilty and unworthy. She feels that she deserves to be punished for wrongs she has committed. She feels regretful and unhappy about life, and seems plagued by anxiety and worry about the future. She feels hopeless at times and feels that she is a condemned person. She has difficulty managing routine affairs and the item content she endorsed suggests a poor memory, concentration problems, and an inability to make decisions. She appears to be immobilized and withdrawn and has no energy for life. According to her self-report, there is a strong possibility that she has seriously contemplated suicide. She feels somewhat self-alienated and expresses some personal misgivings or a vague sense of remorse about past acts. She feels that life is unrewarding and dull, and finds it hard to settle down.

Interpersonal Relations   She appears to be somewhat passive-dependent in relationships. She may manipulate others through her physical symptoms, and become hostile if sufficient attention is not paid to her complaints.

She appears to be rather shy and inhibited in social situations, and may avoid others for fear of being hurt. She has very few friends, and is considered by others as "hard to get to know." She is quiet, submissive, conventional, and lacks self-confidence in dealing with other people. Individuals with this passive and withdrawing lifestyle are often unable to assert themselves appropriately, and find that they are frequently taken advantage of by others.

Behavioral Stability   There are likely to be long-standing personality problems predisposing her to develop physical symptoms under stress. Her present disorder could reflect, in part, an exaggerated response to environmental stress. Social introversion tends to be a very stable personality characteristic. Her generally reclusive interpersonal behavior, introverted lifestyle, and tendency toward interpersonal avoidance would likely be evident in any future test results.

Diagnostic Considerations   Individuals with this profile type are often seen as neurotic, and may receive a diagnosis of Somatoform Disorder. Actual organic problems such as ulcers and hypertension might be part of the clinical picture. Some individuals with this profile have problems with abuse of pain medication or other prescription drugs.

Treatment Considerations   Her view of herself as physically disabled needs to be considered in any treatment planning. She tends to somatize her difficulties and to seek medical solutions rather than to deal with them psychologically. She seems to tolerate a high level of psychological conflict and may not be motivated to deal with her problems directly. She is not a strong candidate for insight-oriented psychotherapy. Psychological treatment may progress more rapidly if her symptoms are dealt with through behavior modification techniques. However, with her generally pessimistic attitude and low energy resources, she seems to have little hope of getting better.

The item content she endorsed indicates attitudes and feelings that suggest a low capacity for self-change. Her potentially high resistance to change might need to be discussed with her early in treatment in order to promote a more treatment-expectant attitude. In any intervention or psychological evalua-tion program involving occupational adjustment, her negative work attitudes could become an important problem to overcome. She holds a number of at-titudes and feelings that could interfere with work adjustment.

Note: This MMPI-2 interpretation can serve as a useful source of hypotheses about clients. This report is based on objectively derived scale indexes and scale interpretations that have been developed in diverse groups of patients. The personality descriptions, inferences and recommendations contained herein need to be verified by other sources of clinical information since individual cli-ents may not fully match this prototype. The information in this report should most appropriately be used by a trained, qualified test interpreter. The infor-mation contained in this report should be considered confidential.

Conclusions from the Minnesota Report
Narrative for Case 136

The Minnesota Report narrative for Case 136 addressed many of the prob-lems this woman was experiencing and described several important personal-ity features she appears to possess. First, the validity paragraph pointed out an interesting aspect of her self-report that requires some discussion. Even though she reported a number of problems and acknowledged several chronic personality problems, she had a very high L score, which suggests caution in interpreting her clinical profile. The nature of her scale elevations on the clini-cal scales (D and Pt) probably confirms the interpretation of scale L as rigidity of her personal adjustment.

The symptomatic pattern in her narrative report addressed her depressed mood and intense psychological distress. Moreover, her self-report also focused on a prominent pattern of somatization that could prove resistant to treat-ment. Her personal history offers some suggestion of complicating somatic predisposition (she was described as being "frail" and having had numerous medical problems in the past). A therapist attempting to engage her in psycho-logical treatment should be aware that she may tend to somatize psychologi-cal conflict rather than deal with it on a psychological level.

Central to her adjustment problems appears to be her passive-dependent personality style, low self-esteem, and poor self-concept. The Minnesota Report narrative, drawing both from the clinical scales configuration and the MMPI-2 content scales, particularly Low Self-Esteem, points to the pervasive, chronic nature of her problems. These self-esteem problems are salient in her inability to "resist" drugs when they are offered to her. Her MMPI profile and LSE scores are quite consistent with that of a long-suffering, codependent behavior pattern often found in spouses of alcoholics.

Two problematic features, noted in the narrative, were drawn from the MMPI-2 content scales WRK and TRT. She appears to endorse many symptoms and attitudes suggestive of an inability to change her behaviors toward more productive work attitudes and positive self-change in therapy. It is likely that, early in her treatment, a therapist would need to address these possibly negative indicators that could signal both treatment and work failures.

The computer-based interpretation of the MMPI-2 profiles provided a clear description of the two individuals described in the case histories.

Psychological Test Results: Rorschach Interpretation

The Rorschach scoring summaries for Cases 135 and 136 are included, in full, in the appendix at the end of the book. The Rorschach protocols have also been interpreted by John Exner, using the Exner Comprehensive Rorschach Interpretation System, and are included in the following summaries.

Interpretive Summary of the Rorschach— Case 135

Although this 23-year-old man usually has about as much capacity for control and tolerance for stress as do most adults, those features have now become more limited because of some situationally related stress. This experience has created a form of stimulus overload that has had an impact on both his thinking and his feelings. As a consequence, he has become more vulnerable to impulsive behavior, both ideational and emotional. He tends to feel much more helpless and unable to form meaningful responses than is usually the case, and his psychological functioning has become much more complex because of this. He tends to be confused about his feelings and uncertain about his ability to contend with this situation.

He is an extremely self-centered person who exaggerates his own personal worth considerably. In effect, he harbors a narcissistic-like feature that he usually expects those around him to reinforce. He prefers to be dependent upon others who become crucial in allowing him to form and maintain deep and mature interpersonal relationships. In reality, he is less interested in others than are most people, perceiving them mainly as a source on which he can depend. He is quite defensive about his self-image and often takes a more authoritarian approach to those who pose challenges to him.

He is the type of person who invests feelings into most of his decision-making perations and is less concerned with the modulation of his own emotional displays than are most adults. In other words, when he discharges his feelings, they tend to be overly intense and possibly overly influential in his decisions.

He is quite aware of acceptable and conventional behaviors; however, his exquisite self-centeredness often caused him to disregard them in favor of more idiographic patterns of behavior that are in concert with his own needs and wants. He tends to look on the environment negatively and often attempts to deal with it in a pseudointellectual manner that permits him to justify his own activities. He is usually very unwilling to accept responsibility for any behavioral errors, preferring instead to rationalize the causes of problems as being the responsibility of the external world.

Overall, he is the type of person who has a strong need to be in control of his environment. It is unlikely that he would seek out any form of psychological intervention unless he could feel assured that it was directly beneficial to him and in a model over which he had control. He is not very insightful and has no strong interest in changing.

Interpretive Summary of the Rorschach— Case 136

The test data suggests that this 25-year-old woman is quite immature. She does not have good capacities for control or tolerance for stress, and those limitations have become reduced even further by the presence of situationally related stress. As such, she is extremely vulnerable to impulsiveness, both ideational and emotional, and will have considerable difficulty functioning in all but the most highly structured situations.

Basically, she is very passive and dependent kind of person who probably finds the demands of adulthood to be much more hectic and complex than she is able to deal with easily. She has learned to be very cautious in processing information and works hard to avoid processing errors. When she translates information that she has processed, however, she is often prone to be more individualistic than conventional in her interpretation of it. It seems reasonable to speculate that she is the type of person who would prefer more mature interactions, but has been unable to establish them, and as a result has settled on a more peripheral coexistence with her world.

Her self-image is much more negative than positive. She often perceives others as having more assets and capacities than she, and tends to feel quite inadequate. She often ruminates about her own negative characteristics, and this ruminative tendency will frequently give rise to experiences of depression.

She is the type of person who prefers to think things through before forming or implementing a decision, but much of her thinking is unfortunately more detached from reality than focused on it. In fact, flights into fantasy have become a major defensive tactic for her. In other words, whenever the world becomes too harsh or ungiving, she is prone to replace it with a fantasy existence that is more easily managed. She dislikes responsibility and tries to avoid making major decisions whenever possible, relying instead on those around her for that task. She sets very low goals for herself and has come to view the future much more pessimistically than do most adults.

Overall, she is the type of person who seems to have resigned herself to roles in life in which she can be passively dependent on those around her. Her expectations are low, and she seems to anticipate that life will be a series of crises in which she will become the victim. She would like to experience more positive interactions with others but does not expect that this will evolve. She is the sort of person who can benefit considerably from long-term developmental forms of intervention.

Limitations of Computer-Based MMPI-2 Interpretation

In spite of their acceptability, ease of use, and relative accuracy, computer-based reports should not be used as the sole source of clinical information. The Minnesota Report should be used with appropriate cautions. Several factors need to be considered: the limited range of available correlates; the prototypal match of the particular patient being evaluated; and the degree of accuracy in predicting and describing personality.

The Limited Range of Available Test Correlates

Over the past 50 years investigators have attempted to catalog empirical correlates for the various MMPI scales and indexes. Unfortunately, the actuarial base for the MMPI does not, even now, provide extensive replicated correlates for the full range of possible profile configurations. Given this fact, it is likely that the clinical experience of the program developer will determine the makeup of many of the reports generated. The decisions concerning which component to employ in the development of a computer-interpretation program clearly influences the accuracy and generalizability of the report. As Fowler (1987) noted, it is therefore important when choosing a computer-based interpretation program to evaluate carefully the expertise of the system developer. Most MMPI computer-interpretation programs, in order to be comprehensive and interpret all cases, must extrapolate from the available research information base. For example, solid actuarial data do not exist for a 1-9-6 MMPI profile code; consequently, the interpretation needs to be based on the component scales. The computer program developer might follow a scale-by-scale interpretation strategy or one that involves extracting elements from the component codes, 1–9, 9–6, or 1–6. Whichever approach is taken will result in somewhat different narrative reports.

Determining the Prototypal Match

Does the report fit the patient? This decision rests with the system user. At present, computerized personality test reports are not designed to stand alone in a clinical psychological assessment. They are resources that can be used by a trained psychologist or psychiatrist in conjunction with other sources of clinical assessment information to understand the client's symptoms and problems. As resource material the automated MMPI report can provide a useful summary of hypotheses, descriptions, and test inferences about patients in a rapid and efficient manner. Narrative reports, since they are based on modal or typical descriptions of the profile type, should be verified for goodness of fit by the clinician through other sources of information.

An interesting paradox presents itself. We are most comfortable with a computer-based report (or a clinician-derived report) when it meet the expectations we have developed about the patient from our clinical interview. We usually then consider the computer narrative "a good match" because it confirmed our expectations; however, we tend to consider suspect reports that do *not* match our expectations and that seem to be presenting disparate information.

There is, of course, the possibility that the report contains information that is correct, but the clinician was unaware of it. Thus, even seemingly inaccurate reports might provide the clinician with leads to potentially fruitful material. A relatively common situation that occurs in clinical settings is the incorrect impressions generated by high-Pd or 4–9 clients. These people commonly present well and make favorable impressions and are generally adept at influencing others in interpersonal interaction. In such cases, the MMPI-2 might actually be more accurate (less vulnerable to interpersonal influence) than the practitioner's early impressions.

Butcher Treatment Planning Inventory

The BTPI scales provide extensive information on patient characteristics that could affect the psychotherapy process, particularly those characteristics that could prevent or delay therapy-related change. At the beginning of therapy, the full form of the BTPI, 210 items, can provide the practitioner with extensive information on the client's treatment readiness and mental health symptoms. In the early stages of psychotherapy, it can highlight initial treatment foci, whether psychological symptoms, process factors, or interpersonal variables. The BTPI Symptom Monitoring Form, 80 items, can also be administered at different points during the course of psychotherapy to evaluate changes in symptom expression and attitudes toward treatment progress. Although the BTPI was developed as a means of obtaining an easy and rapid summary with manual scoring procedures referred to as the QuikScore™ system using a paper-and-pencil format (see Butcher, 2005), computer scoring and interpretation software is available to score and interpret the results of the test. Both the computer-interpreted Full Form of the BTPI and the Symptom Monitoring Form will be illustrated. For further information contact:

MHS Inc.
    P.O. Box 950
    North Tonawanda, NY 14120–0950
    or
    MHS Inc.
    3770 Victoria Park Ave.
    Toronto, Ontario M2H 3M6
    http://www.mhs.com/

The case to be described is a businessman who was experiencing a severe depressive disorder and was being evaluated in a pretreatment psychological evaluation.

Case History

Referral Problem

Charles V., a 39-year-old restaurant owner, was evaluated in an outpatient private practice treatment setting for symptoms of depression and inability to sleep. He has been encouraged to seek psychological treatment for his depressed mood by his wife and his family physician, who also prescribed an antidepressant medication (Paxil) for him. He has been experiencing depression and sleep disorder for the past 6 months. He attributes his depression primarily to difficult business circumstances over the past year and to family stress (problematic family relationships): his father and a brother have become very angry at him for what they view as his failures to help the family. There is also a family history for depression: both Charles' father and grandfather had been hospitalized for mood disorders. Charles had a prior incident of depression when he was 19 years old, when he was seen by a counselor in college.

Charles has been taking antidepressant medication for the past 3 months but his mood symptoms have persisted and he has been experiencing some side effects such as nausea, diarrhea, dry mouth, constipation, and decreased appetite. He has been experiencing early awakening and difficulty falling asleep for several months and has also been taking Ambien for help in sleeping. He reportedly is reluctant to continue taking sleeping medication because of the drowsiness, dizziness, headaches, and lightheadedness he has experienced, along with some difficulty with coordination.

He is married and has two children, a boy age 10 and a girl age 8. His wife, who he sees as usually very supportive, also works with him in their family business. His mother, who was a strong supporter of Charles and his family,

Cluster 1: Validity

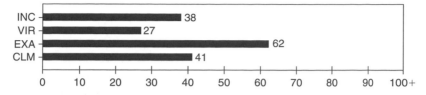

Cluster 2: Treatment Issues

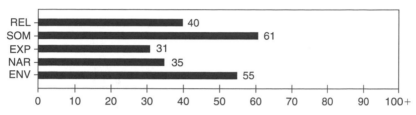

Cluster 3: Current Symptoms

Composite Scales

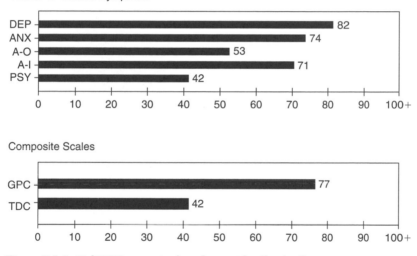

Figure 7.5. Initial BTPI computer-based report for Charles V.

died a year earlier. His father, who had been divorced from his mother for several years, has borrowed a substantial amount of money from Charles. Both Charles and his wife, because of business difficulties, have discontinued this financial support and have been criticized by his father and a brother for not helping them more. This situation has resulted, at times, in Charles feeling like he has failed the family.

His performance on the Full Form of the BTPI is shown on the profile in Figure 7.5. His performance on the BTPI as summarized by the MHS computer interpretation system is as follows.

Computer-Based BTPI Report

Validity of the Report   Charles approached the BTPI items in a clearly frank and open manner, producing a valid review of his state of thinking about his problem situation. Although possibly somewhat exaggerated in intensity, his report of symptoms on other BTPI scales is likely to be a valid indicator of his current psychological symptoms.

Charles has presented a number of problems on the BTPI. Although the test protocol is not likely to be invalid, he has reported more symptoms and problems than most people do. The therapist might profitably focus on these problem areas to provide the client an opportunity to further explore them.

His low scores on VIR reflect an openness that is consistent with being self-disclosing in psychological treatment.

Treatment Issues   Individuals who score high on the SOM scale are reporting physical distress at this time. They seem to feel that their problems are primarily physical, and they tend to ignore emotional conflict. They show some tendency to channel psychological conflict into physical symptoms such as headache, pain, or stomach distress. They tend to be concerned over their health and seem to reduce their activities as a result of their physical concerns. They tend to view themselves as tired and worried that their health is not better.

Some individuals with this BTPI pattern have low self-esteem and a poor self-concept. These characteristics can negatively affect efforts at self-improvement and require particular sensitivity on the part of the therapist to motivate the client to sustain effort toward the treatment plan.

Current Symptoms   Charles has reported an extreme number of symptoms that reflect a likely mood disorder. He feels very depressed and lacks the energy to pursue his daily activities. He feels as though his current life is so filled with unpleasantness that he has difficulty just getting by. He reports that he is having problems sleeping and feels tired all the time. Mood symptoms are common among psychotherapy clients and may reflect a general demoralization as well as specific mood disorder. Depression (DEP) was the most common peak score in the Minnesota Psychotherapy Assessment Project sample: 37% of the sample had T scores > 64, and 23% of these cases had DEP as their peak Current Symptom scale score.

In addition, he has also reported other psychological symptoms on the BTPI items that need to be taken into consideration in evaluating his mood state. He also appears to be very anxious at this time. He is reporting great difficulty as a result of his tension, fearfulness, and inability to concentrate effectively. He seems to worry over even small matters to the point that he can't seem to sit still. His daily functioning is severely impaired because of his worries and an inability to make decisions.

Along with the problems described above, there are other symptoms reflected in his BTPI response pattern that need to be considered in assessing his current symptomatic picture. He appears to have low self-esteem and usually takes a subservient role in interpersonal situations. He readily takes blame for problems he has had no part in originating in order to placate other, more dominant persons. He turns anger inward and appears to punish himself unreasonably at times.

Treatment Planning   His symptom description suggests some concerns that could become the focus of psychological treatment if the client can be engaged in the treatment process. The provision of test feedback about his problem description might prove valuable in promoting accessibility to therapy.

The therapist needs to be alert to the client's typical reliance upon somatic defense mechanisms in dealing with interpersonal conflict. His avoidance mechanisms could create difficulty in his dealing effectively with conflicts that occur in his interpersonal relations.

Severe depressive symptoms as he has reported need to be targeted for attention in early treatment sessions. Clients with such mood problems may respond to cognitive-behavioral or dynamic treatment strategies, providing that clear emotional support is given at this time to lower his mood symptoms.

The therapist needs to keep in mind that he appears to be prone to react to stressful situations with catastrophic reactions.

Progress Monitoring   Charles obtained a General Pathology Composite (GPC) T score of 77. He has endorsed a broad range of mental health symptoms on the BTPI. His elevated GPC index score indicates that he acknowledged a number of mental health symptoms that require attention in psychological treatment. For a statistically significant change, based on 90% confidence interval, a subsequent GPC T score must be above 83 or below 71.

Charles obtained a Treatment Difficulty Composite (TDC) T score of 42. Overall, his TDC index score is well within the normal range, indicating that he has not acknowledged many of the personality-based symptoms addressed by the BTPI to assess difficult treatment relationships. For a statistically significant change, based on a 90% confidence interval, a subsequent TDC T score must be above 49 or below 35.

Special Issues to Address in Therapy   The client has endorsed item content that likely bears some critical importance to his progress in psychological treatment. The Special Problem items are printed out if the client responded in the critical direction. The item endorsement frequencies for the item are also provided for the Normative Sample (N) and the Clinical Sample (C). These issues noted below should be followed up in an early treatment session.

Note: He has endorsed some item content related to suicidal thinking that should be addressed in early treatment sessions.

158. (T) I feel so disappointed with the way things have turned out in my life that I wish I were dead. (N% = 5.8) (C% = 13.2)

It should be noted in discussing treatment goals with him that he has endorsed some item content associated with the development of a substance use or abuse problem.

44. (T) At times I think that I drink too much alcohol. (N% = 22.0) (C% = 18.0)

162. (T) I usually have a drink to pick up my spirits at the end of the day. (N% = 13.2) (C% = 5.3)

164. (T) I really enjoy drinking alcohol. (N% = 29.3) (C% = 23.8)

Treatment Setting

Charles was referred for outpatient psychotherapy on a twice-weekly basis for the first 3 months, after which he was seen weekly for 3 additional months. His wife was also interviewed by the therapist in the early stages of treatment. Charles continued to take Paxil during the first 3 months of treatment. The treatment approach taken with Charles was providing emotional support and assisting him in developing more effective problem-resolution strategies through cognitive–behavioral therapy.

Test Administration

Charles was initially administered the BTPI. He was retested with the Symptom Monitoring Form of the test after 3 months, at which point he was beginning to feel as though his depression had lessened and he was beginning to sleep better. His performance on the Symptom Monitoring Form of the BTPI as summarized by the MHS computer interpretation system is shown in Figure 7.6.

Initial Symptom Monitoring Report Narrative

Current Symptoms   Charles has reported an extreme number of symptoms that reflect a likely mood disorder. He feels very depressed and lacks the energy to pursue his daily activities. He feels as though his current life is so filed with unpleasantness that he has difficulty just getting by. He reports that is having problems sleeping and feels tired all the time. Mood symptoms are common among psychotherapy clients and may reflect a general demoralization as well as a specific mood disorder. Depression (DEP) was the most common peak score in the Minnesota Psychotherapy Assessment Project sample: 37% of the sample had T-scores > 64, and 23% of these cases had DEP as their peak Current Symptom scale score.

He has presented other symptoms through the BTPI items that require consideration if these attitudes are to be sufficiently understood. He appears to have low self-esteem and may take a subservient role in interpersonal situations. He seemingly takes blame for problems he has had no part in originating in order to placate other, more dominant persons. He turns anger inward and appears to punish himself unreasonably at times.

Along with the problems described above, there are other symptoms reflected in his BTPI response pattern that need to be considered in assessing

Scales

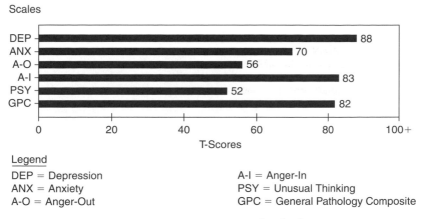

Legend

DEP = Depression   A-I = Anger-In
ANX = Anxiety   PSY = Unusual Thinking
A-O = Anger-Out   GPC = General Pathology Composite

Figure 7.6. First retest Symptom Monitoring Form for Charles V.

his current symptomatic picture. He also appears to be very anxious at this time. He is reporting great difficulty as a result of his tension, fearfulness, and inability to concentrate effectively. He seems to worry over even small matters to the point that he can't seem to sit still. His daily functioning is severely impaired because of his worries and an inability to make decisions.

Progress Monitoring   The General Pathology Composite (GGPC) T score of 82 places Charles in the 99th percentile when compared to the normative sample. He has acknowledged having an extensive number of mental health symptoms on the BTPI that should be addressed in treatment. His GPC index score indicates a large number of mental health symptoms across several problem areas that require attention in order to obtain a clear focus on psychological treatment issues. For a statistically significant change, based on 90% confidence interval, a subsequent GPC T score must be above 88 or below 76.

As treatment progressed and Charles began to show improvement, he was retested again 3 months later prior to termination from treatment, when he began to feel that he had resolved the problems that prompted his depression and no longer required therapy or medication. Charles gained a perspective on his relationship with his father and brother and resolved his guilt over ignoring their demands for further financial support. His performance on the BTPI as summarized by the MHS computer interpretation system is as follows (Fig. 7.7).

Second Symptom Monitoring
Report Narrative

Current Symptoms   Some individuals with his pattern of responses have low self-esteem problems and tend to be somewhat self-punitive.

Scales

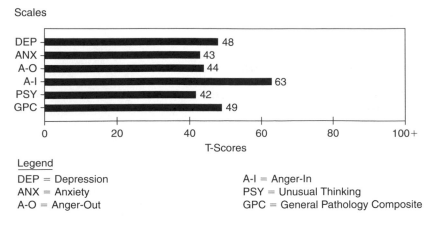

Legend

DEP = Depression   A-I = Anger-In
ANX = Anxiety   PSY = Unusual Thinking
A-O = Anger-Out   GPC = General Pathology Composite

Figure 7.7. Second retest Symptom Monitoring Form for Charles V.

Progress Monitoring   The General Pathology Composite (GPC) T score of 49 places Charles in the 58th percentile when compared to the normative sample. Overall, his GPC index score is well within the normal range, suggesting that he has not acknowledged many mental health symptoms. For a statistically significant change based on a 90% confidence interval, a subsequent GPC T score must be above 55 or below 43.

Control over Access to Computerized Narrative Reports

Patients are typically fascinated with computer-based personality test reports. Many patients will ask for a copy of their computerized report for their own records. For many reasons this is not a good idea. The most important reason for not providing reports to clients is that the computerized report is typically written for professionals and employs language not usually understandable by laypersons. Consequently, reports are easily misinterpreted unless the user is trained in interpreting the test.

Summary

Computer-based personality test interpretation has gained considerable acceptance over the past few decades. Clinicians are finding the computer-generated personality reports to be valuable additions to the pretreatment psychological assessment study. This chapter has discussed a number of issues concerning computer-based MMPI-2 and BTPI interpretation and provided a detailed description of the Minnesota Report and BTPI interpretive systems, along with clinical cases illustrating their utility. Illustrations of computerized reports were given. Possible limitations or special considerations in using computer-based MMPI-2 or BTPI reports were discussed.

8

Providing the Client Feedback with the MMPI-2

This chapter addresses the interrelated topics of the client's "need to know" and the therapist's "need to provide" pertinent personality information to the client in the early stages of treatment. A number of topics are addressed, beginning with the client's need to have objectively based information about himself or herself. Second, a viewpoint detailing the therapist's duty to provide psychological test feedback to potential or ongoing therapy clients is covered. Next, a description and illustration of a method for conducting test feedback sessions using the MMPI-2 or BTPI with clients will be described. And, finally, some of the pitfalls and limitations in the feedback process of which the therapist-diagnostician needs to be aware will be detailed.

As noted in Chapter 1, the field of personality assessment provides both methods and substantive empirical support for treatment-oriented evaluation and provision of test feedback for clients in therapy (Finn & Kamphuis, 2006). Finn and his colleagues (Finn & Tonsager, 1992) have provided a model for providing test feedback to clients that is referred to as therapeutic assessment following observations that some clients seemed to markedly improve after receiving detailed information about their personality and problem situation. This finding has also been reported by other assessment psychologists, including Fischer, in her work in *collaborative psychological assessment* (Fischer, 1985/1994, 2000), and Handler (1995). More will be said of the research in providing test feedback to clients later in this chapter.

Feedback as the Therapist's Duty

People in psychological distress who seek professional help make a number of assumptions about the qualities and the qualifications of their potential therapists. They assume that their therapists, in order to be "entitled" to the title they hold and the function they fulfill, possess knowledge of psychology and psychological problems, are generally savvy about life, have experience working with individuals with similar problems, and are ethical and devoted to helping others. Prospective clients further assume that the "knowledge base" of the therapist involves training and the use of some professional skills that could aid them in their troubles. In fact, therapists, whether they attempt to project it or not, are usually viewed with considerable respect and regard. Indeed, much of the "curative power" of a psychotherapist, at least in the early stages of treatment, is inherent in the *a priori* beliefs and assumptions held by the client. The client may or may not be aware that the specific training and academic backgrounds associated with different professions that engage in psychological treatment qualify them to apply some procedures but not others.

For example, having a medical background enables a psychiatrist to prescribe medications for a client but may not prepare him or her well in psychological assessment. A background in clinical or counseling psychology may lead the therapist to use different techniques, such as psychological tests, to help understand the problem situation, but it does not enable them to prescribe medications, except in some limited circumstances. Whatever the background of therapists, as far as clients are concerned, they all have in common the ability and capability to understand personal problems and to relate to them a systematic and consistent view of *what is the matter with them* and *how they might proceed to remedy the problem(s)*. In short, clients expect the therapist to give them direct feedback about their problems that will assist them in their recovery. This expectation translates into an important duty on the part of the therapist—the necessity to provide detailed information about the client's personality and problems at appropriate times in the treatment process. Yet many therapists and psychotherapeutic schools do not meet this basic need.

The therapist's requirement to provide feedback is variously interpreted by different schools of psychotherapy. Some approaches to treatment give extensive, in-depth psychological feedback to the client early in the therapy; others may only indirectly address the task of providing personality and interpersonal data for the client to incorporate into his or her treatment plan. Perhaps the most extreme viewpoint is the psychoanalytic view, which follows the strategy of providing limited feedback and limited direction early in the therapy; interpretations often do not enter into treatment directly until it is rather far along. Other theoretical views, such as the client-centered approach, provide minimal feedback and operate on the assumption that individuals will, under the conditions of unconditional positive regard and assurance of the therapist, eventually develop a consistent view of themselves without much directive feedback from the therapist.

Feedback as a Clinical Approach

One of the most important and clinically useful applications of personality assessment involves its use in providing personality and symptom information to individual clients. An MMPI-2 or BTPI profile interpretation or computerized clinical report, since it is usually based on established empirical correlates, provides objective, "external" information for appraising the client. Providing the client feedback on his or her problems early in treatment or in the pretreatment diagnostic assessment can provide very valuable clues to:

1. The extent and nature of the problems that the individual is currently experiencing, in comparison with those of other clients
2. Whether the individual is likely to be experiencing problems that require psychological intervention
3. The direction therapy needs to take with potential clients in order to provide valuable entry into the treatment process

In presenting personality test feedback to clients several factors, such as those that follow, need to be taken into account.

Timeliness of the Feedback

The psychological status or mood of the client receiving the feedback needs to be gauged in order to determine how and when the feedback should be presented. Providing test information to clients requires that the client be in sufficient contact with reality and have a "receptive" attitude toward the session and be able to perceive the test information accurately. Clients who are angry about the referral or are uncooperative with the evaluation may be particularly antagonistic in receiving test feedback. Clients who are extremely depressed may be unable to attend to or process information accurately in a single session early in treatment. In some cases, it might be advisable to present feedback over several sessions, "in manageable bits," or to defer feedback until later in treatment, when the client has acquired sufficient energy and emotional resources to deal with it. There is not necessarily a standard time or point in the treatment to provide test feedback. The earlier in the course of care that feedback is provided, the sooner the information can become a part of the therapy process. However, the clinician needs to judge the client's readiness to be presented with and incorporate test results.

Client Expectation

The setting in which the test was given is important to consider; for example, if the test was administered as part of a court-ordered evaluation, the test feedback is likely to be viewed differently by the client than if an assessment measure was given at the client's request. Consequently, the amount of detail and the level of the test inference need to be adapted to fit various situations. In providing feedback to bright, psychologically normal individuals receiving adoption counseling, the clinician would likely employ a different subset of adjective descriptors than those used with disturbed clients in an inpatient treatment context. Published sources such as Graham (2006) or Greene (2000) contain information about relevant MMPI-2 scale descriptors for varied groups. The clinician needs to decide on the appropriate reference group for the subject and select the test correlates accordingly. For example, it may be more relevant for the assessment of some groups, such as college students in a counseling setting, to refer to Drake and Oetting's (1959) code book or Graham's (2006) correlates rather than using correlates developed on an inpatient population in a Veterans Affairs hospital, such as Gilberstadt and Duker's (1965). On the other hand, the more recent set of MMPI-2 correlates in outpatient settings by Graham and colleagues (1999) or among therapy clients by Butcher, Rouse, and Perry (2000) may be quite appropriate.

Ability of the Client to Incorporate Personal Feedback

The client's level of intellectual functioning should be taken into account in deciding the amount and type of feedback to provide. For example, if the client is a well-educated person, more specific and detailed information as to the test findings and implications can be given; however, most people have neither the background nor the interest in the technical elements of the test to dwell on psychometric properties. The presentation should be varied to suit each individual's general fund of information and psychological sophistication.

Likely Length of Treatment

There is a more pressing need to provide test feedback early in therapy if treatment is to be brief (e.g., lasting 8 to 10 sessions) than if the therapy is to be of several months' duration; however, since most therapies are brief (lasting fewer than 25 sessions, per Butcher, 1997, and Koss & Butcher, 1986), feedback should not be delayed for too long, lest treatment terminate before the client has been able to learn about his or her test results.

Research on Using Test Feedback in Therapy

The nature of the therapeutic relationship is commonly accepted as a critical factor affecting therapy process and outcome. Multiple theorists and researchers (e.g., Frank, 1959, 1995; Orlinsky, Grawe, & Parks, 1994) have addressed the ways in which the relational aspect of the therapeutic dyad potentially affects treatment outcome. For those practitioners who provide both assessment and intervention services, the act of performing psychological assessment provides a point at which to begin building the "therapeutic alliance" with the client. One of the most commonly accepted definitions of this concept (which, like "resistance," has its roots firmly in psychoanalytic theory) is based on Bordin (1979). Bordin delineated three elements of an alliance: agreed-upon goals, one or more tasks that are assigned, and the establishment of bonds between the therapist and client.

Attention to this notion of "alliance" is important for several reasons, not the least of which being the fact that research points to its having an impact on therapy outcome (e.g., Horvath, 2001; Martin, Garske, & Davis, 2000). Multiple measures have been employed to assess clients' perceptions of their affiliation with their therapists. These include the Working Alliance Inventory (Horvath & Greenberg, 1989), the California Psychotherapy Alliance Scale (Gaston, 1991), and the Helping Alliance Questionnaire-II (Luborsky et al., 1996).

Several researchers have examined the utility of so-called "therapeutic assessment" models. One of the more popular models is Finn and Tonsager's Therapeutic Model of Assessment (TMA; 1992, 1997). TMA espouses the use of a comprehensive evaluation phase during which multiple modes of assessment are employed. Such modes of assessment may include self-reports, structured or unstructured interviews, tasks of performance, and inventories and other types of free-response tasks. According to Finn and Tonsager, throughout the assessment process there is a critical focus on such factors as developing and maintaining an empathetic connection with the individual, cooperating with him/her around the identification of individualized goals, and communicating assessment findings in a manner that addresses and emphasizes them. It is clear that this model encompasses elements more traditionally associated with formal psychotherapy, thereby blurring the boundaries between assessment and intervention in a way that is intended to promote alliance building in a helpful way.

Finn (1996a, b) has created a manual making specific recommendations around turning MMPI-2 assessment into a therapeutic endeavor by employing a TMA. His manual discusses the MMPI-2 as a therapeutic intervention in and of itself. He also posits that the general method of principles he describes can be applied, with modifications as needed, to other instruments and test batteries. He frames completion of the MMPI-2 as an intervention and discusses the notion that clients will be most engaged in completing the MMPI-2 when they are treated as collaborators whose ideas and cooperation are critical to the assessment process. He also emphasizes the importance of ensuring that test results be used to address clients' personal goals and that feedback be used to help them understand and manage their life problems. His model suggests that an initial interview, lasting 30 or 60 minutes, be used to build rapport and frame the assessment as a collaborative process. A significant component of this involves exploring with the client what he or she hopes to learn on the basis of the assessment. When clients raise reservations about undergoing MMPI-2 assessment, these are validated and addressed directly. At the end of this initial meeting, the MMPI-2 is introduced.

After the client has completed it, and in preparing for the feedback session, the assessor interprets and organizes the test findings. Next, he or she determines how to tailor the feedback to the client, considering which are the most relevant findings, what the client might already know about himself or herself, what the client might agree with when it comes to the findings, how the client might react to information that differs from pre-assessment notions about himself or herself, and how the findings relate to the client's overall goals. Once again, there is strong emphasis on using the test results to facilitate empathy. Finn makes specific recommendations regarding setting the client at ease and working with her or him to elaborate on the test findings. Finn cautions against creating a situation in which the assessor and client argue about test findings. He also advises against making the error of not telling a client about an important finding because it is anticipated that the client will reject the information.

Finn's model has been applied by other researchers as well. Ackerman, Hilsenroth, Baity, and Blagys (2000) examined the relationship between the therapeutic alliance as developed during psychological assessment and the degree of alliance reported as of a third or fourth psychotherapy session. Specifically, they compared the ratings obtained within the context of TMA with those obtained when a more traditional information-gathering model was employed. Their findings showed that client-rated alliance measured just after an assessment feedback session was significantly correlated with the degree of alliance measured during a third psychotherapy session. Moreover, those clients with whom TMA had been employed were significantly less likely to terminate before starting formal psychotherapy, as compared with clients in the control group. The researchers concluded that although the TMA approach required more upfront time for conducting a multifaceted and collaborative evaluation with clients, it constituted a worthwhile investment in the therapeutic relationship that paid off over time.

Hilsenroth, Peters, and Ackerman (2004) took this research a step further. Rather than looking only at the therapeutic alliance established at the initial stages of treatment, they investigated the degree to which therapeutic alliance brought about by psychological assessment developed over the full course of subsequent psychotherapy. Specifically, they were interested in whether the type of alliance created during psychological assessment was similar to the alliance formed during formal psychotherapy; they described theirs as the first study to examine the therapeutic alliance longitudinally, from the point of assessment through the end of treatment. They hypothesized that there would be a significant and positive relationship between the therapeutic alliance ratings by client and therapist during the assessment phase and the alliance ratings given early in formal psychotherapy. They also postulated that there would be significant and positive correlations between the therapeutic alliance during the assessment phase and ratings late in formal psychotherapy. Further, they hypothesized that there would be a stronger alliance for those for whom a collaborative assessment model was followed, as compared to those for whom there was "assessment as usual." Their participants were 42 psychotherapy clients admitted to a psychodynamic psychotherapy treatment team at a university-based community outpatient clinic. All clients participated in at least nine sessions of psychotherapy, and a full range of DSM-IV diagnoses was represented among them. The mean number of sessions attended was 25. The therapists were 18 advanced doctoral students in clinical psychology and one licensed psychologist. Clients' psychological evaluations using TMA consisted of a total of four meetings. The client met with the clinician for three meetings and then completed a battery of self-report measures during the fourth. The "assessment instruments" included a semistructured diagnostic interview, interview follow-up, and a collaborative feedback session. During the collaborative feedback session, clients first were to be given feedback that closely matched their own preconceptions of themselves, and then they were to be presented with information that was progressively more discrepant as the session wore on, in keeping with Finn and Tonsager's model. Clinicians encouraged a dialogue with their clients to facilitate empathy and collaboration.

Results showed that alliance ratings at all measurement points were indicative of a high alliance, showing a sense of connection between client and therapist across the treatment course. Notably, the clients reported alliance scores during assessment that were as high as or higher than those at other points in treatment. Client alliance measured early in the assessment phase was significantly and positively related to alliance later in treatment, even after controlling for the effect of alliance early in formal psychotherapy. It also appeared that the collaborative interactions developed during TMA enhanced client ratings of alliance.

Researchers have investigated therapeutic assessment models other than TMA as well. For example, Tryon (1990) found relationships between continuation into treatment following an initial intake interview and such factors as active collaboration, development of insight, and focus on interpersonal functioning during the intake. In their study of clients with chronic mental illness, Svensson and Hansson (1999) found that client ratings of the therapeutic alliance early in cognitive therapy were significantly correlated with enhanced examination of important and powerful interpersonal themes during an assessment phase.

Procedures for Providing
Psychological Test Feedback to
the Client Entering Treatment

The following guidelines might be useful in conducting a test feedback session.

Step 1: Explain Why the Test
was Administered

Clients may not know why they have been given a particular personality measure such as the MMPI-2 or BTPI, so it is a good idea to explain why this had been recommended in the first place. During this introduction, the therapist can explain that he or she would like to use every means available to try to understand the client fully (clients actually like this!). The therapist may then indicate that an objective test can provide a valuable external source of information about the client's problems.

Step 2: Describe What Test was Used
and How it was Used

Most people do not know much about psychological testing. In some communities where tests are widely employed, there may be preconceived ideas about tests or misconceptions about their use. It is important to establish the credibility and objectivity of the particular test in question for the client by providing some background on the instrument. For example, clients can be advised that the MMPI-2 is the most widely used psychological test and that it (or its predecessor MMPI) has been used in clinical settings since 1940. Its respected status as the personality test used in the majority of clinical settings in the United States can be noted. The MMPI-2 is also the most widely used personality instrument in the world, with more than 32 translations and broad use in over 46 other countries (and there were over 115 translations of the original MMPI).

Step 3: Describe How the Test Works

In a few words, describe how the scales were developed and highlight the extent of empirical scale development and validation. Beginning with the test profiles:

1. Point out what an "average" or typical performance on each scale would be.
2. Point out where the elevated score range is on the clinical profile (e.g., above a T score of 65). Explain that this means that 92% of people fall below that

score. Next, as an example, show the profile presented in Figure 8.1. The profile in this graph shows how clinically depressed clients compare to the normative sample in terms of elevations on the MMPI-2 Depression scale, or scale 2.

Next, point out that the profile patterns have been widely studied for diverse groups of clients. It may be helpful to use the client's own profile as an illustration in showing the scale score average range, elevation differences, their meaning, and so on.

Step 4: Describe How the Validity Scales Work

Briefly describe the validity indicators and discuss the strategies the client used in approaching the test content. Focus on areas of self-presentation and on how the client seems to be viewing the problem situation at this time. Discussion of the validity pattern is one of the most important facets of test feedback, since it provides the therapist with an opportunity to explore the client's motivation for treatment and his or her initial accessibility to treatment. On the MMPI-2, clients with elevated L or K (T > 60) that is greater than the T score for F would be viewed, for example, as defensive, self-protective, and not entering into the treatment process with the goal of self-revelation. In cases of high initial treatment resistance, the therapist can explore possible factors influencing this reluctance and can discuss the potentially negative outcomes from such resistance with the client. For example, a high score on the Closed-Mindedness Scale of the BTPI suggests that there is likely to be resistance to treatment change.

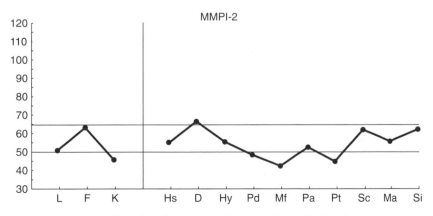

Figure 8.1. MMPI-2 clinical profile showing that the client is likely to be experiencing depression.

Step 5: Point Out the Most Significant Departures from the Norms on the Clinical Scales

It is important to give the client a clear understanding that his or her responses have been compared with those of thousands of other individuals who have taken the MMPI-2 under a range of conditions. Describe the client's highest-ranging clinical scores in terms of prevailing attitudes, symptoms, problem areas, and the like. It is also valuable to discuss the individual's low points on the profile, to provide a contrast with other personality areas in which he or she does not seem to be having problems. Avoid low base rate predictions: MMPI-2 correlates or descriptions that are low in occurrence should not be included in the feedback. It is often useful and desirable in treatment feedback sessions to use the psychological test indexes as a basis for predictions about future behavior of the client. In providing personality feedback it is important to avoid using psychological jargon by translating clinical words into language that the client can readily understand; such determination should involve consideration of the client's educational background, culture, and other relevant factors. The personality descriptions and symptoms presented by the client through the item responses are crucial concepts to communicate, and it is important that they be conveyed clearly. However, the therapist should not try to communicate everything at once. Instead, he or she should be selective in choosing the most pertinent features to highlight and emphasize.

It is possible that the client will have little insight into his or her behavior at this point and thus will have problems "seeing" or accepting feedback about some issues or characteristics. In this instance, it is critical that the therapist avoid getting into an argument with the individual in order to "drive home" the results. The goal here is to present tentative findings from the test that have high validity and generalizability and that might prove useful in the individual's treatment. Clearly, a shouting match is unlikely to achieve that goal.

Step 6: Seek Responses from the Client During the Feedback Session

The client should also be afforded the opportunity to ask questions about his or her scores and clear up any points of concern. A person will sometimes become fixed on an irrelevant or inconsequential point or seemingly incorrect interpretation. It is important that the misconceptions be cleared up and that the individual become aware of the most salient elements of his or her test performance. Providing an active interchange over issues raised by the test can promote a treatment-oriented atmosphere that encourages self-knowledge on the part of the client.

Step 7: Appraise the Client's Overall Acceptance of the Test Feedback

It is a good idea to obtain a closing summary from clients to show how they believe the test characterized their problems. The clinician can evaluate whether there were aspects of the test results that were particularly surprising or distressing and whether there were aspects of the interpretation to which the client objected. Neither of these cases indicates that the test was necessarily "wrong"; rather, they highlight points at which test indices disagree with the individual's self-perception. The information exchange occurring in the feedback session may actually provide excellent material and foci from which to proceed directly in the treatment process.

With some clients, it is a good idea to schedule more than one test feedback session to get an idea of how the person has incorporated, rejected, or elaborated upon the feedback. We have often been amazed with the "hearing loss" associated with high elevations on scales of the MMPI-2 such as the Pd scale. High-Pd individuals do not take feedback to heart; they do not incorporate outside opinions readily and tend to distort the information in a manner that enables them to minimize their problems. In a second feedback session, the therapist might begin by having the client summarize conclusions drawn from the previous session. This provides the therapist with an opportunity to reiterate points that may have been ignored or forgotten and to correct inaccurate perceptions. In addition, after a few days' consideration, many clients will raise questions they were hesitant to ask the first time around.

An outline of the suggested steps for providing client feedback is provided in Table 8.1, to be used as a reference guide in test feedback sessions.

An Approach for Providing Feedback

The case example that follows may be useful in illustrating how test feedback sessions can provide useful information to clients and help them to gain insight into problems or issues they might address in psychological treatment.

Case Example: Interpretation of Feedback in Couple Counseling

Clients' Names: Charles V. and Betty S.

Referral

The clients were referred by Dr. R. for an evaluation with the MMPI-2. His client of 3 years, Betty S., and her friend, Charles V., were seeking information

Table 8.1   Guidelines for Providing Assessment Feedback to Clients

Step 1: Explain Why the Test Was Administered

- Explain the rationale behind your giving test feedback to the client.
- Indicate that you want to provide information about the problem situation that is based on how the client responds to various questions.
- Explain that personality characteristics and potential problems revealed in the test scores are compared to those of other people who have taken the test, and that feedback gives the client perspective on his or her problems that can be used as a starting point in therapy.

Step 2: Describe What the Test Is and its Uses

- Describe the MMPI-2 or BTPI and provide the client with an understanding of how valid and accurate the test is for clinical problem description. For example, explain that the MMPI-2 was originally developed as a means of obtaining objective information about clients' problems and personality characteristics.
- Indicate that the MMPI-2 is the most widely used clinical test in the United States, has been translated into many languages, and is used in many other countries for evaluating client problems.
- Explain that the MMPI-2 has been developed and used with many different client problems and provides accurate information about problems and issues with which the client is dealing.

Step 3: Describe How the Personality Test Works

- Begin by providing a description of several elements of the MMPI-2 or BTPI. Use the client's own test profiles to provide a basis for visualizing the information that you are going to provide.
- Explain that a scale is a group of items or statements that measure certain characteristics or problems, such as depression or anxiousness.
- Describe what an "average" score would look like on the profile. Show how scores are compared on the profile, and indicate that higher scores reflect more of the characteristics and problems that the client is experiencing.
- Point out where the elevated score range is and what a score at T = 65 or T = 80 means in terms of the number of people obtaining scores in this range.
- If available, use an average or typical profile from a relevant clinical group from the published literature to illustrate how people with particular problems score on the measure. For example, if the client has significant depression, showing a group mean profile of depressed clients provides a good comparison group.

Step 4: Describe How the Validity Scales on the Test Work

- Discuss the strategies that the client used in approaching the test content. Focus on the person's self-presentation and on how he or she is viewing the problem situation at this time.
- Keep in mind that discussion of the client's validity pattern is one of the most important facets of test feedback, because it provides the therapist with an opportunity to explore the client's motivation for and accessibility to treatment.

Step 5: Point out the Client's Most Significant Departures from the Norm on the Clinical Scales

- Indicate that the client's responses have been compared with those of thousands of other individuals who have taken the test under different conditions. Describe your client's highest-ranging clinical scores in terms of prevailing attitudes, symptoms, or problem areas.
- Emphasize the individual's highest point(s) on the test profiles.
- Point out where the scores fall in relation to the "average" scores.

(continued)

Table 8.1 *(continued)*

- Provide understandable descriptions of the personality characteristics revealed by the prominent scale elevations.
- Discuss the individual's low points on the profile to provide a contrast with other personality areas in which he or she does not seem to be having problems. Avoid descriptions that are low in occurrence, and avoid using psychological jargon.

Step 6: Seek Responses from the Client During the Feedback Session

- Encourage the client to ask questions about the scores and clear up any points of concern.

Step 7: Appraise Client Acceptance of the Test Feedback

- Ask the client to summarize how he or she feels that the test performed in terms of characterizing personal problems.
- Evaluate whether there were aspects of the test results that were particularly surprising or distressing and whether there were aspects of the interpretation to which the client objected.

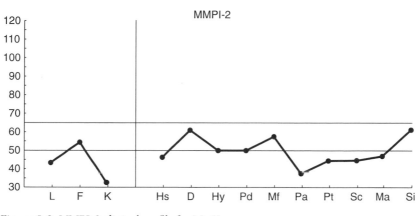

Figure 8.2. MMPI-2 clinical profile for Mr. V.

about their personality adjustment, with specific interest in obtaining test results that might address possible personality differences and "congruencies" between them. Ms. S. was employed as an executive in a large corporation, and Mr. V. was vice president of a bank. They had been dating for a brief period and had recently moved in together, looking toward the possibility of establishing a more permanent relationship.

Testing

Mr. V. and Ms. S. were administered the MMPI-2 and scheduled for their first feedback sessions on separate days a week later. His MMPI-2 profiles are given in Figures 8.2 and 8.3; her profiles are shown in Figures 8.4 and 8.5.

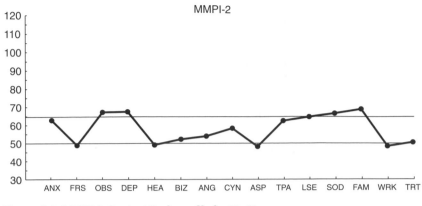

Figure 8.3. MMPI-2 Content Scale profile for Mr. V.

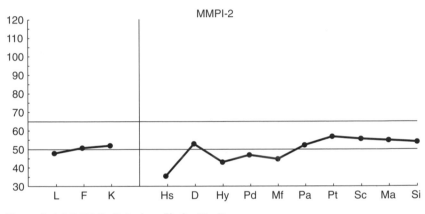

Figure 8.4. MMPI-2 clinical profile for Ms. S.

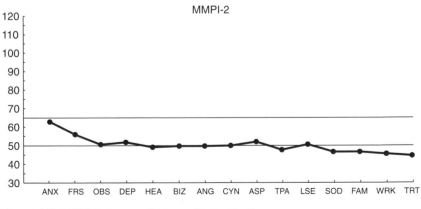

Figure 8.5. MMPI-2 Content Scale profile for Ms. S.

Observations

Mr. V. and Ms. S. were seen individually for their initial feedback session for approximately an hour and a half. They were both highly motivated to discuss the reasons for referral, to provide a description of their present situation, and to learn about their test results. Both presented themselves as being collaborative with regard to the evaluation process. After completion of the individual sessions, a joint feedback session was scheduled.

Psychological Evaluation

Mr. V.'s approach to the psychological evaluation was open and cooperative. He responded in a manner characteristic of individuals entering into a treatment-oriented evaluation. He reported a number of problems that he was experiencing, largely the result of what he viewed as present-day stressors with his family and career. He appeared to be interested in reporting accurate information about himself.

The MMPI-2 profile appeared to be a genuine representation of his present problems. He reported difficulties centering on feelings of low mood and indecisiveness; he seemed to be depressed and to have negative self-attitudes. His depression can be characterized as greater than that of most people. He reported problems with the physical symptoms of depression, such as sleep and appetite disturbance, as well as the social manifestations of low mood. Whereas many of these symptoms may represent a response to stressors that he was experiencing, there were indications that he had personality characteristics of a longstanding nature that predisposed him to negative evaluations and low moods. Individuals with MMPI-2 patterns like his tend to be passive and nonassertive in relationships, and they are apt to be highly conventional as well. They dislike taking risks and resist change. Mr. V. was likely to be quite shy and to prefer a few friends rather than large crowds. His high elevations on the MMPI-2 content scales DEP, OBS, and SOC further confirmed his tendencies toward low mood, obsessive thinking, and social maladjustment.

Ms. S's MMPI-2 was valid as well. She approached the testing in a frank and open manner, although she may have had some concerns about being evaluated. She viewed herself as being "under the gun," since Mr. V. had strongly pressed her to participate in the evaluation. This concern did not, however, result in a distorted profile. The testing appears to be a valid representation of her current psychological functioning.

In the interview and on the MMPI-2, Ms. S. reported few psychological problems. Her overall performance was well within the normal range and did not reflect significant adjustment problems at this time. She appeared to be a generally happy, self-satisfied woman who enjoyed sufficient self-esteem. Although her adjustment at the time of the evaluation appeared good, there was some suggestion that she may have been predisposed to transitory problems. Two trends were suggested. First, she appeared to be a somewhat rigid and perfectionistic person who was prone to guilt and self-punishment. She may have been somewhat prone to developing anxious states when under outside pressure. There was some suggestion that she would become easily bored and need to seek stimulation and activity more than most people. The second area in which she might create problems for herself lay in a tendency to be impulsive and to act before contemplating her actions. She was regarded as likely to experience guilt and remorse in response to actual acting-out behavior she might engage in. She may have been prone to irritable moods at times. Her high score on the MMPI-2 content scale ANX supports the view that she is at times prone to anxiety.

Interpersonal Relations

Interpersonally, Mr. V. and Ms. S. appeared to have rather different styles of interacting with others. Mr. V. was shy, inhibited, and concerned with social interactions. Mr. V. appeared to be overly concerned, even hypersensitive, about what others thought of him. Ms. S., on the other hand, appeared to meet people easily and enjoy social interaction; she seemed adept at negotiating interpersonal relationships. They appeared to be "polar opposites" in terms of social interests and abilities. This might have led to some periods of conflict and result in their placing different strains on the relationship. If they maintained their security and trust in the relationship, however, this set of differences need not have become a point of difficulty.

Trust

There seemed to be a strong element of mistrust in Mr. V.'s current thinking. He was an insecure, uncertain man who appears to need a great deal of reassurance, especially about what others think of him. Some of the depression and low self-esteem may result from his being insecure and feeling inadequate. He appeared to become threatened easily. It was possible that Ms. S.'s social confidence and "impulsivity" would actually threaten Mr. V.

Summary and Recommendations

The relationship between Ms. S. and Mr. V. appeared to have some points of difficulty that may have needed to be addressed. Their different modes of interacting and the potential tendency for Mr. V. to become threatened, alienated, and mistrustful were apt to present sources of conflict. Mr. V.'s proneness to feeling inadequate and his low self-esteem made him vulnerable to negative mood states such as suspicion, mistrust, and depressed affect. He appeared not to have much confidence in himself or in the future. It was likely that he could benefit from psychological treatment that would help to alleviate his low moods and engender more self-efficacy.

No recommendations were made with regard to Ms. S.'s treatment. She appeared to have gained substantially from her present therapy and planned to continue her treatment in the coming months. All things considered, she appeared to be functioning well in her present situation.

Feedback Sessions

Test Feedback with Mr. V   Mr. V. was seen first in an initial session. He was very motivated to receive the test feedback. The session was structured so that he would secure feedback on his MMPI-2 *only* in the individual session and that Ms. S.'s profile would not be discussed. Later, a joint session was scheduled to discuss their profiles together, since they had both requested a session where the information concerning their personality testing could be shared.

Mr. V. was a bright, well-educated man who was quite interested in how the MMPI-2 was originally developed and how the test correlates were researched. He asked a number of questions about the profile, such as, "What percentage of average people score in the 'critical' range?" When the personality descriptions based on the MMPI-2 were shared with him, he appeared to accept the characteristics, such as "depressed," "shy," and "socially withdrawn," painfully and with quiet acknowledgment. He also thought that the feeling of inadequacy and insecurity that the test-based hypotheses addressed were mostly appropriate for his social/personal life and did not apply to his professional behavior. He indicated that he was quite successful and prided himself in his work competence (a contention that was supported by his WRK Content Scale score). He did acknowledge that tendencies toward perfectionism and self-critical behavior caused him some problems at times. He also acknowledged that the test was accurate with regard to his feeling low and felt that the recommendations for his treatment were possibly very useful. He agreed to accept a referral for a therapist to explore some sources of his low mood and personal discomfort.

Test Feedback with Ms. S.   Ms. S. was quite enthusiastic about receiving feedback on her test profile, although she seemed very nervous about "what was going to be revealed." She admitted that she was somewhat concerned about the testing because Mr. V. had pushed for the evaluation (in her mind, possibly because she *was* in therapy). She clearly felt that there was "a lot riding" on the results because she loved Mr. V. and wanted to reassure him.

She did not show initial inquisitiveness about the test itself but wanted to get quickly to the results. When she was told that her test scores were generally within normal limits and reflected a generally good adjustment with no serious psychological problems, she appeared to be pleasantly surprised and said, "It certainly wouldn't have been like that a couple of years ago!" She also acknowledged that she did have a tendency to "lose it" now and then and become extremely anxious and self-doubting on those occasions. She also felt that the test finding that she was somewhat rigid and set in her ways was "right on."

The treatment recommended in the report reflected the view that she was probably sufficiently improved and did not need much further therapy. She, too, had thought that her treatment was reaching an end, but she was still working on some issues and did not foresee a time for termination in the near future.

Joint Feedback Session

The couple arrived arm-in-arm for the joint feedback session, and both seemed to be looking forward to discussing the tests together. The session actually began in a somewhat anticlimactic atmosphere, since they had both already shared the test information in great detail. The session started with each summarizing their conclusions from the individualized sessions, she with her notebook in hand, since she had taken careful notes on the feedback. In sum, most of the points seemed to have been correctly digested and were accurately reiterated, especially by Ms. S., who was a practiced hand after having been in treatment for 3 years. Mr. V. plodded through his points, showing some clear indecisiveness with regard to his "feelings of insecurity and inadequacy."

A large portion of the time was devoted to the issue of alienation and mistrust in interpersonal relationships. The differences between their abilities to trust were discussed. This seemed to be a persistent personality problem for Mr. V. In fact, his lack of trust was one important reason he had been insistent upon her having a psychological evaluation in the first place. He appeared to show both insight and acceptance of this problem and acknowledged that it may have had some bearing in previous relationships in which he was intimately involved. This was the first time they had objectively discussed this problem even though it had clearly had an impact on their relationship in the past. Much of the remaining time in the feedback was spent exploring ways he might appropriately seek reassurance from her when he feels threatened and possible ways she might try to alleviate or circumvent his developing "feelings of uncertainty."

It is interesting that the feedback sessions that began as a part of the diagnostic assessment evaluation wherein the assessment psychologist was not anticipated to be involved in the treatment ended with a clear "blending" of the diagnostic study and therapy-oriented content. At the end of the joint session, Mr. V.'s need to initiate a therapeutic contact was reiterated. He was clearly motivated to obtain treatment and did follow up on the referral.

Cautions, Limitations, and Pitfalls in Providing Feedback

There are possible negative effects of providing test feedback to clients at the beginning of treatment, which we now examine (see also discussion by Pope, Sonne, & Greene, 2006).

1. *Prematurely setting the therapist's "switches" and foreclosing on other possibilities in treatment.* Test data should be presented as "provisional" information rather than as revelations about how the client has always been or will always be. Psychological tests can provide hypotheses about the person's problems, symptoms, and behavior that the therapist and client can further explore in the sessions ahead.

2. *Giving more intense, more detailed, or more divergent information than the client can incorporate.* The amount of information to be provided needs to be carefully appraised before feedback is given. The therapist should gauge how much feedback to provide and how detailed the information for this client can be, so as to avoid overwhelming the client. Before proceeding, the therapist should determine the extent of symptom exaggeration and the severity of the client's plea for help as reflected in the profile. Careful appraisal of the validity scales, especially the F score in the MMPI-2, will provide clues to symptom exaggeration that may accompany many initial test administrations. The possibility that the client has presented a large number of problems in an effort to "tell it all" should be considered. Symptom "extremity" may need to be soft-pedaled or otherwise carefully explained so that the client does not become demoralized by too much input too early in treatment. The therapist may choose to spread the test findings over more than one session or defer some aspects of the test information until a stronger treatment relationship is established.

3. *Selective perception of information.* Clients often seize on descriptions of characteristics that are of lesser relevance to the treatment and ignore other points, possibly those that are less favorable or more emotionally painful, that the therapist wishes to make. It is important to order the hypotheses by levels of importance to the treatment to ensure that the important themes do not get lost in the session. Clients sometimes sit passively in the sessions while the "oracle" reads the descriptions—not really absorbing important points because their attention gets fixed on one point, and also not asking questions. In this way, the individual may selectively attend to minutiae and miss major points.

4. *Selective remembering.* One potentially helpful strategy for providing client feedback involves providing the test information over two sessions. In the first session, the material is discussed and the client is afforded the opportunity to absorb the information. In the second scheduled session, the therapist begins by asking the client to recall the main themes that he or she remembers from the previous feedback session. Afterward, the therapist has the opportunity to follow up, correcting any misconceptions the client might have and reiterating important points that were "lost" in the interim period. As noted earlier, this technique is particularly valuable with some types of individuals (e.g., the high-Pd or -Ma person, who tends to gloss over or ignore problems).

5. *Control over test materials and protocols.* Clients will frequently ask for copies of their profiles or other test results. For most therapists, test materials such as the MMPI-2 profiles and computer-based reports are working materials

or notes that the psychologist employs in developing hypotheses about client problems. They are not readily understandable by laypersons and therefore should not be made available to them to keep. Clients who are not trained in the use of psychological tests and gain copies of these materials can, in the quiet of their homes, make grand misinterpretations of this type of data. Requests for copies of test protocols by the client can usually be handled by telling them, "I can't release profiles or computer-generated narratives, but any time you would like to discuss them further we can," and by providing them with a clear rationale for this decision.

6. *Perception of confrontation.* When providing MMPI-2 test feedback, there is the danger that a confrontational style will be employed. In this type of clinical interaction, the "expert" is providing secret and inaccessible information to the client, who has the role of passive and probably defensive listener. It is easy for a feedback session to gravitate to a "tell all" or "tell it like it is" format, in which the client quickly becomes as defensive as a trapped animal. In a self-protective mode, the besieged client fights back against the therapist's "assault." An extreme example of this confrontational style, and one with an extremely unprofessional thrust, was reported to the author. A psychiatrist was using computerized MMPI reports as a confrontation technique in group treatment sessions with disturbed, acting-out adolescents. He typically gave the computer-generated output to clients and had them read them aloud in group sessions. Not only is this technique likely to be unproductive, as few adolescents would accept such interpretations even if accurate, but the clinician was flirting with malpractice litigation if such aggressive confrontations produced negative outcomes, such as acting-out behavior or suicide.

7. *The implication of specific medication or dosage levels from personality test profiles.* The MMPI-2 has been used as a pre/post measure in numerous drug treatment studies; however, there is insufficient research to use scale scores or elevation levels to guide medication prescription practices. For example, high elevations on D do reflect the presence of significant depressive symptoms. It is also correct to say that many clients with this profile respond to antidepressant medication. However, it is not possible to say, with any degree of certainty, that an antidepressant medication *should* be administered. It is also possible that lithium would be the treatment of choice for some clients with high D scores, because depressive-phase clients with bipolar disorders can produce a spike D profile. The MMPI-2 profile can provide some clues to symptoms, but the clinician needs to consider the other criteria on which appropriate medication prescriptions will be based.

Summary

This chapter addressed the importance of providing feedback on personality characteristics and psychological symptoms to clients early in the treatment process. Factors important to the feedback process, such as timeliness, receptivity of the client, and ability of the individual to incorporate information were discussed. A suggested approach for providing psychological test feedback was outlined. The process of providing test feedback was described and illustrated with a diagnostic case involving a couple seeking information about their compatibility and possible need for treatment. Finally, several cautions or limitations to the client feedback process were described, as a means of sensitizing the clinician to potential problems that may emerge in the course of interpreting test profiles to clients.

9

Case Analyses

This chapter presents four examples of how MMPI-2 and BTPI test findings are incorporated when creating client's treatment plans. In the first case, the assessment efforts centered on the MMPI-2, which significantly informed the consequent treatment plan recommendations. For the next two cases presented, the BTPI was at the heart of this endeavor. For the final case, both instruments were incorporated into the evaluation (including the computer based interpretation of the Minnesota Report and BTPI) and treatment planning processes. Each case illustrates particular therapy challenges that may be faced with clients and highlights some of the issues that arise when objective assessment instruments are incorporated into clients' treatment plans.

MMPI-2: Craig

Presenting Complaint

Craig was a 30-year-old, Caucasian, married, employed man who presented to the urgent care department at a hospital, reportedly at the insistence of a supervisor from work who wanted him to be evaluated. Craig reported that he was embroiled in a custody battle for his two young daughters from a previous marriage. He was not pleased that his supervisor had "made" him seek help, but he was willing to consider taking a medication that would help him "relax" and "be mellow" at work, despite his contention that the personal stressors were not affecting his work in any way. The urgent care staff arranged for him to be evaluated by a psychologist.

During the interview, Craig provided additional background information. He had married his high school sweetheart when both were 18 years old. The couple had quickly had twin daughters and then settled into what Craig felt was a happy relationship. Then, after 10 years of marriage, Craig's wife had shocked him by announcing one day that she no longer loved him and wanted to end their relationship so that she could marry another man. Craig had felt devastated by the request, which had caught him completely off guard. When it became clear that she could not be dissuaded from divorce, Craig had agreed to separate, with the stipulation that he would have joint custody of the twins. Although she initially had agreed, she had unexpectedly sued for sole custody of the twins several months later, claiming that Craig was guilty of neglect. Craig had adamantly denied the claim and insisted on maintaining his parental rights. A messy legal battle ensued, during which Craig's contact with his daughters was severely restricted.

As part of the initial evaluation, Craig did also meet with a psychiatrist and receive a prescription for an anxiolytic medication. The psychologist spoke with him about considering adjunctive psychotherapy. Craig was leery but willing to consider it. He consented to take the MMPI-2 and discuss the findings with the psychologist during a feedback session.

MMPI-2 Results

Craig left none of the MMPI-2 items blank, producing a raw Cannot Say score of 0. His validity configuration revealed that he approached the instrument in a rather defensive way. He responded to the items on the L scale (T = 56) in particular in a manner suggesting a person who is attempting to present a somewhat positive impression of himself by claiming to be more virtuous than the average person. This response style is associated with putting one's best foot forward even in the face of problems or adversity.

The sole elevation on Craig's clinical scales came on Pa (T = 72). At that level, scale correlates include readily apparent sensitivity and suspiciousness. People with similar elevations feel persecuted and concerned about others' motives.

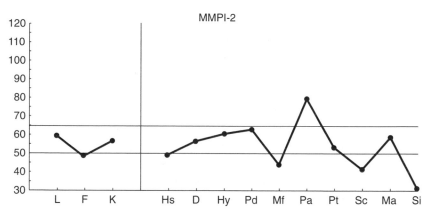

Figure 9.1. MMPI-2 Validity and Clinical Scales profiles for Craig.

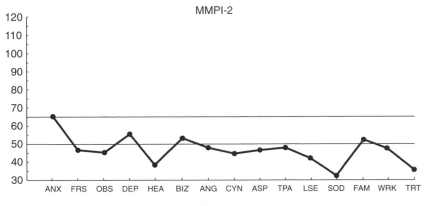

Figure 9.2. MMPI-2 Content Scales profile for Craig.

They tend to be mistrustful and even openly hostile, viewing the world as a threatening place in which others are trying to harm them or exert undue control. They are inclined to feel misunderstood, blamed, and unfairly punished.

Craig, consistent with his approach of minimizing problems, produced no high elevations on any of the content scales. His ANX score (T = 62) did point to possible anxiety symptoms in the form of tension and nervousness. However, the level of the score suggested that these were not especially salient features of his clinical picture. On TRT, the MMPI-2 score geared especially toward treatment planning matters, Craig's score was T = 35.

Treatment Plan Development

Craig's manner of responding to the MMPI-2 was not unexpected in light of his life events at the time of the evaluation; it would be understandable for him to put his best foot forward to an unrealistic degree within the context of the legal battle. His response style suggested that he might be rigid and moralistic, with limited tolerance for beliefs that he considered unconventional. As was shared with him during the feedback session, these qualities could make it challenging for him to accept new ideas, especially those that he perceived as quite different from what he thought to be "right."

In addition, although Craig's profile suggested that he was not experiencing disabling psychopathology, it did reveal the possibility of poor tolerance for pressure and stress. Furthermore, it indicated a desire to give the outward appearance of adequacy, control, and effectiveness despite stressors. As was discussed with Craig in the feedback session, despite feeling very distressed, he was apt to resist letting others know when he was genuinely struggling and how upset he might actually be. Craig alluded to the fact that he had been aware of a need for intervention for quite some time but he had elected not to pursue it because of a desire to "tough it out" and deal with his problems "like a man." He also admitted that he probably would not have presented for treatment at all, had his boss not insisted.

Perhaps most significantly, Craig's clinical profile was associated with a high level of interpersonal mistrust. Treatment within the context of this type of profile is very challenging due to associated problems in developing a supportive, collaborative relationship. Craig was likely to resist being open with his therapist out of deep concerns about trust. He could also be expected to be highly sensitive to perceived slights and to take exception with his therapist's challenging him. This would make a therapeutic relationship with Craig especially vulnerable to rupture, possibly resulting in abrupt and premature termination of care.

The MMPI-2 results pointed to a high potential for a negative outcome from psychotherapy. The psychologist discussed this with Craig and presented him with the option of returning for additional supportive contact during which he might target his "trust issues." However, Craig declined to schedule a follow-up appointment at that time. He stated that he would "think about it" and call the psychologist at a later date if he wished to return to see her.

BTPI: Jack

Presenting Complaint

Jack was a 51-year-old, Caucasian and Native American, married, unemployed man who presented for a social work evaluation at an outpatient mental health clinic. He had wished to establish care following discharge from an inpatient substance use treatment program. Jack reported that he had abused alcohol, marijuana, and occasionally other illicit drugs for most of his life, beginning in early adolescence. His substance abuse had been problematic in multiple ways: he had been fired from several construction jobs for having too many unexcused absences or for reporting for work while drunk or hung over; his first wife divorced him and their children became estranged from him because of problems related to substance use; he had been jailed several times for DUI citations and had also been convicted of domestic assault for slapping his current wife while drunk; and he was significantly in debt. At the time of the intake evaluation, he had been abstinent from alcohol and illicit drugs for 30 days and was distressed because his legal history was preventing him from finding work. He indicated a desire for his providers to assist him in maintaining his abstinence and getting his life back on track. He had also requested assistance from his social worker in applying for disability benefits, given his impression that he was too distressed to function capably at a job and needed other means of financial support.

Jack's social worker had referred him for a psychological evaluation to assist her with differential diagnosis and treatment planning. As part of that process, Jack completed the BTPI and agreed to have the results provided both to him and to his social worker.

BTPI Results

Jack completed all of the BTPI items. He endorsed a high number of symptoms on the BTPI (Fig. 9.3). Although BTPI normative data (Butcher, 1998) indicate that high EXA scores are relatively common among psychotherapy clients, Jack's score (T = 92) indicated that he was experiencing symptoms and attitudes unlikely to be endorsed by most people, including those who are engaged in therapy. Clients can produce scores in this range for several reasons, including exaggerating problems so as to call others' attention to the extreme nature of their distress, randomly responding to items, and falsely claiming symptoms for the purposes of secondary gain. Irrespective of the reason for the elevation, an EXA score in the range of Jack's is cause for questioning the validity of Jack's BTPI findings as well as the overall credibility of his self-report.

Jack produced an elevated score on another of the Validity Scales as well. His CLM score (T = 82) is associated with adopting a closed stance in the face of new ideas and alternative suggestions about his behavior. Clients who produce similar elevations tend not to be open to psychological interpretations of their behavior. They may readily dismiss ideas about alternative ways of thinking and behaving, which can get in the way of developing and working toward treatment goals.

Jack's scores were quite elevated on several of the Treatment Issues Scales as well: SOM (T = 83), ENV (T = 73), and REL (T = 70). His SOM score indicated that he worried a great deal about his physical functioning and viewed his problems as having physical causes. His score was associated with being so concerned about his health that he was apt to retrict his activities significantly. His ENV and REL scores indicated that he might have a hard time in connecting with others because of his attitudes about them. His scores were indicative of someone who feels misunderstood and unsupported by the people around him. He was apt to see them as unsympathetic and perhaps even hostile toward him. Clients who produce similar scores feel isolated and alone in the face of a stress-filled world. They also have a hard time connecting with other people. It is especially challenging for them to develop new relationships, generally because of a lack of trust in others.

All but one of Jack's scores on the Current Symptom Scales were highly elevated: for ANX, T = 90; for A-I, T = 87; for DEP, T = 85; and for PSY, T = 82. Thus, he was expected to demonstrate such problems as tension, fearfulness, and worry to such a degree that his daily functioning could be impaired due to indecisiveness. Correlates of elevations on A-I and DEP included low self-esteem, subservience in interpersonal relationships, unreasonable self-punishment,

Cluster 1: Validity

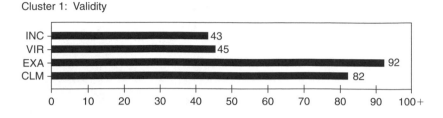

Cluster 2: Treatment Issues

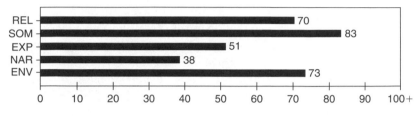

Cluster 3: Current Symptoms

Composite Scales

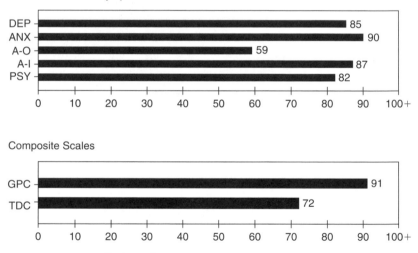

Figure 9.3. BTPI profile for Jack.

depressed mood, and lack of energy. His PSY score was suggestive of highly unusual thinking. Magical and sometimes even delusional beliefs may be present. Clients with scores on PSY as high as Jack's also tend to be quite mistrustful of others and suspicious of their motives.

Jack's significantly elevated scores on most of the Treatment Issues and Current Symptom Scales produced elevated scores on both BTPI composites. His GPC (T = 91) suggested that there were a large number of mental health problems across multiple domains, all of which were potential foci in therapy.

His TDC (T = 72) suggested the presence of many personality-based symptoms that were apt to complicate his treatment relationships.

Treatment Plan Recommendations

Jack did not wish for his social worker to attend his feedback session with the psychologist. The results therefore were reviewed separately with him, although he was aware that they would be communicated to his social worker as well.

The feedback session began with a review of the purpose of the testing and a conversation about his approach to the inventory. His Validity Scales had indicated a strong possibility of his having exaggerated problems and symptoms on the BTPI. Jack's history included a number of factors that made this hypothesis viable, including his desire to apply for disability benefits. However, raising this topic was tricky in light of the indications that Jack might be suspicious of others and may experience them as being largely nonsupportive. The psychologist attempted to present these issues to him in a sensitive yet straightforward way. Jack expressed anger that he was being "accused of lying." He was given an opportunity to process both the BTPI feedback iteself and his reaction to it with the psychologist, and he was encouraged to discuss them with his social worker during a subsequent meeting as well.

Significantly, one of the correlates of Jack's profile was the likelihood of self-medicating in order to deal with somatic and other problems. Clearly, this possibility was particularly significant in light of his substance abuse history. The psychologist spoke with him about the ways in which his attempts to avoid distress could make him vulnerable to relapse and recommended that he target this area in working with his social worker. Jack was accepting of this information and agreed that it would be important for him to work on developing new coping strategies and skills, given his reported commitment to ongoing abstince.

Jack was invited to contact the psychologist later on to discuss any subsequent questions that he had, particularly those that might emerge as he worked with his social worker. He was also encouraged to consider taking the BTPI again after he and his therapist had had some time to address symptom reduction. Because of the questionable validity of his initial profile, the psychologist planned for Jack to complete the Full Form again during any subsequent re-evaluations rather than the Symptom Monitoring Form that excludes the Validity Scales.

BTPI: Stephanie

Presenting Complaint

Stephanie was a 25-year-old, Asian, never-married, unemployed graduate student who presented for an initial evaluation with a psychologist at an outpatient clinic. During the interview, she discussed a history of problematic behaviors related to weight and body image, including binge eating, vomiting, excessive exercising (even when injured), and abusing laxatives. Stephanie reported ambivalence about engaging in psychotherapy; although she was motivated to reduce her distress and improve her self-image, she was concerned about being required to make significant changes.

Toward the end of the first meeting, the psychologist presented a plan for conducting further assessment of Stephanie's difficulties. She discussed how the BTPI could assist with the ensuing treatment planning process, explaining that the BTPI could assist clients and their therapists in understanding symptoms, personality features, areas of potential interpersonal conflict, and other factors that could significantly affect the process and outcome of psychotherapy. Stephanie agreed to complete the BTPI Full Form immediately following her intake appointment, and the psychologist reviewed the results with her at their next appointment.

BTPI Results

Stephanie produced a valid and interpretable BTPI profile (Fig. 9.4). She did not omit any items and was consistent in her item responses. The results were regarded as a credible reflection of her current level of functioning.

Among the Validity Scales, the most notable feature was an elevated score on CLM (T = 69). This score indicated that Stephanie had endorsed item content consistent with being resistant to new ways of thinking. Individuals who produce elevated scores on CLM tend to reject others' interpretations of their behavior and defend against perspectives that differ significantly from their own. Such attitudes can significantly impair clients' receptivity to the ideas and suggestions of their therapists.

On the Treatment Issues Scales, Stephanie had produced a highly elevated score on REL (T = 76). Scores in this range are strongly suggestive of problems in forming relationships with others. People with REL scores in this range are unlikely to trust many people. It can be hard for them to make new friends and to connect with other people in meaningful ways, including care providers.

In addition, Stephanie's elevated score on ENV (T = 65) suggested that she did not regard those people to whom she already was "close" as being particularly caring or encouraging. Her score indicated that she was vulnerable to feeling isolated and even estranged from those on whom she supposedly could count. It also suggested that she would be reluctant to develop new sources of support, be they in the form of treatment providers or friends.

Stephanie scored high on SOM as well (T = 71). Scores at that level are associated with high physical distress and proneness to deal with emotional conflict by channeling it into physical symptoms. Clients with similar SOM scores are inclined to experience stress bodily, often becoming so focused on somatic

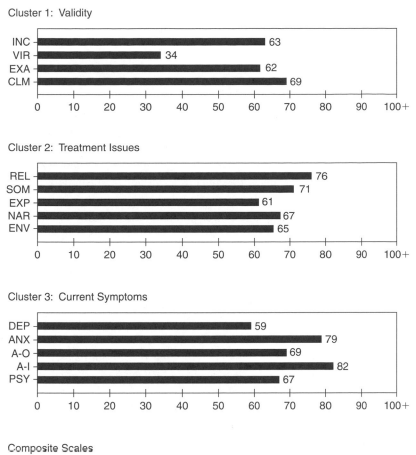

Cluster 1: Validity

INC		63
VIR	34	
EXA		62
CLM		69

Cluster 2: Treatment Issues

REL		76
SOM		71
EXP		61
NAR		67
ENV		65

Cluster 3: Current Symptoms

DEP		59
ANX		79
A-O		69
A-I		82
PSY		67

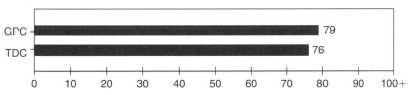

Composite Scales

GPC		79
TDC		76

Figure 9.4. BTPI profile for Stephanie.

complaints that they are unable to deal with problems in a psychologically minded way. In a BTPI normative sample, over one quarter of the psychotherapy clients assessed produced a T score in excess of 64 on SOM, and almost one fifth had it as their highest Treatment Issues Scale.

Stephanie produced elevated scores on ANX (T = 79), A-O (T = 69), and PSY (T = 67). The elevations on A-O and PSY suggest tendencies to direct anger toward others to an unreasonably extent and also to be mistrustful of them. Such feelings often extend to therapists. The elevated score on ANX is associated with catastrophic thinking and decision-making problems. Those qualities had the potential to impede Stephanie's ability to take action around her treatment targets.

Treatment Plan Development

During a feedback session that took place soon after the testing, the psychologist reviewed with Stephanie the BTPI findings. The feedback focused especially on the indications of personality-based treatment resistance that were reflected in the results and began creating a plan for addressing them. Although Stephanie expressed doubt about some of the conclusions drawn on the basis of the BTPI, she reported overall acceptance of their accuracy because they were based on her own responses to the questionnaire and did not represent merely her therapist's "opinion."

Stephanie agreed that it was hard for her to trust others and that she had been reluctant to seek help before because of uncertainty about whether anyone could understand her. She stated that she was similarly concerned about whether this provider could be helpful given her reticence to commit to ongoing care. Nonetheless, she did tentatively agree to work with the psychologist on a "trial" basis over a limited number of sesions. They determined that, during that time, they would work actively on building their relationship, observing interpersonal concerns, discussing them openly as they emerged, and trying to work through them without delay. The psychologist also spoke frankly with Stephanie about how receptivity to different ideas would be important if Stephanie were to be able to engage in many treatment elements (e.g., cognitive restructuring exercises). Moreover, because of Stephanie's impression of having a nonsupportive environment, they identified some goals related to expanding her support network and perhaps making different use of the social supports that she already had.

Stephanie and her therapist determined that they would work together in psychotherapy for approximately 3 months, after which time they would formally re-examine Stephanie's progress. As part of this process, Stephanie would repeat the psychological evaluation with the BTPI. Given that she had produced a valid profile on the intial evaluation, it could have been appropriate for Stephanie to complete only the Symptom Monitoring Form at time 2, particularly if she and the psychologist were interested solely in that aspect of the clinical picture. However, Stephanie's Treatment Issues configuration at time 1 suggested that it would be valuable to have her complete the Full Form again at time 2, given the relevance to her treatment plan of the initial elevations on REL and ENV. By having her repeat the Full Form, she and the psychologist would be able to monitor any change in these areas, or lack of thereof, and address the related issues accordingly.

MMPI-2 and BTPI: Raymond

Presenting Complaint

Raymond was a 40-year-old, Caucasian, never-married, gay man who was requesting psychotherapy upon transferring his mental health care because of a change in his health insurance benefits. He had previously been diagnosed by a psychologist with Anxiety Disorder Not Otherwise Specified and Major Depressive Disorder, Recurrent. During his initial appointment, he reported having recently endured multiple stressors, including a layoff from his job, a costly legal battle with his former employer, and the breakup of a 2-year romantic relationship. As a consequence of all of those events, Raymond had just moved back in with his parents. Raymond reported that his symptoms had been under reasonably good control until the spate of stressful events. At the time of the initial interview, he was already scheduled to be psychiatrically evaluated so that he could establish an appropriate medication regimen. To better assess Raymond's current level of functioning and prepare a viable psychological treatment plan for him, he was asked to complete both the MMPI-2 and the BTPI Full Form following the intake interview.

MMPI-2 Results

Raymond produced a valid MMPI-2 profile. He answered all of the items on the inventory, producing a raw CS score of 0. The validity configuration indicated that he approached the test in a basically forthright manner, being willing to report problems and symptoms, but also being choosy about those that he endorsed. Thus, it was regarded as unlikely that the profile represented either a significant overestimate or a significant underestimate of the problems that he was experiencing.

There were four Clinical Scales with elevations above T = 65 (Fig. 9.5 and 9.6). These were on scales 6 (Pa), 7 (Pt), 4 (Pd), and 8 (Sc). There was no single configural code type for Raymond's pattern of elevations. The highest elevation occurred on scale 6, suggesting the presence of paranoid symptoms. As noted in Chapter 3, scale 6 is important from a treatment planning perspective in that it assesses for ideas of reference, feelings of persecution, rigidity, and excessive interpersonal sensitivity. Clients with elevations on the scale tend to demontrate interpersonal mistrust, inflexibility with regard to change, and negative attitudes about people in positions of authority (including therapists). Generally, high-Pa scorers are not regarded as good therapy candidates, as they are prone to feel misunderstood and to terminate therapy early.

Likewise, Raymond's elevated score on Pd suggested the possibility that he was not anxious enough about his current situation to make changes. In therapy

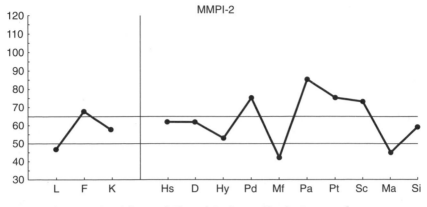

Figure 9.5. MMPI-2 Validity and Clinical Scales profiles for Raymond.

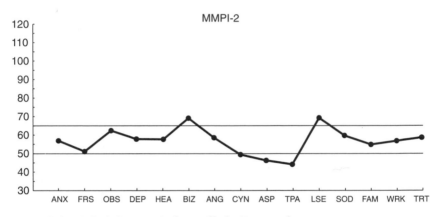

Figure 9.6. MMPI-2 Content Scales profile for Raymond.

relationships, high scorers on Pd are manipulative, aggressive, and deceptive. They can act out in therapy and engage in destructive behavior. They, too, are prone to leave therapy prematurely.

Of course, as noted in Chapter 2, it is critical to examine the MMPI-2 configuation of scores rather than looking at each elevation in isolation. Raymond produced elevations on other MMPI-2 clinical scales associated with more favorable treatment indicators. His elevations on Pt and Sc suggested possible motivation for relief from such symptoms as anxiety and emotional distress. Although those with elevations on Sc can also feel misunderstood and may not respond well to therapy, those with elevations on Pt and D (on which Raymond's score was moderately elevated at T = 62) often do. In addition, Raymond's score was not elevated on the TRT content scale, which was developed specifically to assess potential to cooperate with treatment. His WRK score was similarly within normal limits. Raymond's content scales had included elevated scores only on BIZ and LSE (both at T = 70). The BIZ scale measures schizotypal symptoms, cognitions, and behaviors as well as overly psychotic ones. LSE gauges the degree to which individuals hold negative, self-deprecatory views of themselves.

Minnesota Report for Raymond's Initial MMPI-2

Profile Validity   His MMPI-2 clinical profile is probably valid. The client's responses to the MMPI-2 validity items suggest that he cooperated with the evaluation enough to provide useful interpretive information. The resulting clinical profile is an adequate indication of this present personality functioning.

Symptomatic Patterns   The clinical scale prototype used to develop this report incorporates correlates of Pd and Pa. Because these scales are not well defined in the clinical profile (the highest scales are relatively close in elevation), interpretation of the clinical profile should not ignore the adjacent scales in the profile code. Individuals with this MMPI-2 clinical profile tend to be chronically maladjusted. The client is apparently immature and self-indulgent, manipulating others for his own ends. He may behave in an obnoxious, hostile, and aggressive way, and he may rebel against authority figures. Despite these difficulties with others, he refuses to accept responsibility for his problems. He may have an exaggerated or grandiose idea of his own capabilities and personal worth. He is likely to be hedonistic and may overuse alcohol or drugs. He appears to be quite impulsive, and he may act out against others without considering the consequences. He is also likely to be suspicious, aloof, and unapproachable. Paranoid features and externalization of blame are likely to be present in his clinical picture.

The client seems to have a rather limited range of cultural interests and tends to prefer stereotyped masculine activities to literary and artistic pursuits or introspective experiences. Interpersonally, he may be somewhat intolerant and insensitive.

In addition, the following description is suggested by the client's scores on the content scales. He may feel somewhat estranged and alienated from people. He is suspicious of the actions of others, and he may tend to blame them for his negative frame of mind. He views the world as a threatening place, sees himself as having been unjustly blamed for others' problems, and feels that he is getting a raw deal out of life.

He endorsed a number of extreme and bizarre thoughts, suggesting the presence of delusions and/or hallucinations. He apparently believes that he has special powers or a special "mission" in life that others do not understand or accept.

An understanding of the client's underlying personality, as represented by his scores on the PSY-5 scales, can provide a clinical context in which to view the extreme psychological symptoms he is presently experiencing. He apparently holds some unusual beliefs that appear to be disconnected from reality. His high score on the PSYC (Psychoticism) scale suggests that he often feels alienated from others and might experience unusual symptoms such as delusional beliefs, circumstantial and tangential thinking, and loose associations. According to his score on NEGE (Negative Emotionality/Neuroticism), he tends to view the world in a highly negative manner and usually develops a worst-case scenario to explain events affecting him. He tends to worry to excess and interprets even neutral events as problematic. His self-critical nature prevents him from viewing relationships in a positive manner.

Profile Frequency   Profile interpretation can be greatly facilitated by examining the relative frequency of clinical scale patterns in various settings. The client's high-point clinical scale score (Pa) occurred in 9.6% of the MMPI-2 normative sample of men. However, only 3.0% of the sample had Pa as the peak score at or above a T score of 65, and only 2.2% had well-defined Pa spikes. This elevated MMPI-2 profile configuration (4–6/6–4) is very rare in samples of normals, occurring in less than 1% of the MMPI-2 normative sample of men.

The relative frequency of this MMPI-2 high-point Pa score is high in various outpatient settings. In the large NCS Pearson outpatient sample, this high-point clinical scale score (Pa) occurred in 13.6% of the men. Moreover, 8.1% of the male outpatients had this high-point scale spike at or above a T score at or above a T score of 65, and 5.2% had well-defined Pa high-point scores in that range. This elevated MMPI-2 profile configuration (4–6/6–4) occurred in 2.8% of the men in the NCS Pearson outpatient sample.

He scored relatively high on APS, suggesting the possibility of a drug- or alcohol-abuse problem. The base rate data on this profile type among residents in alcohol and drug programs should also be evaluated. His high-point MMPI-2 score, Pa, is the third highest peak score among alcohol- and drug-abusing populations. Over 14.5% of the men in substance-abuse treatment programs had this pattern, perhaps reflecting guardedness about their problems (McKenna & Butcher, 1987).

Profile Stability   The relative elevation of his clinical scale scores suggests that his profile is not as well defined as many other profiles. There was no difference between the profile type used to develop the present report (involving Pd and Pa) and next highest scale in the profile code. Therefore, behavioral elements related to elevations on Pt should be considered as well. For example, intensification of anxiety, negative self-image, and unproductive rumination could be important in his symptom pattern.

Interpersonal Relations   He is probably having difficult interpersonal relationships. He appears to be sullen, resentful of others, and quite uncompromising in interpersonal style. His manipulative and self-serving behavior may cause great difficulties for people close to him. He may go into a rage because of his poor impulse control and low frustration tolerance. He tends to blame others for problems he has helped to create.

Diagnostic Considerations   An individual with this profile is usually viewed as having a Personality Disorder, probably a Paranoid or Passive-Aggressive Personality. Symptoms of a delusional disorder are prominent in his clinical pattern. His scores on the content scales suggest that his unusual thinking and bizarre ideas need to be taken into consideration in any diagnostic formulation.

He appears to have a number of personality characteristics that have been associated with substance use or abuse problems. His scores on the addiction proneness indicators suggest that there is a possibility of his developing an addictive disorder. Further evaluation for the likelihood of a substance use or abuse disorder is indicated.

Treatment Considerations   Individuals with this profile tend not to seek psychological treatment on their own, and they are usually poor candidates for psychotherapy. They resist psychological interpretation, tend to argue with others, and tend to rationalize or blame others for their problems. They tend to leave therapy prematurely and blame the therapist for their own failings.

BTPI Full Form Results

Raymond answered all of the items on the BTPI. His Validity Scale scores were generally in the average range, suggesting that he had responded to the inventory in a consistent and open fashion. The results were taken to be an accurate representation of his current functioning (Fig. 9.7). Only his EXA score (T = 65) was above average. Nonetheless, his score was congruent with normative data suggesting that around 22% of psychotherapy clients have EXA as their highest Validity Scale score and at a level above T = 64 (Butcher, 1998). Raymond's high EXA score was interpreted as representing an attempt to communicate acute distress on the inventory, though it was not so high as to suggest a strong likelihood of malingering.

Raymond's scores were also above average on two of the Treatment Issues scales. His SOM score (T = 65) was suggestive of the use of somatic defenses and the development of physical complaints (including headaches, other pain, and stomach distress) in the face of psychological stressors. As previously noted, clients who produce elevated scores on SOM are prone to worry about their health and disinclined to deal with emotional conflict in a psychologically minded way. They tend to focus largely on the physical aspects of their problems. Raymond's ENV score (T = 62) was also somewhat elevated, though only mildly so. It indicated that he may have doubts about the quality of his social support network, though his score did not suggest that this area was the biggest source of concern for him.

Cluster 1: Validity

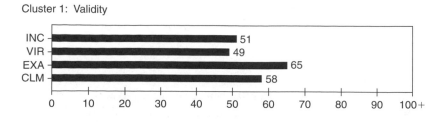

Cluster 2: Treatment Issues

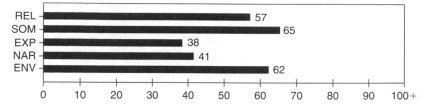

Cluster 3: Current Symptoms

Composite Scales

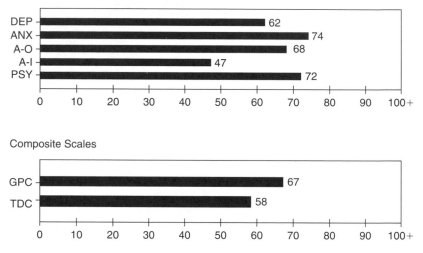

Figure 9.7. BTPI profile for Raymond.

With regard to the Current Symptom Scales, Raymond's highest elevations were on ANX (T = 74) and PSY (T = 72). Thus, he was apt to be tense, fearful, and agitated. There was also potential for him to have trouble with his thought processes. His PSY score was elevated to a range that suggested the presence of magical thinking, odd beliefs, and possibly delusions. The score is also suggestive of wariness in dealing with others, out of concern that their intentions are suspect.

Raymond also produced an above-average score on A-O (T = 68). This score is consistent with feelings of aggressiveness and irritability toward others.

Clients with comparable A-O scores can feel as though the world around them is highly antagonistic. They can be quite resentful and demonstrate problems in controlling their tempers at times.

Raymond's Initial BTPI Interpretive Report

Validity of the Report   The BTPI™ scales are likely to be a valid indication of Raymond's treatment-related attitudes because he approached the item content in an open, consistent manner. The therapist is likely to find the present symptom review a credible picture of the client's current functioning.

Raymond has reported a number of symptoms and problems, more than most people do. This high degree of symptom expression could result from a felt need to have the therapist pay immediate attention to his problems. The potential sources of his high number of problems should be carefully evaluated to determine whether they are the appropriate focus of therapy.

High symptom endorsement, as shown by his elevated EXA score, is relatively common among clients engaged in psychotherapy. About 22% of clients in the Minnesota Psychotherapy Assessment Project had EXA as their highest Validity Scale score, with a T score > 64. There is a tendency for women in therapy to report significantly more problems than men in therapy do.

Treatment Issues   Individuals who score high on the Somatization of Conflict (SOM) scale are reporting a considerable amount of physical distress at this time. They seem to feel their problems are, for the most part, physical, and they do not like to deal with emotional conflict. They have a tendency to channel conflict into physical symptoms such as headache, pain, or stomach distress. They tend to worry about their health and seem to be reducing their life activities substantially as a result of their physical concerns. They view themselves as tired and worried that their health is not better.

The use of somatic defenses and the development of physical problems under psychological conflict are prominent mechanisms in outpatient therapy. Over a quarter (28%) of the clients in the Minnesota Psychotherapy Assessment Project produced high scores (T > 64) on the SOM scale. In addition, SOM led other Cluster 2 scales as the most frequent peak score (with 19% of the clients having a peak SOM T score > 64).

Current Symptoms   Raymond appears to be extremely anxious at this time. He is reporting great difficulty as a result of this tension, fearfulness, and inability to concentrate effectively. He seems to worry a great deal and feels that he can't seem to sit still at times. His daily functioning is severely impaired because of his worries and an inability to make decisions. The elevation he obtained on the Anxiety (ANX) scale is relatively common among psychotherapy clients. The ANX scale was the second most frequent peak score in the Minnesota Psychotherapy Assessment Project, with 28% of the cases having T scores > 64 (6% of these with ANX as the peak Current Symptom scale score). However, peak ANX elevations were more prominent for women (9%) than for men (2%).

In addition, he has presented a number of other serious problems through the BTPI items that require careful evaluation at this time. He has also obtained a high score on the PSY scale. Scores in this range reflect very unusual thinking. Individuals with extreme scores such as his are reporting that their minds are not working well and that they are having difficulty with their thought processes. Unusual and magical thoughts are characteristic of their belief systems. He also appears to be extremely mistrustful and suspicious of others. There is some possibility that his unusual thoughts are delusional in nature.

Along with the problems described above, there are other symptoms reflected in his BTPI response pattern that need to be considered in assessing his current symptomatic picture. His responses to the BTPI items suggest that he is likely to be somewhat aggressive and irritable toward other people. He feels as though he lives in a world full of antagonism and reports feeling so tense and irritable that he thinks he is "going to explode." He reports behavior that suggests he has temper control problems and may feel angry and resentful of other people.

Treatment Planning   His symptom description suggests some concerns that could become the focus of psychological treatment if the client can be engaged in the treatment process. The provision of test feedback about his problem description might prove valuable in promoting accessibility to therapy.

His reliance upon somatic defense mechanisms and his need to view conflicts in medical terms need to be the dealt with in therapy if he is going to be able to effectively resolve conflicts that occur in his interpersonal relations.

Treatment planning should proceed with the understanding that the client maintains the view that he lives in a very unsupportive environment. This perceived lack of a supportive context for change, whether real or imagined, can prove frustrating to the client's efforts at self-improvement.

His intense anxiety and high tension would likely be good target symptoms to address in therapy. He appears to be experiencing some disabling cognitions and may need to explore these vulnerabilities in some detail to alleviate the sources of this anxious states. Directing treatment toward tension reduction and focusing upon more-effective stress management strategies would likely serve to improve his life adjustment.

His rigid beliefs and opinionated interaction style are likely to challenge the therapist as treatment proceeds.

Progress Monitoring   Raymond obtained a General Pathology Composite (GPC) T score of 67. His GPC index score indicates that he has endorsed a number of mental health symptoms that may require consideration in psychological treatment planning. For a statistically significant change, based on a 90% confidence interval, a subsequent GPC T score must be above 73 or below 71.

Raymond obtained a Treatment Difficulty Composite (TDC) T score of 58. Overall, his TDC index score is well within the normal range, indicating that he has not acknowledged many of the personality-based symptoms addressed by the BTPI to assess difficult treatment relationships. For a statistically significant change, based on a 90% confidence interval, a subsequent TDC T score must be above 65 or below 51.

Special Issues to Address in Therapy The client has endorsed item content that likely bears some critical importance to his progress in psychological treatment. The Special Problem items are printed out if the client responded in the critical direction. The item endorsement frequencies for the item are also provided for the Normative Sample (N) and the Clinical Sample. These issues noted below should be followed up in an early treatment session.

He has endorsed item content indicating that he has concerns over his anger to the point of openly expressing aggression toward another person. The potential that he might act out in an aggressive or violent manner should be explored in early treatment sessions.

205. (T) My temper sometimes flares up to the point that I cannot control what I do or say. (N% = 27.3) (C% = 31.7).

Initial Treatment Plan Development

During Raymond's feedback session, the psychologist presented the MMPI-2 and BTPI findings. In discussing current symptoms, they had highlighted especially the correlates of MMPI-2's scale 7 and BTPI's SOM, ANX, and A-O. The psychologist reviewed with Raymond the finding that although his MMPI-2 D and BTPI DEP scores had been slightly above average (both at T = 62), there was not strong evidence of significant depression. They concurred that his recent stressors had not seemed to cause a significant exacerbation of his depressive symptoms. Raymond indicated that because his own experience of symptoms matched the symptom feedback, both the test results and the psychologist seemed credible.

Raymond and his therapist also discussed how Raymond's MMPI-2 TRT and BTPI TDC T scores were within the normal range, indicating that he had not acknowledged through these scales many of the personality-based problems associated with difficult treatment relationships. Nonetheless, it was noted that Raymond's MMPI-2 and BTPI profiles included other, less favorable indicators of his willingness to participate actively and collaboratively in psychotherapy. They discussed these openly. Raymond was predictably guarded in the face of this feedback but was willing to consider that he might demonstrate feelings of persecution, rigidity, and excessive interpersonal sensitivity. The therapist noted ways in which those factors could affect their therapeutic relationship and his participation in treatment.

Raymond indicated that he was uncomfortable enough about his anxiety and anger to address them in therapy. After considering various options, he and his therapist agreed to target his anger symptoms primarily via involvement in an psychoeducational and skills-focused anger management group. They also decided to hold adjunctive individual sessions that could reinforce his application of the anger management skills and additionally provide opportunities to target anxiety management more specifically. The two discussed the potential for Raymond to be especially guarded and defensive in dealing with the group therapist and his fellow group members. Raymond was able to acknowledge apprehension about joining a group of unknown individuals. However, he felt that the knowledge that both he and the other group members were struggling with similar problems would help him ally with them. Also, the psychologist had made a point of recommending a psychoeducation group rather than a process-oriented one, so that the focus would be more on skill acquisition and practice and less on personal feedback.

Raymond and the therapist specifically discussed the potential for him to be unwilling to try out new ways of thinking and behaving and to give up too quickly in the face of challenging treatment goals. They created specific aims around this; for example, Raymond agreed to apply each new skill at least three times, regardless of outcome, so that he could not quit after a single unsuccessful attempt.

The feedback discussion was experienced as helpful by both client and therapist as they crafted Raymond's initial treatment plan. Given that the MMPI-2 and BTPI findings had underscored those problems that seemed most pertinent to Raymond, he experienced the evaluation as helpful. They also steered his therapist and him toward early symptom targets. Because the inventories had also highlighted significant interpersonal themes, they fostered open discussion of potentially uncomfortable topics that might otherwise have been avoided.

Over the ensuing 3 months, Raymond completed the anger management group, missing occasional sessions for questionable reasons but ultimately being able to "graduate" from the group with his cohort. He also participated reasonably actively in individual therapy appointments during that time. Following the termination of his group, Raymond agreed to be re-evaluated to assess the changes in his symptom picture.

MMPI-2 Retest Results

At follow-up, Raymond again produced a valid MMPI-2 profile. He completed all items and reported a moderate level of symptoms, suggesting neither indiscriminate item endorsement nor significant reluctance to report problems via his responses.

His second MMPI-2 profile was somewhat different from the first (Figs. 9.8 and 9.9). Among the clinical scales, he produced T scores above 65 only on Pt and Sc. This 7–8 code type is associated with intense anxiety and needs related to crisis management. As noted in Chapter 3, people with this profile tend to be crisis-prone and lack the ability to bounce back from significant stressors and events. They tend to respond best to problem-focused treatment rather than insight-oriented approaches.

Minnesota Report for Raymond's Retest MMPI-2

Profile Validity   This client's approach to the MMPI-2 was open and coopera-
tive. The resulting clinical and content scale profiles are valid and is probably a good indication of his present level of personality functioning. This cooperative performance may be viewed as a positive indication of his involvement with the evaluation.

Symptomatic Patterns   The MMPI-2 clinical profile configuration that includes scales Pt and Sc was the prototype used to develop this report. This scale configuration is not well defined. Interpretation of the profile should take into con-
sideration other clinical profile elements, particularly the scales that are close in elevation to the prototype scales. The client's profile suggests that he feels somewhat fearful and tense. He may also tend to be overideational, often feeling guilty, insecure, and inadequate to deal with life. He may have periods of intense anxiety and disorganization.

The client seems to have a rather limited range of cultural interests and tends to prefer stereotyped masculine activities to literary and artistic pursuits or in-

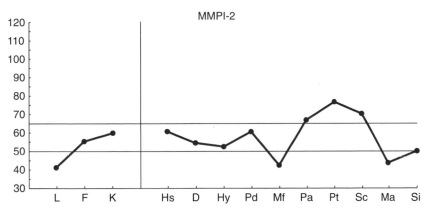

Figure 9.8. Retest MMPI-2 Validity and Clinical Scales profiles for Raymond.

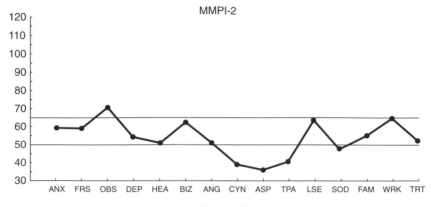

Figure 9.9. Retest MMPI-2 Content Scales profile for Raymond.

trospective experiences. Interpersonally, he may be somewhat intolerant and insensitive.

In addition, the following description is suggested by the client's scores on the content scales. The client's recent thinking is likely to be characterized by obsessiveness and indecision.

Long-term personality factors identified by his PSY-5 scale elevations may help provide a clinical context for the symptoms he is presently experiencing. He tends to view the world in a highly negative manner and usually develops a worst-case scenario to explain events affecting him. He tends to worry to excess and interprets even neutral events as problematic. His self-critical nature prevents him from viewing relationships in a positive manner.

Profile Frequency   It is usually valuable in MMPI-2 clinical profile interpretation to consider the relative frequency of a given profile pattern in various settings. The client's MMPI-2 high-point clinical scale score (Pt) was found in only 4.9% of the MMPI-2 normative sample of men. Only 3.1% of the sample had Pt as the peak score at or above a T score of 65, and only 1.6% had well-defined Pt spikes. This elevated MMPI-2 profile configuration (7–8/8–7) is rare in samples of normals, occurring in 1.5% of the MMPI-2 normative sample of men.

The relative frequency of this MMPI-2 high-point score is informative. In the NCS Pearson outpatient sample, 7.7% of the males had this MMPI-2 high-point clinical scale score (Pt). Moreover, 6.5% of the male outpatients had the Pt score of 65, and 3.3% had well-defined Pt spike scores in that range. This elevated MMPI-2 profile configuration (7–8/8–7) was found in 3.6% of the men in the NCS Pearson outpatient sample.

Profile Stability   The relative elevation of his highest clinical scale scores suggests some lack of clarity in profile definition. Although his most elevated clinical scales are likely to be present in his profile pattern if he is retested at a later date, there could be some shifting of the most prominent scale elevations in the profile code. The difference between the profile type used to develop the present report (involving Pt and Sc) and the next highest scale in the profile was 3 points. So, for example, if the client is tested at a later date, his profile might involve more behavioral elements related to elevations on Pa. If so, then on retesting, externalization of blame, mistrust, and questioning the motives of others might become more prominent.

Interpersonal Relations He appears to be somewhat passive-dependent in relationships, and he tends to be a follower in social activities. Feelings of insecurity and fear of rejection cause him considerable anxiety at times. Rocky relationships are common among individuals with this profile.

Diagnostic Considerations He reported a number of psychological concerns, anxiety, and unusual thoughts that should be taken into consideration in any diagnostic formulation.

Treatment Considerations Individuals with this profile often exhibit anxiety and tension that require symptom relief. Although they may seek psychological treatment for their fears and concerns, they tend to intellectualize and ruminate a great deal and may have difficulty focusing on specific problems. Their poor social skills may become the focus of treatment.

He harbors many negative work attitudes that could limit his adaptability in the workplace. His low morale and lack of interest in work could impair future adjustment to employment, a factor that should be taken into consideration in treatment.

Unlike in his first MMPI-2 profile, Raymond's content scales included elevations on OBS (T = 70) and WRK (T = 65) at the time of the reassessment. Elevations on OBS are associated with anxiety in the form of an obsessive-compulsive style. Associated features include a ruminative cognitive style and engagement in repetitive behaviors. WRK elevations are associated with a perceived inability to focus on productive activities, including those associated with traditional jobs. They are associated with decision-making problems, low expectations for success, being quick to give up in the face of adversity, and general dislike for work endeavors. His LSE score at time 2 was at T = 64.

BTPI Symptom Monitoring Form Results

Because both of Raymond's MMPI-2 profiles and his initial BTPI profile had all been regarded as valid, with no cause to suspect the accuracy of his self-report, he was administered the BTPI Symptom Monitoring Form at follow-up. This form provided data only for the Current Symptom Scales of DEP, ANX, A-O, and A-I, in addition to calculating a new GPC. Raymond's GPC T score on the BTPI

Full Form had been 67. In order for there to have been a statistically significant reduction in his symptoms (based on a 90% confidence interval), this index score would have needed to fall below T = 61 at follow-up.

Raymond's Retest BTPI Interpretive Report

Current Symptoms   His moderate elevation on the Unusual Thinking (PSY) scale needs to be evaluated further. There is some possibility that his unusual beliefs reflect unusual thought content. He appears to be somewhat mistrustful and suspicious of others. There is some possibility that his unusual thoughts reflect intractable beliefs.

Progress Monitoring   The General Pathology Composite (GPC) T score of 50 places Raymond in the 62nd percentile when compared to the normative sample. Overall, his GPC index score is well within the normal range, suggesting that he has not acknowledged many mental health symptoms. For a statistically significant change, based on a 90% confidence interval, a subsequent GPC T score must be above 56 or below 44.

Similar to his second MMPI-2, Raymond's new BTPI profile showed significant changes in his symptoms (Fig. 9.10). His PSY score remained above average at T = 62, though it was significant reduced from its value (T = 72) at the initial evaluation. His remaining Current Symptom Scale scores all fell in the average range, including ANX (T = 58) and A-O (T = 47). Importantly, his GPC fell to T = 50, which was within the normal range for the normative sample.

Revisions to the Treatment Plan

Raymond reported having felt more comfortable with the assessment process the second time around. During his feedback session following the re-evaluation, he evidenced openness to hearing the results. The psychologist shared that the BTPI re-evaluation findings in particular suggested substantial reductions in Raymond's psychiatric symptoms since the initial testing. These results were consistent with the observations that he reported to his therapist in recent sessions, which he had based on his own impressions of his functioning and also on information from family and friends. He and the psychologist discussed how the findings were additionally congruent with his group and individual therapists' observations about changes in his symptoms. Raymond reported being pleased about having experienced treatment as helpful and having noted objective evidence of enhanced functioning over time. Raymond stated that it also was validating for him to have the BTPI data corroborate his impression.

Nevertheless, the feedback session also included a discussion of suggestions of persisting distress on the second MMPI-2. That profile may even have indicated some exacerbation of symptoms. This was not unexpected for either Raymond or

Scales

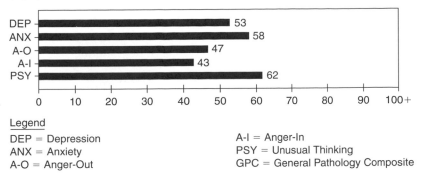

Legend

DEP = Depression
ANX = Anxiety
A-O = Anger-Out

A-I = Anger-In
PSY = Unusual Thinking
GPC = General Pathology Composite

Summary of Scale Scores

The following table presents raw scores, T-scores, and interpretive guidelines for all obtained scores. Please refer to the BTPI™ Technical Manual for more information on the interpretation of these results.

Scales	Raw Score	T-Score	Guideline
Depression	4	53	Average
Anxiety	6	58	Average
Anger-Out	3	47	Average
Anger-In	2	43	Average
Unusual Thinking	4	62	Above Average
General Pathology Composite	201	50	Average

Figure 9.10. Retest on the BTPI (Symptom Monitoring Profile) for Raymond.

his therapist, as related to recent events in his personal life. His father had been diagnosed with Alzheimer's disease in the weeks prior to the re-evaluation. Because Raymond's mother was herself in poor health and Raymond was an only child who again was living in his childhood home, it seemed inevitable that he would bear most of the responsibility for caring for both parents. Although his father's functioning was still quite good on most days, there were also times when it dropped off precipitously; at those times, Raymond was faced with crisis management responsibilities for which he often felt ill prepared.

Raymond and his therapist decided to revise his treatment plan to address the apparent need for further skill development, focusing on how he best could handle the types of emergencies and predicaments that his father's illness produced. They targeted resource planning, worked further on cognitive restructuring, and also incorporated new relaxation-oriented strategies into the behavioral interventions. They also arranged for further evaluation of his current psychotropic medication needs.

10

Postscript: Objective Personality
in Psychological Treatment

Patients in psychological treatment usually expect a high level of expertise and understanding from their therapist, not simply a sympathetic listener. They anticipate that the therapist will be competent to evaluate their problems in a nonjudgmental way and will employ objective, scientific means of helping them resolve their problems. Furthermore, when people go to a psychotherapist, they anticipate that the therapist will provide them with more information and insight into their problems than they can get from a friend or relative.

For therapy to proceed as clients actually expect, the therapist must have a good understanding of the client's problems, personality characteristics, needs, motivations, aspirations, and social relationships. Without a sound psychological assessment the treatment situation is likely to be superficial and disjointed and may drift aimlessly toward an unsuccessful outcome. One thesis of this book is that psychological treatment works best when it proceeds from a clear understanding of the patient's contribution to his or her personality problems, symptomatic behavior, and familial and social conflicts. The use of the personality-based measures like the MMPI-2 and BTPI introduces new, relevant material into the treatment sessions in an objective way.

This book addresses the processes and strategies for employing an assessment methodology for understanding the individual's perception of his or her problems—responses to objective questionnaires. We have presented the view that many important aspects of the patient's behavior can become incorporated into the treatment process by using objective personality information available through the MMPI-2 and BTPI.

Assessment of Treatment Readiness and Psychological Accessibility

The MMPI-2 and BTPI can provide the therapist with clues to whether the individual is ready for treatment and is willing to approach the task of self-discovery with honesty. Test indicators that are helpful in assessing client reluctance or inability to cooperate with treatment are described in Chapters 2 and 3 on the MMPI-2 and Chapter 6 on the BTPI. As described earlier, these validity indicators are among the most useful means available to the clinician for determining treatment readiness. The way in which the client approaches the task of self-disclosure in response to the test items provides valuable information about treatment readiness or openness to change.

Clues to the individual's motivation for treatment can be obtained from the MMPI-2, as well as possible negative factors that could interfere with treatment, such as a tendency to feel threatened and to form hasty conclusions about people in authority. It may be valuable to discuss possible negative factors with the client early in treatment to head off beliefs or behaviors that can threaten treatment before they become fatal issues in therapy.

Amenability to change is also measurable with personality assessment tools like the MMPI-2 and BTPI. The prospects of a failed outcome to the therapy might be shared with the client early in therapy, perhaps to provoke a better outcome by challenging the patient and forewarning the therapist of potential perils ahead.

Building Rapport in Therapy

Clinicians find that sensitive, tactful test interpretation can be shared with clients early in therapy and can actually improve the treatment relationship because it reassures the patients that they are not going to be embarrassed or harmed by the process of self-discovery with the therapist. Many patients approach treatment with the fear that even the therapist, when he or she "finds out" about them, will despise or reject them. The evaluation stage of treatment, if properly and sensitively handled by the therapist, can serve to teach clients that disclosing "secrets" about themselves is important and that the treatment situation is a safe place in which to discuss their private thoughts. Finn and Butcher (1991) describe the value of the MMPI-2 in building rapport with the client. The substantial research support for the value of personality tests to enhance the rapport between patient and therapist has been described by Finn and his colleagues (Finn & Kamphuis, 2006; Finn & Martin, 1997).

The Need for Treatment

One of the most important functions of the MMPI-2 in treatment planning is that it provides the therapist with a perspective on the extent and nature of the patient's symptom pattern. It provides the clinician with an objective "outside opinion" concerning the nature of the problems the individual is experiencing and gives important information about the person's contribution to his or her problems. An important facet of the personality evaluation is that the scale scores provide summaries of symptoms and attitudes that indicate the relative strength or magnitude of the problems experienced. The clinical and supplementary scales of the MMPI-2 can assist the therapist in uncovering feelings or problems of which the patient might be unaware. For example, the extent of manifest depression might not be evident in initial interviews since many individuals, even in a therapist's office, attempt to "put on a good face" and not acknowledge the full extent of their problems. Many people are able to admit to problems through their response to personality questionnaires that they would not voluntarily report in a face-to-face context.

The hypothesis and descriptions generated from MMPI-2 scores provide information about how the client compares with the numerous other clinical groups and patient problem types. Information on the relative importance of the various problems the individual is experiencing in the overall clinical picture is valuable in charting the course of treatment and provides clues in the initial session to possible hidden or unseen problems. For example, if significant elevations on the Pa scale are prominent in the client's profile, the clinician and patient need to be aware of the possibility that the treatment can be threatened by early and intense problems in their relationship.

The MMPI-2 can provide information about the general quality of the individual's adjustment as well as the prevalence of long-term problems versus more situationally based difficulties, which would be beneficial for the therapist to assess early in treatment. Are the problems longstanding and chronic, or are the individual's problems situational in scope? The tasks of setting treatment goals and attempting to project a course of therapy are made easier if the therapist and patient have a clear idea of the overall "shape" of the problems for which the patient is seeking help. Discussing the past "courses" of similar problems in the patient's experience is also very helpful to client and therapist. In some cases, more realistic, obtainable treatment goals can be developed if both therapist and client are fully aware that there are unresolvable issues or personality factors that are not going to be manageable in the treatment plan or in the time available for therapy.

The MMPI and MMPI-2 have a substantial research base underlying their use; Rouse et al. (1997) found more than a thousand research studies on the two forms of the instrument. The MMPI-2 has been shown to be valuable in treatment planning since different MMPI-based profile types appear to respond to treatments differently (Sheppard, Smith, & Rosenbaum, 1988).

The Role of Personality in Treatment Success

The hypotheses and descriptions about the client's social relationships reflected in the BTPI can be of value in forewarning the therapist that the patient's social perceptions and typical styles of interacting with other people may be problematic. For example, information provided in the treatment process indicators can suggest potential process difficulties. Elevated scores on the SOM scale can suggest that the client is not open to behavioral change. An elevated score on the ENV scale of the BTPI can suggest that the client lives in (or perceives himself or herself to live in) an unsupportive environment that is not conducive to behavioral changes. Particularly valuable to the therapist in the early stages of therapy are clues to the presence of such detrimental factors as a debilitating lack of confidence in social relationships and feelings of isolation or alienation from others (i.e., through the MMPI-2 Si scale score). Such feelings of social distance may be particularly difficult to overcome in relationship-oriented psychotherapy. The advance knowledge that one's client possesses such beliefs or attitudes can warn the therapist that problems can occur in the development of a treatment relationship and need to be averted. The therapist might be able to structure the treatment situation in such a way as to prevent the client from feeling isolated, which would cause further withdrawal or premature termination of treatment.

Another factor that can negatively affect treatment is the possibility that the client possesses an unrecognized substance abuse problem. Rouse et al. (1999) examined the effectiveness of the MMPI-2 in detecting substance abuse among outpatients in psychotherapy. They found all of the MMPI-2 substance abuse scales (particularly MAC-R and AAS) to be effective at detecting substance abuse problems in the psychotherapy sample (10.2% were diagnosed as having substance abuse problems). The growing problem of substance abuse in contemporary society makes it likely that addictive disorders will occur in situations where it is least expected—in your client who was referred to you for a very different problem! Addictive disorders are difficult enough to deal with in settings where they are expected. When they occur in settings or clients for which the base rate expectancy is low, they can have a highly detrimental effect on the treatment situation. Clinicians who see a broad variety of clients in their practice usually discover early in their careers that not all people with addictive disorders recognize their problems and promptly check in at the local alcohol or drug program. Most of us have had the unfortunate situation of discovering, perhaps well into the treatment, that our client's real problem was not the initial referral issue but actually a matter of substance abuse. The MMPI-2 at initial assessment can provide the clinician with clues to whether the individual is likely to have a problem with alcohol or drugs. Regardless of the setting or the particular reason for referral, the clinician is well advised, given the pervasiveness of substance abuse in society, to view addictive disorder routinely as a potential problem and to evaluate this possibility in pretreatment assessment.

Other forms of acting-out behavior can be quite disruptive to psychological treatment as well. Several MMPI-2 profile types (i.e., the high Pd, the high Ma, or the 49 profile type) manifest a high potential for acting out in impulsive, destructive ways—for example, by violence toward family members or engaging in reckless sexual behavior. Such characteristics need to be carefully monitored and addressed in treatment to head off calamity.

Other character traits that can result in difficulties in treatment can also be appraised by the MMPI-2 and BTPI. For example, pathological distrust can deter the development of a treatment relationship in the initial stages of therapy and result in early termination if not dealt with adroitly. Another factor, assessed by prominent Pt scale elevations on the MMPI-2, is unproductive rumination. Individuals with very high elevations on Pt are likely to be overly ideational and obsessive and possess a seemingly unrelenting rigidity that is difficult to "re-route" in insight-oriented treatment because they have problems implementing new behaviors or viewing themselves in different ways. The BTPI can assess the extent to which a client's view of his or her relationships is unsupportive of his or her actions.

Communication of Information to the Client

The MMPI-2 and BTPI are excellent vehicles for providing personality information in a feedback session to clients because the information provided represents a summary of the broad range of problems the client has in comparison with many other patient groups. In addition, because the information is from an "outside" source, the therapist can present the findings in a comfortable, perhaps even professional and provocative, manner in order to challenge the patient or raise issues that the patient has not felt comfortable addressing. The MMPI or BTPI scale summary forms and the computer-generated narrative are good didactic materials for presenting test feedback to the client. Information about how insightful the client is, and whether he or she is able to incorporate test feedback information, is also often available from the test profile. For example, a person with a very high Hs scale score on the MMPI-2 or the SOM scale on the BTPI may be engaging in a flight into physical symptoms and may be unable to absorb information about personality problems.

Clients can usually grasp the meaning and significance of their prominent MMPI-2 scores. As noted earlier, the patient expects to obtain this type of information from the therapist and usually appreciates the feedback when it is appropriately given.

MMPI-2 personality descriptors are valuable in therapy since they provide names for relevant and powerful emotions the patient may be feeling. Finn and Butcher (1991) describe the *naming* function of MMPI-2 interpretation with clients and illustrate the process by which the client can learn to describe feelings in the relatively safe interpersonal context of therapy.

Tracking Progress in Treatment

Personality inventories can be very valuable tools for documenting how a person can change over time in treatment. Administering the instrument at the beginning of treatment to establish a baseline of self-reported problems and personality characteristics and retesting at a later date can provide valuable information for the treatment. The initial testing can serve as an interesting backdrop for evaluating changes in personality and problem "hang-ups" over the course of treatment. Patients appreciate feedback and are usually reassured when the therapist conducts progress evaluations by readministering the MMPI-2 during the course of therapy or as it ends.

The BTPI is particularly well suited for monitoring symptomatic status as therapy proceeds. A Symptom Monitoring Form (80 items) is available for evaluating symptom expression in a brief format. The computer-based scoring and interpretation program provides a quick summary of mood or symptomatic status of the client throughout the treatment process. The program provides a comparative analysis of change in symptom status over several administrations.

Limitations of Personality Assessment Strategies

The MMPI-2

The MMPI-2 contains 567 items and requires about 1.5 hours to administer, but the resulting scores provide the therapist with a considerable amount of information on measures that have a substantial "track record" in treatment assessment. This length does not present much of a problem for most applications because many clinical settings make it a routine practice to administer the full instrument to all patients at intake. In some clinical practices, however, it may be viewed as problematic to administer a questionnaire of this length on several occasions, or even in an initial assessment, because of a lack of space or inexperience in testing. Sometimes the therapist is employed in a setting that is simply not conducive to testing. It has been our experience that if the therapist explains the purpose of the test and indicates the importance of the results for treatment planning, most clients cooperate well with the evaluation. Concerning the question of office space for test administration or time to take the test, it is important not to fall into the practice of allowing clients to take the test home to complete it. This is not a recommended practice because professional ethics call for a tight control of psychological test materials. More problematic, however, is the fact that if the test is administered away from the office setting, you can never be sure that the inventory was completed by the client.

If the client is unable to respond to the full 567-item version of the MMPI-2 because of item restrictions, some have suggested altered or shortened versions. For example, a 180-item short version was suggested by Dahlstrom and Archer (2000). However, research has shown that this form does not assess the MMPI-2 constructs in a valid, reliable manner (Gass & Gonzalez, 2003) and it is not recommended for use in making decisions about clients. Moreover, a new shortened version of the MMPI-2 (the MMPI-RF) has been developed based on highly altered measures that bear little resemblance to the traditional MMPI-2 clinical scales (see Butcher, Hamilton, et al., 2006; Nichols, 2006). This new version has not been validated in a psychological treatment setting.

Another issue of concern to therapists using the MMPI-2 in treatment planning is the possibility that the instrument does not address all questions for which we seek answers and will not address some important areas of interest in treatment evaluation and planning. The highly structured nature of the MMPI-2 dictates that there are areas of personality, environment, or treatment dynamics that remain untouched by the personality assessment. The clinician must be alert to the need for verification of test-based impressions and scores, as well as the need to look beyond the particular profile for other possible relevant treatment variables. The BTPI contains 210 items regarding treatment that were developed specifically for treatment planning.

The issue that psychological tests may bias the therapist against the client was raised earlier. The argument that tests should not be used in treatment planning because they provide information that could close the therapist's mind to the client and prejudice the therapist against the person was not considered relevant; the benefits that accrue from the appropriate use of the test far outweigh any possible negative "mind-sealing" effects of test usage. The view described here that MMPI-2–based descriptors are used as hypotheses or provisional interpretations to be introduced, discussed, and verified in therapy sessions reduces the likelihood that particular test findings will be given the significance of "revealed truths" and will become fruitful treatment topics.

The MMPI-2 has become the most widely used objective personality instrument for assessing individuals in clinical settings. The original MMPI enjoyed considerable success in guiding clinicians through difficult assessment situations and in providing psychotherapy researchers with a valuable, objective outcome measure. The MMPI-2 promises to be an even more relevant and valuable instrument for treatment evaluation because the nonworking items in the original instrument have been deleted and broader, more therapy-relevant content and scales have been included.

The BTPI

Unlike the MMPI-2, the BTPI was specifically designed to address problems and issues facing clients in the treatment process. However, the research base available for this instrument is not as extensive as that for the MMPI-2, which has a long and rich tradition of use in the field of psychological assessment. Although initial research has demonstrated the utility of the BTPI in assessing clients in psychological treatment, further research will be needed to provide client information across the variety of treatment settings in which personality assessment has been shown to contribute to understanding of client problems.

References

Ackerman, S. J., Hilsenroth, M. J., Baity, M. R., & Blagys, M. D. (2000). Interaction of therapeutic process and alliance during psychological assessment. *Journal of Personality Assessment, 75*, 82–109.

Altman, H., Gynther, M. D., Warbin, R. W., & Sletten, I. W. (1973). Replicated empirical correlates of the MMPI 8–9/9–8 code type. *Journal of Personality Assessment, 37*, 369–371.

American Psychological Association (1986). *American Psychological Association guidelines for computer-based tests and interpretations.* Washington, D.C.: American Psychological Association.

Apfeldorf, M., & Huntley, P. J. (1975). Application of MMPI alcoholism scales to older alcoholics and problem drinkers. *Journal of Studies on Alcohol, 37*, 645–653.

Arbisi, P., & Ben-Porath, Y. S. (1995). An MMPI-2 infrequency scale for use with psycho-pathological populations: the Infrequency-Psychopathology Scale, F(p). *Psychological Assessment, 7*, 424–431.

Arbisi, P., & Ben-Porath, Y. S. (1997). Characteristics of the MMPI-2 F(p) Scale as a function of diagnosis in an inpatient sample of veterans. *Psychological Assessment, 9*, 102–105.

Arbisi, P. A. (2006). Use of the MMPI-2 in personal injury and disability evaluations. In J. N. Butcher (Ed.), *MMPI-2: the practitioner's handbook* (pp. 407–441). Washington, D. C.: American Psychological Association.

Arbisi, P. A., Ben-Porath, Y. S., & McNulty, J. L. (2003). Empirical correlates of common MMPI-2 two-point codes in male psychiatric inpatients. *Assessment, 10* (3), 237–247.

Archer, R. P., Gordon, R. A., Zillmer, E. A., & McClure, S. (1985). Characteristics and correlates of MMPI change within an adult psychiatric inpatient setting. *Journal of Clinical Psychology, 41*(6), 739–746.

Archer, R. P., Griffin, R., & Aiduk, R. (1995). Clinical correlates for ten common code types. *Journal of Personality Assessment, 65*, 391–408.

Arnold, P. D. (1970). *Recurring MMPI two-point codes of marriage counselors and "normal" couples with implications for interpreting marital interaction behavior.* Unpublished doctoral dissertation. University of Minnesota.

Arnow, B. A., Blasey, C., Manber, R., Constantino, M. J., Markowitz, J. C., Klein, D. N., Thase, M. E., Kocsis, J. H., & Rush, A. J. (2007). Dropouts versus completers among chronically depressed outpatients. *Journal of Affective Disorders, 97*(1–3), 197–202.

Atlis, M. M., Hahn, J., & Butcher, J. N. (2006). Computer-based assessment with the MMPI-2. In J. N. Butcher (Ed.), *MMPI-2: the practitioner's handbook* (pp. 445–476). Washington, D.C.: American Psychological Association.

Bagby, R. M., Marshall, M. B., Basso, M. R., Nicholson, R. A., Bacchiochi, J., & Miller, L. S. (2005). Distinguishing bipolar depression, major depression, and schizophrenia with the MMPI-2 clinical and content scales. *Journal of Personality Assessment, 84,* 89–95.

Bagby, R. M., Marshall, M. B., Bury, A., Bacchiocci, J. R., & Miller, L. (2006). Assessing underreporting and overreporting styles on the MMPI-2. In J. N. Butcher (Ed.), *MMPI-2: the practitioner's handbook* (pp. 39–69). Washington, D.C.: American Psychological Association.

Barefoot, J. C., Dahlstrom, W. G., & Williams, R. B. (1983). Hostility, CHD incidence, and total mortality: a 25-yr follow-up study of 255 physicians. *Psychosomatic Medicine, 45*(1), 59–63.

Barron, F. (1953). An ego strength scale which predicts response to psychotherapy. *Journal of Consulting Psychology, 17,* 327–333.

Barthlow, D. L., Graham, J. R., Ben-Porath, Y. S., & McNulty, J. L. (1999). Incremental validity of the MMPI-2 content scales in an outpatient mental health setting. *Psychological Assessment, 11*(1), 39–47.

Barthlow, D. L., Graham, J. R., Ben-Porath, Y. S., & McNulty, J. L. (2004). Construct validity of the MMPI-2 college maladjustment (Mt) scale. *Assessment, 11*(3), 251–262.

Beck, T., & Steer, R. A. (1990). *Beck Anxiety Inventory Manual.* San Antonio, TX: The Psychological Corporation.

Beck, A. T., Steer, R. A., & Brown, G. (1996). *Beck Depression Inventory, Second Edition: manual.* San Antonio, TX: The Psychological Corporation.

Beck, A. T., Steer, R. A., Epstein, N., & Brown, G. (1990). Beck Self-Concept Test. *Psychological Assessment, 2*(2), 191–197.

Ben-Porath, Y., Hoestetler, K., Butcher, J. N., & Graham, J. R. (1989). New subscales for the MMPI-2 Social Introversion (Si) Scale. *Psychological Assessment: A Journal of Consulting and Clinical Psychology, 1,* 169–174.

Ben-Porath, Y., Slutsky, W., & Butcher, J. N. (1989). A real-data simulation of computerized adaptive administration of the MMPI. *Psychological Assessment: A Journal of Consulting and Clinical Psychology, 1,* 18–22.

Ben-Porath, Y., Waller, N.G., Slutsky, W., & Butcher, J. N. (1988). *A comparison of two methods for adaptive administration of MMPI-2 Content Scales.* Paper presented at the 96th Annual meeting of the American Psychological Association, August 1988, Atlanta, Georgia.

Ben-Porath, Y. S. (1997). Use of personality assessment instruments in empirically guided treatment planning. *Psychological Assessment, 9*, 361–367.

Ben-Porath, Y. S. (2003, October). *Psychometric characteristics of the RC scales.* Paper presented at the 38th Annual Symposium on Recent Developments in the Use of the MMPI-2/MMPI-A, Cleveland, Ohio.

Ben-Porath, Y. S., Butcher, J. N., & Graham, J. R. (1991). Contribution of the MMPI-2 Content Scales to the differential diagnosis of psychopathology. *Psychological Assessment, 3*, 634–640.

Ben-Porath, Y. S., McCully, E., & Almagor, M. (1993). Incremental validity of the MMPI-2 Content Scales in the assessment of personality and psychopathology by self-report. *Journal of Personality Assessment, 61*, 557–575.

Ben-Porath, Y. S. & Tellegen, A. (in press). *The MMPI-2 RF.* Minneapolis, MN: Pearson Assessments.

Berry, D.T.R., Adams, J. J., Smith, G. T., Greene, R. L., Sekirnjak, G. C., Wieland, G., & Tharpe, B. (1997). MMPI-2 clinical scales and 2-point code types: impact of varying levels of omitted items. *Psychological Assessment, 9*, 158–160.

Beutler, L. E. (1995). Integrating and communicating findings, In L. E. Beutler & M. R. Berren (Eds.), *Integrative assessment of adult personality* (pp. 25–64). New York: The Guilford Press.

Beutler, L. E., Engle, D., Mohr, D., Daldrup, R. J., Bergan, J., Meredith, K., & Merry, W. (1991). Predictors of differential and self-directed psychotherapeutic procedures. *Journal of Consulting and Clinical Psychology, 59*, 333–340.

Boerger, A. R., Graham, J. R., & Lilly, R. S. (1974). Behavioral correlates of single scale MMPI code types. *Journal of Consulting and Clinical Psychology, 42*, 398–402.

Bordin, E. S. (1979). The generalizability of the psychoanalytic concept of the working alliance. *Psychotherapy: Theory, Research, and Practice, 16*, 252–260.

Bosquet, M., & Egeland, B. (2000). Predicting parent behaviors from antisocial practices content scale scores of the MMPI-2 administered during pregnancy. *Journal of Personality Assessment, 74*(1), 146–162.

Brandwin, M. A., & Kewman, D. G. (1982). MMPI indicators of treatment response to spinal epidural stimulation in patients with chronic pain and patients with movement disorders. *Psychological Reports, 51*(3, Pt. 2), 1059–1064.

Brems, C., & Lloyd, P. (1995). Validation of the MMPI-2 Low Self Esteem Content Scale. *Journal of Personality Assessment, 65*(3), 550–556.

Brody, S. (1994). Traditional ideology, stress, and psychotherapy use. *Journal of Psychology, 128*, 5–13.

Burisch, M. (1984). Approaches to personality inventory construction. *American Psychologist, 39*, 214–227.

Butcher, J. N. (Ed.) (1972). *Objective personality assessment: changing perspectives.* New York: Academic Press.

Butcher, J. N. (1985). Current developments in MMPI use: an international perspective. In J. N. Butcher & C. D. Spielberger (Eds.), *Advances in personality assessment*, Vol. 4. Hillsdale, NJ: Lawrence Erlbaum Press.

Butcher, J. N. (1987a). Computerized clinical and personality assessment using the MMPI. In J. N. Butcher (Ed.), *Computerized psychological assessment*. New York: Basic Books.

Butcher, J. N. (Ed.). (1987b). *Computerized psychological assessment*. New York: Basic Books.

Butcher, J. N. (1989a, August). *MMPI-2: issues of continuity and change*. Paper presented at the 97th Annual Convention of the American Psychological Association, New Orleans, Louisiana.

Butcher, J. N. (1989b). *User's guide for the Minnesota Personnel Report*. Minneapolis, MN: National Computer Systems.

Butcher, J. N. (Ed.) (1996). *International adaptations of the MMPI-2*. Minneapolis, MN: University of Minnesota Press.

Butcher, J. N. (1997a). Assessment and treatment in the era of managed care. In J. N. Butcher (Ed.), *Personality assessment in managed care: using the MMPI-2 in treatment planning* (pp. 3–12). New York: Oxford University Press.

Butcher, J. N. (1997b). *Personality assessment in managed health care*. New York: Oxford University Press

Butcher, J. N. (2000a). Revising psychological tests: lessons learned from the revision of the MMPI. *Psychological Assessment, 12*(3), 263–271.

Butcher, J. N. (2000b). Dynamics of personality test responses: the empiricist's manifesto revisited. *Journal of Clinical Psychology, 56*(3), 375–386.

Butcher, J. N. (Ed). (2000c). *Basic sources for the MMPI-2*. Minneapolis: University of Minnesota Press.

Butcher, J. N. (2004). Personality assessment without borders: adaptation of the MMPI-2 across cultures. *Journal of Personality Assessment, 83*(2), 90–104.

Butcher, J. N. (2005). *Butcher Treatment Planning Inventory (BTPI): technical manual*. Toronto, ON: Multi-Health Systems, Inc.

Butcher, J. N. (2005a). Exploring universal personality characteristics: an objective approach. *International Journal of Clinical and Health Psychology, 5*, 553–566.

Butcher, J. N. (2005b). *A beginner's guide to the MMPI-2* (2nd ed.). Washington, D.C.: American Psychological Association.

Butcher, J. N. (2005c). *User's guide for the MMPI-2 Minnesota Report: adult clinical system* (4th ed.). Minneapolis, MN: Pearson Assessments.

Butcher, J. N. (Ed.) (2006a). *MMPI-2: a practitioner's guide*. Washington, D.C.: American Psychological Association.

Butcher, J. N. (2006b). Assessment in clinical psychology: a perspective on the past, present challenges, and future prospects. *Clinical Psychology: Science and Practice, 13*, 205–209.

Butcher, J. N., Berah, E., Ellertsen, B., Miach, P., Lim, J., Nezami, E., Pancheri, P., Derksen, J., & Almagor, M. (1998). Objective personality assessment: computer-based MMPI-2 interpretation in international clinical settings. In C. Belar (Ed.), *Comprehensive clinical psychology: Sociocultural and individual differences* (pp. 277–312). New York: Elsevier.

Butcher, J. N., Cabiya, J., Lucio, E. M., & Garrido, M. (2007). *Assessing Hispanic clients using the MMPI-2 and MMPI-A*. Washington, D.C.: American Psychological Association.

Butcher, J. N., Dahlstrom, W. G., Graham, J. R., Tellegen, A., & Kaemmer, B. (1989). *Manual for the Restandardized Minnesota Multiphasic Personality Inventory: MMPI-2. An interpretive guide*. Minneapolis, MN: University of Minnesota Press.

Butcher, J. N., & Finn, S. (1983). Objective personality assessment in clinical settings. In M. Hersen, A. E. Kazdin, & A. S. Bellack (Eds.), *The clinical psychology handbook*. New York: Pergamon Press.

Butcher, J. N., Graham, J. R., Ben-Porath, Y. S., Tellegen, Y. S., Dahlstrom, W. G., & Kaemmer, B. (2001). *Minnesota Multiphasic Personality Inventory-2: manual for administration and scoring* (revised ed.). Minneapolis, MN: University of Minnesota Press.

Butcher, J. N., Graham, J. R., Kamphuis, J. & Rouse, S. (2006). Evaluating MMPI-2 research: considerations for practitioners. In J. N. Butcher (Ed.), *MMPI-2: the practitioner's handbook* (pp. 15–38). Washington, D.C.: American Psychological Association.

Butcher, J. N., Graham, J. R., Williams, C. L., & Ben-Porath, Y. (1990). *Development and use of the MMPI-2 Content Scales*. Minneapolis, MN: University of Minnesota Press.

Butcher, J. N., Hamilton, C. K., Rouse, S. V., & Cumella, E. J. (2006).The deconstruction of the Hy scale of MMPI-2: failure of RC3 in measuring somatic symptom expression. *Journal of Personality Assessment, 87*(1), 199–205.

Butcher, J. N., & Han, K. (1995). Development of an MMPI-2 scale to assess the presentation of self in a superlative manner: the S Scale. In J. N. Butcher & C. D. Spielberger (Eds.), *Advances in personality assessment*, Vol. 10 (pp. 25–50). Hillsdale, NJ: LEA Press.

Butcher, J. N., & Herzog, J. (1982). Individual assessment in crisis intervention: observation, life history, and personality approaches. In D. Spielberger & J. N. Butcher (Eds.), *Advances in personality assessment* (pp. 115–166). New York: Lawrence Erlbaum, Inc.

Butcher, J. N., & Hostetler, K. (1990). Abbreviating MMPI item administration: past problems and prospects for MMPI-2. *Psychological Assessment: A Journal of Consulting and Clinical Psychology, 2*, 12–21.

Butcher, J. N., Keller, L. S., & Bacon, S. (1985). Current developments and future directions in computerized personality assessment. *Journal of Consulting and Clinical Psychology, 53*, 803–815.

Butcher, J. N., & Owen, P. (1978). Survey of personality inventories: recent research developments and contemporary issues. In B. Wolman (Ed.), *Handbook of clinical diagnosis*. New York: Plenum.

Butcher, J. N., & Pancheri, P. (1976). *Handbook of cross-national MMPI research*. Minneapolis, MN: University of Minnesota Press.

Butcher, J. N., Perry, J., & Hahn, J. (2004). Computers in clinical assessment: historical developments, present status, and future challenges. *Journal of Clinical Psychology, 60*, 331–346.

Butcher, J. N., & Rouse, S. V. (1996). Personality: individual differences and clinical assessment. *Annual Review of Psychology, 47*, 87–111.

Butcher, J. N., Rouse, S. V., & Perry, J. N. (1998). Assessing resistance to psychological treatment. *Measurement and Evaluation in Counseling and Development, 31*, 95–108.

Butcher, J. N., Rouse, S. V., & Perry, J. N. (2000). Empirical description of psychopathology in therapy clients: correlates of the MMPI-2 scales. In J. N. Butcher (Ed.), *Basic sources on the MMPI-2* (pp. 487–500). Minneapolis: University of Minnesota Press.

Butcher, J. N., & Williams, C. L. (2000). *Essentials of MMPI-2 and MMPI-A interpretation* (2nd ed.) Minneapolis, MN: University of Minnesota Press.

Caldwell, A. B. (2006). Maximal measurement or meaningful measurement: the interpretive challenges of the MMPI-2 Restructured Clinical (RC) scales. *Journal of Personality Assessment, 87*(2), 193–201.

Carson, R. C. (1969). Interpretive manual to the MMPI. In J. N. Butcher (ed.), *MMPI: research developments and clinical applications*. New York: McGraw-Hill.

Castro, J. (1993, May 31). What price mental health? *Time*, 59–60.

Cernovsky, Z. (1984). ES scale level and correlates of MMPI elevation: alcohol abuse vs. MMPI scores in treated alcoholics. *Journal of Clinical Psychology, 40*(6), 1502–1509.

Chall, J. S., & Dale, E. (1995). *Readability revisited: the new Dale-Chall readability formula*. Cambridge, MA: Brookline Books.

Cheatham, H. E., Shelton, T. O., & Ray, W. (1987). Race, sex, causal attribution, and help-seeking behavior. *Journal of College Student Personnel, 26*, 559–568.

Chodzko-Zajko, W. J., & Ismail, A. H. (1984). MMPI interscale relationships in middle-aged males before and after an 8-month fitness program. *Journal of Clinical Psychology, 40*(1), 163–169.

Clark, M. E. (1993, March). *MMPI-2 Anger and Cynicism scales: interpretive cautions*. Paper presented at the 28th annual symposium on recent developments in the use of the MMPI/MMPI-2/MMPI-A. St. Petersburg Beach, FL.

Clark, M. E. (1996). MMPI-2 Negative Treatment Indicators Content and Content Component Scales: clinical correlates and outcome prediction for men with chronic pain. *Psychological Assessment, 8*, 32–47.

Clavelle, P., & Butcher, J. N. (1977). An adaptive typological approach to psychological screening. *Journal of Consulting and Clinical Psychology, 45*, 851–859.

Clements, R., & Heintz, J. M. (2002). Diagnostic accuracy and factor structure of the AAS and APS scales of the MMPI-2. *Journal of Personality Assessment, 79*(3), 564–582.

Colligan, R. C., Osborne, D., Swenson, W. M., & Offord, K. P. (1983). *The MMPI: a contemporary normative study*. New York: Praeger.

Connell, J., Grant, S., & Mullin, T. (2006). Client-initiated termination of therapy at NHS primary care counseling services. *Counseling & Psychotherapy Research, 6*(1), 60–67.

Cook, W. W., & Medley, D. M. (1954). Proposed hostility and pharisaic-virtue scales for the MMPI. *Journal of Applied Psychology, 381*, 414–418.

Craig, R. J. (2005). Assessing contemporary substance abusers with the MMPI MacAndrews Alcoholism Scale: a review. *Substance Use & Misuse, 40*, 427–450.

Dahlstrom, W. G. (1980). Altered versions of the MMPI. In *Basic readings on the MMPI* (pp. 386–393). Minneapolis, MN: University of Minnesota Press.

Dahlstrom, W. G., & Archer, R. P. (2000). A shortened version of the MMPI-2. *Assessment, 7*(2), 131–137.

Dahlstrom, W. G., Welsh, G. S., & Dahlstrom, L. E. (1975). *A MMPI handbook*, Vol. 2. Minneapolis, MN: University of Minnesota Press.

Dale, E., & Chall, J. S. (1948). A formula for predicting readability. Columbus, OH: Ohio State University Bureau of Educational Research (Reprinted from *Educational Research Bulletin, 27*, 11–20), 34–54.

Dawes, R. M., Faust, D., & Meehl, P. E. (1989). Clinical versus actuarial judgment. *Science, 24*, 1668–1674

Derogatis, L. R. (1994). *Brief Symptom Inventory: administration, scoring and procedures manual*. Minneapolis, MN: National Computer Systems.

Drake, L. E., & Oetting, E. R. (1959). *A MMPI codebook for counselors*. Minneapolis, MN: University of Minnesota Press.

Drake, L. E. (1946). A social I-E scale for the MMPI. *Journal of Applied Psychology, 30*, 51–54.

Eyde, L., Kowal, D., & Fishburne, J. (1987). *Clinical implications of validity research on computer based test interpretations of the MMPI*. Paper given at the Annual Meeting of the American Psychological Association, New York, New York.

Faull, R., & Meyer, G. J. (1993, March). *Assessment of depression with the MMPI-2: distinctions between Scale 2 and the DER*. Paper presented at the midwinter meeting of the Society for Personality Assessment, San Francisco.

Finn, S. E. (1996a). Assessing feedback integrating MMPI-2 and Rorschach findings. *Journal of Personality Assessment, 67*(3), 543–557.

Finn, S. E. (1996b). *Using the MMPI-2 as a therapeutic intervention*. Minneapolis, MN: University of Minnesota Press.

Finn, S. E., & Butcher, J. N. (1991). Clinical objective personality assessment. In M. Hersen, A. E. Kazdin, & A.S. Bellack (Eds.), *The clinical psychology handbook* (2nd ed., pp. 362–373). New York: Pergamon Press.

Finn, S. E., & Kamphuis, J. H. (2006). Therapeutic assessment with the MMPI-2. In J. N. Butcher (Ed.), *MMPI-2: the practitioner's handbook* (pp. 165–191). Washington, D.C.: American Psychological Association.

Finn, S. E., & Martin, H. (1997). Therapeutic assessment with the MMPI-2 in managed care. In J. N. Butcher (Ed.), *Personality assessment in managed care: using the MMPI-2 in treatment planning* (pp. 131–152). New York: Oxford University Press.

Finn, S. E., & Tonsager, M. E. (1992). Therapeutic effects of providing MMPI-2 test feedback to college students awaiting therapy. *Psychological Assessment, 4*, 278–287.

Finn, S. E., & Tonsager, M. E. (1997). Information-gathering and therapeutic models of assessment: complementary paradigms. *Psychological Assessment, 9*, 374–385.

Fischer, C. T. (1985/1994). *Individualizing psychological assessment*. Mahwah, NJ: Erlbaum.

Fischer, C. T. (2000). Collaborative individualized assessment. *Journal of Personality Assessment, 74*, 2–14.

Fishburne, J., Eyde, L., & Kowal, D. (1988). "Computer-based test interpretations of the MMPI with neurologically impaired patients." Paper given at the Annual Meeting of the American Psychological Association, Atlanta, Georgia.

Fordyce, W. (1987). *Use of the MMPI with chronic pain patients*. Paper given at the Ninth International Conference on Personality Assessment, Brussels, Belgium.

Fowler, R. D. (1985). Landmarks in computer-assisted psychological test interpretation. *Journal of Consulting and Clinical Psychology, 53*, 748–759.

Fowler, R. D. (1987). Developing a computer based interpretation system. In J. N. Butcher (Ed.), *Computerized psychological assessment*. New York: Basic Books.

Fowler, R. D., Jr., & Athey, E. B. (1971). A cross-validation of Gilberstadt and Duker's 1–2–3–4 profile type. *Journal of Clinical Psychology, 27*, 238–240.

Frank, J. D. (1959). The dynamics of the psychotherapeutic relationship: determinants and effects of the therapist's influence. *Psychiatry, 22*, 17–39.

Frank, J. D. (1995). Psychotherapy or rhetoric: some implications. *Clinical Psychology: Science and Practice, 2*, 90–93.

Garfield, S. (1978). Research on client variables in psychotherapy. In S. L. Garfield & A. E. Bergin (Eds.), *Handbook of psychotherapy and behavior change. An empirical analysis* (2nd ed., pp. 191–232). New York: Wiley.

Gass, C. S., & Gonazalez, C. (2003). MMPI-2 short form proposal: CAUTION. *Archives of Clinical Neuropsychology, 18*(5), 521–527.

Gass, C. S., & Luis, C. A. (2001). MMPI-2 Short Form psychometric characteristics in a neuropsychological setting. *Assessment, 8*(2), 213–219.

Gaston, L. (1991). Reliability and criterion-related validity of the California Psychotherapy Alliance Scales-Patient Version. *Psychological Assessment, 3*, 68–74.

Gilberstadt, H., & Duker, J. (1965). *A handbook for clinical and actuarial MMPI interpretation*. Philadelphia: Saunders.

Gilmore, J. D., Lash, S. J., Foster, M. A., & Blosser, S. L. (2001). Adherence to substance abuse treatment: clinical utility of two MMPI-2 scales. *Journal of Personality Assessment, 77*(3), 524–540.

Goldberg, L. R., & Jones, R. R. (1969). *The reliability, the generality and correlates of intra-individual consistency in response to structured personality inventories*. Oregon Research Monograph, 9, No. 2.

Gonzalez-Ibanez, A., Mora, M., Gutierrez-Maldonado, J., Ariza, A., & Lourido-Ferreira, M. R. (2005). Pathological gambling and age: differences in personality, psychopathology, and response to treatment variables. *Addictive Behaviors, 30*, 383–388.

Gottesman, I. I., & Prescott, C. A. (1989). Abuses of the MacAndrew MMPI alcoholism scale: a critical review. *Clinical Psychology Review, 9*, 223–242.

Gough, H. G., McClosky, H., & Meehl, P. E. (1952). A personality scale for social responsibility. *Journal of Abnormal and Social Psychology, 47*, 73–80.

Graham, J. R. (1973). *Behavioral correlates of simple MMPI code types*. Paper given at the Eighth Annual Symposium on Recent Developments in the Use of the MMPI, New Orleans, Louisiana.

Graham, J. R. (1979). *Using the MMPI in counseling and psychotherapy. Clinical notes on the MMPI*. Minneapolis, MN: National Computer System.

Graham, J. R. (1989, August). *The meaning of elevated MacAndrew Alcoholism Scale scores for nonclinical subjects*. Paper presented at the 97th Annual Convention of the American Psychological Association, New Orleans, Louisiana.

Graham, J. R. (1990). *MMPI-2: Assessing personality and psychopathology*. New York: Oxford University Press.

Graham, J. R. (2006). *MMPI-2: assessing personality and psychopathology* (4th ed.). New York: Oxford University Press.

Graham, J. R., Ben-Porath, Y. S. & McNulty, J. (1999). *Using the MMPI-2 in outpatient mental health settings*. Minneapolis, MN: University of Minnesota Press.

Graham, J. R., & Strenger, V. E. (1988). MMPI characteristics of alcoholics: a review. *Journal of Consulting and Clinical Psychology, 56*, 197–205.

Gray, H. (2005). An exploration of MMPI-2 extratest correlates for female criminal defendants. *Dissertation Abstracts International: Section B: The Sciences and Engineering, 66*(3-B), 1718.

Grayson, H. M. (1951). *Psychological admission testing program and manual*. Los Angeles: Veterans Administration Center, Neuropsychiatric Hospital.

Green, B. A., Handel, R. W., & Archer, R. P. (2006). External correlates of the MMPI-2 Content Component Scales in mental health inpatients. *Assessment, 13*, 80–97.

Greene, R. L. (2000). *The MMPI-2: an interpretive manual* (2nd ed.). Needham Heights, MA: Allyn & Bacon.

Greene, R. L., Robin, R. W., Albaugh, B., Caldwell, A., & Goldman, D. (2003). Use of the MMPI-2 in American Indians: II. Empirical correlates. *Psychological Assessment, 15*(3), 360–369.

Grove, W. M., & Meehl, P. E. (1996). Comparative efficiency of informal (subjective, impressionistic) and formal (mechanical, algorithmic) prediction procedures: the clinical-statistical controversy. *Psychology, Public Policy, and Law, 2*(2), 293–323.

Gynther, M. D. (1972). *A new replicated actuarial program for interpreting MMPIs of state hospital inpatients*. Paper given at the Seventh Annual Symposium on Recent Developments in the Use of the MMPI, Mexico, 1972.

Gynther, M. D., Altman, H., & Sletten, I. W. (1973). Development of an empirical interpretive system for the MMPI: some after-the-fact observations. *Journal of Clinical Psychology, 29*, 232–234.

Gynther, M. D., Altman, H., & Warbin, R. W. (1972). A new empirical automated MMPI interpretive program: the 2–4/4–2 code type. *Journal of Clinical Psychology, 28*, 498–501.

Gynther, M. D., Altman, H., & Warbin, R. W. (1973a). A new actuarial-empirical automated MMPI interpretive program: the 2–7/7–2 code type. *Journal of Clinical Psychology, 29*, 229–231.

Gynther, M. D., Altman, H., & Warbin, R. W. (1973b). A new actuarial-empirical automated MMPI interpretive program: the 6–9/9–6 code type. *Journal of Clinical Psychology, 29*, 60–61.

Gynther, M. D., Altman, H., Warbin, R. W., & Sletten, I. W. (1972). A new actuarial-empirical automated MMPI interpretive program: rationale and methodology. *Journal of Clinical Psychology, 28*, 173–179.

Gynther, M. D., Altman, H., Warbin, R. W., & Sletten, I. W. (1973). A new actuarial-empirical automated MMPI interpretive program: the 1–2/2–1 code type. *Journal of Clinical Psychology, 29*, 54–57.

Halbower, C. C. (1955). *A comparison of actuarial versus clinical prediction to classes discriminated by MMPI.* Unpublished doctoral dissertation, University of Minnesota.

Han, K., Weed, N., Calhoun, R., & Butcher, J. N. (1995). Psychometric characteristics of the MMPI-2 Cook-Medley Hostility Scale. *Journal of Personality Assessment, 65,* 567–586.

Handler, L. (1995). The clinical use of figure drawings. In C. Newmark (Ed.), *Major psychological assessment instruments* (pp. 206–293). Boston: Allyn & Bacon.

Harkness, A. R. (1992). Fundamental topics in the personality disorders: candidate trait dimensions from lower regions of the hierarchy. *Psychological Assessment, 4,* 251–259.

Harkness, A. R., McNulty, J. L., & Ben-Porath, Y. S. (1995). The Personality Psychopathology Five (PSY-5): constructs and MMPI-2 scales. *Psychological Assessment, 7,* 104–114.

Harkness, A., McNulty, J., Ben-Porath, Y., & Graham, J. R. (1999). *MMPI-2 Personality Psychopathology 5 (PSY-5) Scales. MMPI-2 test reports.* Minneapolis, MN: University of Minnesota Press.

Harkness, A.R., McNulty, J. L., Ben-Porath, Y. S., & Graham, J. R. (2002). *The Personality Psychopathology Five (PSY-5) scales: gaining an overview for case conceptualization and treatment planning.* Minneapolis, MN: University of Minnesota Press.

Harris, R. E., & Lingoes, J. C. (1955, 1968). *Subscales for the MMPI: an aid to profile interpretation.* Unpublished manuscript. The Langley Porter Neuropsychiatric Institute.

Hatchett, G. T., Han, K., & Cooker, P. G. (2002). Predicting premature termination from counseling using the Butcher Treatment Planning Inventory. *Assessment, 9,* 156–163.

Hathaway, S. R. (1980). Scales 5 (Masculinity–Femininity) 6 (Paranoia), and 8 (Schizophrenia). In W. G. Dahlstrom & L. E. Dahlstrom (1980). *Basic readings on the MMPI.* Minneapolis: University of Minnesota Press.

Hathaway, S. R., & McKinlay, J. C. (1940). A Multiphasic Personality Schedule (Minnesota): I. Construction of the schedule. *Journal of Psychology, 10,* 249–254.

Hathaway, S. R., & McKinley, J. C. (1943). *The Minnesota Multiphasic Personality Schedule.* Minneapolis, MN: University of Minnesota Press.

Henrichs, T. F. (1987). MMPI profiles of chronic pain patients: some methodological considerations that concern clusters and descriptors. *Journal of Clinical Psychology, 43,* 650–660.

Hilsenroth, M. J., Peters, E. J., & Ackerman, S. J. (2004). The development of therapeutic alliance during psychological assessment: patient and therapist perspectives across treatment. *Journal of Personality Assessment, 83,* 332–344.

Hjemboe, S., Almagor, M., & Butcher, J. N. (1992). Empirical assessment of marital distress: the Marital Distress Scale (MDS) for the MMPI-2. In C. D. Spielberger & J. N. Butcher (Eds.), *Advances in personality assessment* (Vol. 9, pp. 141–152). New Jersey: Lawrence Erlbaum Press.

Hjemboe, S., & Butcher, J. N. (1991). Couples in marital distress: a study of demographic and personality factors as measured by the MMPI-2. *Journal of Personality Assessment, 57,* 216–237.

Hollon, S., & Mandell, M. (1979). Use of the MMPI in the valuation of treatment effects. In J. N. Butcher (Ed.), *New developments in the use of the MMPI*. Minneapolis, MN: University of Minnesota Press.

Horan, W. P., Subotnik, K. L., Reise, S. P., Ventura, J., & Nuechterlein, K. H. (2005). Stability and clinical correlates of personality characteristics in recent-onset schizophrenia. *Psychological Medicine, 35*, 995–1005.

Horowitz, L. M., Alden, L. E., Wiggins, J. S., & Pincus, A. L. (2000). *Inventory of Interpersonal Problems manual*. Odessa, FL: Psychological Corporation.

Horowitz, L. M., Rosenberg, S. E., Baer, B.A., Ureño, G., & Villaseñor, V. S. (1988). Inventory of interpersonal problems: psychometric properties and clinical applications. *Journal of Consulting and Clinical Psychology, 56*(6), 885–892.

Horvath, A. (2001). The alliance. *Psychotherapy, 38*, 365–372.

Horvath, A. O., & Greenberg, L. S. (1989). Development and validation of the Working Alliance Inventory. *Journal of Counseling Psychology, 36*, 223–233.

Hostetler, K., Ben-Porath, Y., Butcher, J. N., & Graham, J. R. (1989). *New subscales for the MMPI-2 Social Introversion scale*. Paper presented at the Society for Personality Assessment, New York.

Jacobson, N. S., & Truax, P. (1991). Clinical significance: a statistical approach to defining meaningful change in psychotherapy research. *Journal of Consulting and Clinical Psychology, 59*, 12–19.

Johnson, J. H., Butcher, J. N., Null, C., & Johnson, K. (1984). Replicated item level factor analysis of the full MMPI. *Journal of Personality and Social Psychology, 47*, 105–114.

Johnson, M. E. (1988). Influences of gender and sex role orientation on help-seeking attitudes. *Journal of Psychology, 122*, 237–241.

Jung, K. (1922). *Psychological types*. New York: Harcourt, Brace & World.

Kamphuis, J., & Finn, S. (2002) Incorporating base rate information in daily clinical decision making. In J. N. Butcher (Ed.), *Clinical personality assessment* (2nd ed., pp. 257–269). New York: Oxford University Press.

Keane, T. M., Malloy, P. F., & Fairbank, J. A. (1984). Empirical development of an MMPI subscale for the assessment of posttraumatic stress disorder. *Journal of Consulting and Clinical Psychology, 52*, 888–891.

Keller, L. S., & Butcher, J. N. (1991). *Use of the MMPI-2 with chronic pain patients*. Minneapolis, MN: University of Minnesota Press.

Kelly, C. K., & King, G. D. (1978). Behavioral correlates for within-normal limit MMPI profiles with and without elevated K in students at a university mental health center. *Journal of Clinical Psychology, 34*, 695–699.

Kleinmuntz, B. (1961). The College Maladjustment Scale (MT): norms and predictive validity. *Educational and Psychological Measurement, 21*, 1029–1033.

Klump, K., & Butcher, J. N. (1997). Psychological tests in treatment planning: the importance of objective assessment. In J. N. Butcher (Ed.), *Personality assessment in managed health care* (pp. 93–130). New York: Oxford University Press.

Koss, M. P. (1979). MMPI item content: recurring issues. In J. N. Butcher (Ed.), *New developments in the use of the MMPI* (pp. 3–38). Minneapolis, MN: University of Minnesota Press.

Koss, M. P., & Butcher, J. N. (1973). A comparison of psychiatric patients' self-report with other sources of clinical information. *Journal of Research in Personality, 7,* 225–236.

Koss, M. P., & Butcher, J. N. (1986). Research on brief and crisis-oriented psychotherapy. In S. L. Garfield & A. E. Bergin (Eds.), *Handbook of psychotherapy and behavior change* (3rd ed.). New York: Wiley.

Koss, M. P., Butcher, J. N., & Hoffman, N. G. (1976). The MMPI critical items: how well do they work? *Journal of Consulting and Clinical Psychology, 44,* 921–928.

Lachar, D., & Wrobel, T. A. (1979). Validating clinicians' hunches: construction of a new MMPI critical item set. *Journal of Consulting and Clinical Psychology, 47,* 277–284.

Lauterbach, D., Garcia, M., & Gloster, A. (2002). Psychometric properties and predictive validity of the Mt Scale of the MMPI-2. *Assessment, 9*(4), 390–400.

Lazaratou, H., Anagnostopoulos, D. C.,Vlassopoulos, M.,Tzavara, C., & Zelios, G. (2006). Treatment compliance and early termination of therapy: a comparative study. *Psychotherapy and Psychosomatics, 75*(2), 113–121.

Lees-Haley, P. R., Smith, H. H., Williams, C. W., & Dunn, J. T. (1996). Forensic neuropsychological test usage: an empirical survey. *Archives of Clinical Neuropsychology, 11,* 45–51.

Leon, G., Gillum, B., & Gouze, M. (1979). Personality stability and change over a thirty-year-period—middle age to old age. *Journal of Consulting and Clinical Psychology, 47,* 517–524.

Levenson, M. R., Aldwin, C.M., Butcher, J. N., de Labry, L., Workman-Daniels, K., & Bossé, R. (1990). The MAC scale in a normal population: the meaning of "false positives." *Journal of Studies on Alcohol, 51,* 457–462.

Lewandowski, D., & Graham, J. R. (1972). Empirical correlates of frequently occurring two-point MMPI code types: a replicated study. *Journal of Consulting and Clinical Psychology, 39,* 467–472.

Lilienfeld, S. O. (1991). Assessment of psychopathy with the MMPI and MMPI-2. *MMPI-2 News and Profiles, 2,* 2.

Lilienfeld, S. O. (1996). The MMPI-2 Antisocial Practices Content Scale: construct validity and comparison with the Psychopathic Deviate Scale. *Psychological Assessment, 8,* 281–293.

Liu, Y., Shi, W., Ding, B., Li, X., Xiao, K., Wang, X., & Sun, X. (2001). Analysis of correlates in the SAS, the SDS, and the MMPI of stutterers. [Chinese]. *Chinese Journal of Clinical Psychology, 9*(2), 133–134.

Livingston, R. B., Jennings, E., Colotla, V. A., Reynolds, C. R., & Shercliffe, R. J. (2006). MMPI-2 code-type congruence of injured workers. *Psychological Assessment, 18,* 126–130.

Long, C. J. (1981). The relationship between surgical outcome and MMPI profiles in chronic pain patients. *Journal of Consulting and Clinical Psychology, 37*(4), 744–749.

Lubin, B., Larsen, R. M., & Matarazzo, J. (1984). Patterns of psychological test usage in the United States, 1935–1982. *American Psychologist, 39,* 451–454.

Luborsky, L., Barber, J., Siqueland, L., Johnson, S., Najavits, L. Frank, A., & Daley, D. (1996). The Revised Helping Questionnaire-II (HAq-II): psychometric properties. *Journal of Psychotherapy Research and Practice, 6,* 260–271.

MacAndrew, C. (1965). The differentiation of male alcoholic outpatients from non-alcoholic psychiatric outpatients by means of the MMPI. *Quarterly Journal of Studies on Alcohol, 26,* 238–246.

Malec, J. F. (1983). Relationship of the MMPI-168 to outcome of a pain management program at long-term follow-up. *Rehabilitation Psychology, 28*(2), 115–119

Marks, P. A., & Seeman, W. (1963). *The actuarial description of abnormal personality.* Baltimore: Williams & Wilkins.

Marks, P. A., Seeman, W., & Haller, D. L. (1974). *The actuarial use of the MMPI with adolescents and adults.* Baltimore: Williams & Wilkins.

Martin, D. J., Garske, J. P., & Davis, M. K. (2000). Relation of the therapeutic alliance with outcomes and other variables: a meta-analytic review. *Journal of Consulting and Clinical Psychology, 68,* 438–450.

McKenna, T. & Butcher, J. Continuity of the MMPI with alcoholics. (April, 1987). Paper presented at the 22nd Annual Symposium on Recent Developments in the Use of the MMPI. Seattle, Washington.

McNulty, J. L., Ben-Porath, Y.S., & Graham, J. R. (1998). An empirical examination of the correlates of well-defined and not defined MMPI-2 code types. *Journal of Personality Assessment, 71*(3), 393–410.

Meehl, P. E. (1954). *Clinical versus statistical prediction: a theoretical analysis and a review of the evidence.* Minneapolis: University of Minnesota Press.

Meehl, P. E., & Hathaway, S. R. (1946). The K factor as a suppressor variable in the MMPI. *Journal of Applied Psychology, 30,* 525–564.

Megargee, E. E., Cook, P. E., & Mendelsohn, G. A. (1967). Development and validation of an MMPI scale of assaultiveness in overcontrolled individuals. *Journal of Abnormal Psychology, 72,* 519–528.

Megargee, E. I. (2006). *Using the MMPI-2 in criminal justice and correctional settings.* Minneapolis, MN: University of Minnesota Press.

Meilke, S., & Gerritse, R. (1970). MMPI "cookbook" pattern frequencies in a psychiatric unit. *Journal of Clinical Psychology, 26,* 82–84.

Moore, J. E., Armentrout, D. P., Parker, J. D., & Kivlahan, D. R. (1986). Empirically derived pain-patient MMPI subgroups: prediction of treatment outcome. *Journal of Behavioral Medicine, 9*(1), 51–63.

Moras, K., & Strupp, H. H. (1982). Pretherapy interpersonal relations, patients' alliance, and outcome in brief therapy. *Archives of General Psychiatry, 39,* 405–409.

Moreland, K. (1985). *Test–retest reliability of 80 MMPI scales.* Unpublished materials (Available from National Computer Systems, 5605 Green Circle Drive, Minnetonka, MN 55343).

Moreland, K. L., & Onstad, J. (1985, March). *Validity of the Minnesota Clinical Report I: mental health outpatients.* Paper presented at the 20th Annual Symposium on Recent Developments in the Use of the MMPI, Honolulu.

Nichols, D. S. (2006). The trials of separating bath water from baby: a review and critique of the MMPI-2 Restructured Clinical scales. *Journal of Personality Assessment, 87,* 121–138.

Oostdam, E. M., Duivenvoorden, H. J., & Pondaag, W. (1981). Predictive value of some psychological tests on the outcome of surgical intervention in low back pain patients. *Journal of Psychosomatic Research, 25*(3), 579–582.

Orlinsky, D. E., Grawe, K., & Parks, B. K. (1994). Process and outcome in psychotherapy. In A. E. Bergen & S. L. Garfield (Eds.), *Handbook of psychotherapy and behavior change* (pp. 270–376). New York: Wiley.

Ottomanelli, G., Wilson, P., & Whyte, R. (1978). MMPI evaluation of 5-year methadone treatment status. *Journal of Consulting and Clinical Psychology, 46*(3), 579–582.

Pearson, J. S., & Swenson, W. M. (1967). *A user's guide to the Mayo Clinic automated MMPI program.* New York: The Psychological Corporation.

Penk, W. E., Rierdan, J., Losardo, M., & Rabinowitz, R. (2006). The MMPI-2 and assessment of post-traumatic stress disorder (PTSD). In J. N. Butcher (Ed.), *MMPI-2: The practitioner's handbook* (pp. 121–141). Washington, D.C.: American Psychological Association.

Perry, J. N. (1999). *Assessment of psychological treatment planning issues in clients with anxiety disorders.* Unpublished doctoral dissertation. University of Minnesota, Minneapolis.

Perry, J. N. (in press). *Assessment of treatment resistance via questionnaire.* In J. N. Butcher (Ed.), *Clinical personality assessment: practical approaches.* New York: Oxford.

Perry, J. N., & Butcher, J. N. (1999). Butcher Treatment Planning Inventory (BTPI): an objective guide to treatment planning. In M. E. Maruish (Ed.), *The use of psychological testing for treatment planning and outcomes assessment* (2nd ed., pp. 1157–1171). Mahwah, NJ: Erlbaum.

Persons, R. W., & Marks, P. A. (1971). The violent 4–3 MMPI personality type. *Journal of Consulting and Clinical Psychology, 36,* 189–196.

Pettinati, H. M., Sugerman, A. A., & Maurer, H. S. (1982). Four-year MMPI changes in abstinent and drinking alcoholics. *Alcoholism: Clinical & Experimental Research, 6*(4), 487–494.

Pope, K. S., Butcher, J. N., & Seelen, J. (2006). *MMPI/MMPI-2/MMPI-A in court assessment: a practical guide for expert witnesses and attorneys* (3rd ed.). Washington, D.C.: American Psychological Association.

Pope K. S., Sonne, J. L., & Greene, B. (2006). *What therapists don't talk about and why: understanding taboos that hurt us and our clients.* Washington, D.C.: American Psychological Association.

Prochaska, J. O., Velicer, W. F., DiClemente, C. C., & Fava, J. (1988). Measuring process of chance: Applications to the cessation of smoking. *Journal of Consulting and Clinical Psychology, 56,* 520–528.

Raynes, A. E., & Warren, G. (1971). Some distinguishing features of patients failing to attend a psychiatric clinic after referral. *American Journal of Orthopsychiatry, 41,* 581–589.

Regier, D. A., Boyd, J. H., Burke, J. D., Rae, D. S., Myers, J. K., Kramer, M., Robins, C. N., George, L. K., Karno, M., & Locke, B. Z. (1993). One-month prevalence of mental disorders in the United States and sociodemographic characteristics: the Epidemiological Catchment Area study. *Acta Psychiatrica Scandinavica, 88,* 35–47.

Rhodes, R. J. (1969). The MacAndrews alcoholism scale: a replication. *Journal of Clinical Psychology, 25,* 189–911.

Rich, C. C., & Davis, H. G. (1969). Concurrent validity of MMPI alcoholism scales. *Journal of Clinical Psychology, 25,* 425–426.

Rogers, R., Sewell, K. W., Harrison, K. W., & Jordan, M. J. (2006). The MMPI-2 Restructured Clinical scales: a paradigmatic shift to scale development. *Journal of Personality Assessment, 87,* 139–147.

Rosenthal, D., & Frank, J. D. (1958). Psychotherapy and the placebo effect. *Psychological Bulletin, 53,* 294–302.

Rothke, S. E., Friedman, A. F., Jaffe, A. M., Greene, R. L., Wetter, M. W., Cole, P., & Baker, K. (2000). Normative data for the F(p) Scale of the MMPI-2: implications for clinical and forensic assessment of malingering. *Psychological Assessment, 12*(3), 335–340.

Rouse, S., Butcher, J. N., & Miller, M. B. (1999). Assessment of substance abuse in psychotherapy clients: the effectiveness of the MMPI-2 substance abuse scales. *Psychological Assessment, 11,* 101–107.

Rouse, S. V., Greene, R. L., Butcher, J. N., Nichols, D., & Williams, C. L. (submitted). What do the MMPI-2 Restructured Clinical Scales reliably measure? Answers from multiple research settings.

Rouse, S. V., Sullivan, J., & Taylor, J. (1997). Treatment-oriented MMPI/MMPI-2 studies. In J. N. Butcher (Ed.), *Personality assessment in managed health care.* New York: Oxford University Press.

Ryan, W. (1969). *Distress in the city.* Cleveland: Press of Case Western Reserve University.

Schill, T., & Wang, T. (1990). Correlates of the MMPI-2 Anger Content Scale. *Psychological Reports, 67,* 800–804.

Schofield, W. (1950). Changes in response to the Minnesota Multiphasic Personality Inventory following certain therapies. *Psychological Monographs, 64,* whole number 311.

Schwartz, M. F., & Graham, J. R. (1979). Construct validity of the MacAndrew alcoholism scale. *Journal of Consulting and Clinical Psychology, 47,* 1090–1095.

Sellbom, M., Graham, J. R., & Schenk, P. W. (2005). Symptom correlates of MMPI-2 scales and code types in a private-practice setting. *Journal of Personality Assessment, 84,* 163–171.

Serkownek, K. (1975). *Subscales for scales 5 and 0 are of the Minnesota Multiphasic Personality Inventory.* Unpublished Manuscript.

Sheppard, D., Smith, G. T., & Rosenbaum, G. (1988). Use of MMPI subtypes in predicting completion of a residential alcoholism treatment program. *Journal of Consulting and Clinical Psychology, 56,* 590–596.

Shores, A., & Carstairs, J. R. (1998). Accuracy of the MMPI-2 computerized Minnesota Report in identifying fake-good and fake-bad response sets. *Clinical Neuropsychologist, 12,* 101–106.

Sines, J. O. (1966). Actuarial methods in personality assessment. In B. A. Maher (Ed.), *Progress in experimental personality research.* New York: Academic Press.

Skoog, D. K., Andersen, A. E., & Laufer, W. S. (1984). Personality and treatment effectiveness in anorexia nervosa. *Journal of Clinical Psychology, 40*(4), 955–961.

Slesinger, D., Archer, R. P., & Duane, W. (2002). MMPI-2 characteristics in a chronic pain population. *Assessment, 9*(4), 406–414.

Smith, S. R., & Hilsenroth, M. J. (2001). Discriminative validity of the MacAndrew Alcoholism Scale with cluster B personality disorders. *Journal of Clinical Psychology, 57*(6), 801–803.

Strassberg, D. S., Reimherr, F., Ward, M., Russell, S., & Cole, A. (1981). The MMPI and chronic pain. *Journal of Consulting and Clinical Psychology, 49*(2), 220–226.

Streit, K., Greene, R. L., Cogan, R., & Davis, H. G. (1993). Clinical correlates fo MMPI depression scales. *Journal of Personality Assessment, 60*(2), 390–396.

Svensson, B., & Hansson, L. (1999). Relationships among patient and therapist ratings of therapeutic alliance and patient assessment of therapeutic process: A study of cognitive therapy with long-term mentally ill patients. *Journal of Nervous and Mental Disease, 187,* 579–585.

Sweet, J. J., Breuer, S. R., Hazlewood, L. A., Toye, R., & Pawl, R. P. (1985). The Millon Behavioral Health Inventory: concurrent and predictive validity in a pain treatment center. *Journal of Behavioral Medicine, 8*(3), 215–226.

Tellegen, A., Ben-Porath, Y. S., McNulty, J. L., Arbisi, P. A., Graham, J. R., & Kaemmer, B. (2003). *MMPI-2 Restructured Clinical (RC) Scales: development, validation, and interpretation.* Minneapolis, MN: University of Minnesota Press.

Terman, L. M., & Miles, C. C. (1936). *Sex and personality: studies in masculinity and femininity.* New York: Russell and Russell.

Thurstin, A. H., Alfano, A. M., & Sherer, M. (1986). Pretreatment MMPI profiles of A.A. members and nonmembers. *Journal of Studies on Alcohol, 47*(6), 468–471.

Tryon, G. S. (1990). Session depth and smoothness in relation to the concept of engagement in counseling. *Journal of Counseling Psychology, 37,* 248–253.

Turner, J. A., Herron, L., & Weiner, P. (1986). Utility of the MMPI pain assessment index in predicting outcome after lumbar surgery. *Journal of Clinical Psychology, 42*(5), 764–769.

Uomoto, J. M., Turner, J. A., & Herron, L. D. (1988). Use of the MMPI and MCMI in predicting outcome of lumbar laminectomy. *Journal of Clinical Psychology, 44*(2), 191–197.

Walker, D. E., Blankenship, V., Ditty, J. A., & Lynch, K. P. (1987). Prediction of recovery for closed-head-injured adults: an evaluation of the MMPI Adaptive Behavior Scale, and a "quality of life" rating scale. *Journal of Clinical Psychology, 43*(6), 699–707.

Wallace, A., & Liljequist, L. (2005). A comparison of the correlational structures and elevation patterns of the MMPI-2 Restructured Clinical (RC) and clinical scales. *Assessment, 12,* 290–294.

Walters, G. D., Greene, R. L., & Jeffrey, T. B. (1984). Discriminating between alcoholic and non-alcoholic blacks and whites on the MMPI. *Journal of Personality Assessment, 48,* 486–488.

Walters, G. D., Greene, R. L., Jeffrey, T. B., Kruzich, D. J., & Haskin, J. J. (1983). Racial variations on the MacAndrew alcoholism scale of the MMPI. *Journal of Consulting and Clinical Psychology, 51,* 947–948.

Warbin, R. W., Altman, H., Gynther, M. D. & Sletten, I. W. (1972). A new empirical automated MMPI interpretive program: 2–8 and 8–2 code types. *Journal of Personality Assessment, 36,* 581–584.

Weed, N. C., Butcher, J. N., Ben-Porath, Y. S., & McKenna, T. (1992). New measures for assessing alcohol and drug abuse with the MMPI-2: the APS and AAS. *Journal of Personality Assessment, 58,* 389–404.

Wiggins, J. S. (1966). Substantive dimensions of self-report in the MMPI items pool. *Psychological Monographs, 80*(22), whole number 630.

Wilderman, J. E. (1984). *An investigation of the clinical utility of the College Maladjustment Scale.* Unpublished master's thesis, Kent State University, Kent, Ohio.

Williams, J. E., & Weed, N. C. (2004). Review of computer-based test interpretation software for the MMPI-2. *Journal of Personality Assessment, 83*(1), 78–83.

Wisniewski, N. M., Glenwick, D. S., & Graham, J. R. (1985). MacAndrew scale and sociodemographic correlates of adolescent drug use. *Addictive Behaviors, 10,* 55–67.

Wolfson, K. T., & Erbaugh, S. E. (1984). Adolescent responses to MacAndrew Alcoholism scale. *Journal of Consulting and Clinical Psychology, 52,* 625–630.

Woodworth, R. S. (1920). *The personal data sheet.* Chicago: Stoelting.

Young, R. C., Gould, E., Glick, I. D., & Hargreaves, W. A. (1980). Personality inventory correlates of outcome in a follow-up study of psychiatric hospitalization. *Psychological Reports, 46*(3, pt. 1), 903–906.

Yu, L. M., & Templer, D. I. (2004). Personality, psychopathology, and demographic correlates of medical vs behavioral reasons for referral in alcoholic men. *Psychological Reports, 94*(1), 273–276.

Zuckerman, M., Bone, R. N., Neary, R., Mangelsdorff, D., & Brustman, B. (1972). What is the sensation seeker? Personality trait and experience correlates of the Sensation-Seeking Scales. *Journal of Consulting and Clinical Psychology, 39*(2), 308–321.

Appendix
Rorschach Protocol for Case #135 and #136

MMPI-2 in Psychological Treatment

Subject Name: Protocol.136   Age: 25   Sex: F   Race: W   MS: Liv   ED: 14

Interpretive Hypotheses for the Rorschach Protocol
Utilizing the Comprehensive System
(Copyright 1976, 1985 by John E. Exner, Jr.)

The following computer-based interpretation is derived * * exclusively * * from the structural data of the record and does not include consideration of the sequence of scores or the verbal material. It is intended as a guide from whom the interpreter of the total protocol can proceed to study and refine the hypotheses generated from these actuarial findings.

* * * * * *

1. The record appears to be valid and interpretively useful.
2. The subject does not have good capabilities for control and tolerance for stress is somewhat lower than would be expected for the mid-adolescent or adult.
3. However, currently experienced situational related stress has reduced those capacities for control even more, so that there is a considerable likelihood of impulsive-like behaviors or behaviors that are not well formulated and/or implemented.
4. This is the type of person who prefers to delay making responses in coping situations until time has been allowed to consider response possibilities and their potential consequences. Such people like to keep their emotions aside under these conditions.

5. This person tends to use deliberate thinking more for the purpose of creating fantasy through which to ignore the world than to confront problems directly. This is a serious problem because the basic coping style is being used more for flight than to adapt to the external world.

6. This type of person is not very flexible in thinking, values, or attitudes. In effect, people such as this have some difficulty in shifting perspectives or viewpoints.

7. There is a strong possibility that this is a person who prefers to avoid initiating behaviors, and instead, tends towards a more passive role in problem solving and interpersonal relationships.

8. This subject does not modulate emotional displays as much as most adults and, because of this, is prone to become very influenced by feelings in most thinking, decisions, and behaviors.

9. This is an individual who does not experience needs for closeness in ways that are common to most people. As a result, they are typically less comfortable in interpersonal situations, have some difficulties in creating and sustaining deep relationships, and are more concerned with issues of personal space, and may appear much more guarded and/or distant to others. In spite of this guarded interpersonal stance, some of the data suggest a preference for dependency on others which would seem to create a conflict situation. In other words, the subject wants to take from others while remaining distant from them.

10. This subject has as much interest in others as do most adults and children.

11. This subject has more negative self esteem or self value than is common for either adults or children. It is the product of making comparisons of oneself to others, usually peers, and concluding that those external models are more adequate. This creates a tendency to dislike oneself and can become the nucleus from which feelings of inferiority and/or inadequacy evolve. In light of this finding, it is very important to review the overall record carefully to obtain a sense of the self image.

12. This person is prone to much more introspection than is common. When this occurs, much of the focus concerns negative features perceived to exist in the self image. This provokes internal pain. Such a process if often a precursor to feelings of sadness, pessimism, or even depression.

13. This subject is very prone to interpret stimulus cues in a unique and over-personalized manner. People such as this often view their world with their own special set of biases and are less concerned with being conventional and/or acceptable to others.

14. This subject is not as oriented as most people to making conventional and/or socially acceptable responses in those situations where the conventional response is easily identifies.

15. This person makes a marked effort to organize stimuli in a meaningful and integrated way.

16. This is a person who tends to use more time and energy than is necessary to organize each new stimulus field. Such people prefer to have an

abundance of information available before decision making and typically are more perfectionistic in most of their daily behaviors. This is not necessarily a liability. However, they tend to underestimate time which can become a problem in those situations where time factors are important. In that this subject tends to delay and to think things through before making responses, this characteristic could create the appearance of ruminativeness.

17. This person prefers to minimize ambiguity. People like these often try to make a stimulus field overly precise and are excessively concerned with being accurate. This may be a characteristic of an individual who seems more perfectionistically oriented.

18. In spite of the fact that the subject makes an effort to organize stimuli, this person is somewhat conservative in setting goals. Usually people like this want to commit themselves only to objectives which offer a significant probability of success.

*   *   *   End of Report   *   *   *

STRUCTURAL SUMMARY

R = 19   zf = 11   ZSum = 41.0   P = 3   (2) = 5   Fr + rF = 0

LOCATION FEATURES	DETERMINANTS BLENDS	SINGLE	CONTENTS	S-CONSTELLATION (ADULT)
			H = 3, 0	YES . . FV + VF + V + FD > 2
W = 5	M.FV	M = 1	(H) = 0, 0	NO . . Col-Shd Bl > 0
(Wv = 0)	FV.m	FM = 3	Hd = 2, 0	YES . . Ego < . 31, > .44
D = 9	M.FY	m = 0	(Hd) = 1, 0	NO . . MOR > 3
Dd = 5	FM.FC'	C = 0	Hx = 0, 0	YES . . Zd > + − 3.5
S = 1	m.FD	Cn = 0	A = 6, 0	YES . . es > EA
	M.FC	Cf = 1	(A) = 0, 0	NO . . CF + C + Cn > FC
DQ		FC = 0	Ad = 1, 0	YES . . X+ < .70
· · · · · · · · · · · (FQ?)		C' = 0	(Ad) = 0, 0	NO . . S > 3
+ = 8 (0)		C'F = 0	Al = 0, 0	NO . . P < 3 or > 8
o = 11 (2)		FC' = 1	An = 1, 0	NO . . Pure H < 2
v/+ = 0 (0)		T = 0	Art = 1, 0	NO . . R < 17
v = 0 (0)		TF = 0	Ay = 0, 0	5 . . . . . TOTAL
		FT = 0	Bl = 0, 0	
		V = 0	Bt = 0, 1	SPECIAL SCORINGS
		VF = 0	Cg = 0, 2	L1 L2
		FV = 0	Cl = 0, 0	DV = 1 x 1 0 x 2
		Y = 0	Ex = 0, 0	INCOM = 1 x 2 0 x 4
		YF = 0	Fi = 0, 0	DR = 1 x 3 0 x 6
FORM QUALITY		FY = 1	Fd = 0, 1	FABCOM = 0 x 4 0 x 7
		rF = 0	Ge = 0, 0	ALOG = 0 x 5
FQx FQf M Qual.		Fr = 0	Hh = 0, 1	CONTAM = 0 x 7
		FD = 0	Ls = 0, 1	− − WSUM6 = 6
		F = 6	Na = 0, 0	
+ = 0 + = 0 + = 0			Sc = 1, 0	AB = 1 CP = 0
o = 11 o = 4 o = 3			Sx = 0, 0	AG = 0 MOR = 3
u = 6 u = 1 u = 1			Xy = 1, 0	CFB = 0 PER = 1
− = 2 − = 1 − = 0			Idio = 2, 0	COP = 3 PSV = 0
none = 0 none = 0				

RATIOS, PERCENTAGES, AND DERIVATIONS

Zsum-Zest = 41.0 − 34.5	FC:CF + C = 1:1	W:M	= 5:4
	(Pure C = 0)		
Zd = +6.5		W:D	= 5:9
	Afr = 0.58		
------------------		Isolate:R	= 2:19
• EB = 4:1.5 EA = 5.5 •	3r + (2)/R = 0.2		
• >D = −2		2Ab + Art + Ay =	3
• Eb = 6:6 es = 12 •	L = 0.46		
• ------------------ •		An + Xy = 2	
(FM = 4 : C' = 2 T = 0) (Adj D = −1)	Blends:R = 6:19		
(m = 2: V = 2 Y = 2)		H(H):Hd (Hd)	= 3:4
	X+% = 0.58	(Pure H	= 3)
a:p = 3:7	(F+% = 0.67)	(HHd):(AAd)	= 2:0
	X−% = 0.11		
Ma:Mp = 0:4	(Xu% = (0.32)	H + A:Hd + Ad	= 9:5

SCZI2(1) = 1(1)   DEPI = 2   S–CON = 5   HVI = 1 + 2

CARD NO	LOC #		DETERMINANT(S)	(2) CONTENT(S)	POP Z	SPECIAL SCORES
I	1 W+	1	Mp.FVo	H,Cg	4. 0	
	2 Ddo	24	Fo	Id		
II	3 D+	2	FMpu	2 A	5. 5	
	4 Do	4	Fc' −	Hd		PER, MOR
III	5 D+	1	Mpo	2 H, Hh	P 3. 0	
IV	6 Do	3	FV.mpu	Id		DR
	7 Ddo	33	FYo	xy		
V	8 Wo	1	FMao	A	P 1. 0	INC
	9 Do	1	Fo	Hd		MOR
VI	10 Do	3	Fu	A		
VII	11 WS+	1	FMpo	2 A, Ls	2. 5	
	12 Dd+	28	Mp.FYu	H, Cg, Ab	1. 0	
VIII	13 Wo	1	F−	An	4. 5	MOR
	14 Do	3	Fo	A	P	
IX	15 Wo	1	CFu	Art, (Hd)	5. 5	
X	16 D+	11	FMa.FC'o	2 A,Bt	4. 0	
	17 Do	5	Fo	Ad		
	18 DdS+	29	ma.FDu	Sc	6. 0	
	19 Dd	99	Mp.FCo	2 (Hd) , Fd	4. 0	DV

© 1976, 1985 by John E. Exner, Jr.

Abbreviations Used Above:

DQ:	CONTENTS:	SPECIAL SCORES.	
"/" = V/+	"ID" = Idiographic	"CFB" = CONFAB	"FAB" = FABCOM
	Content	"CON" = CONTAM	"INC" = INCOM

MMPI-2 in Psychological Treatment

Subject Name: Protocol.135   Age: 23   Sex: M   Race: W   MS: Liv   ED: 16

Interpretive Hypotheses for the Rorschach Protocol
Utilizing the Comprehensive System
(Copyright 1976, 1985 by John E. Exner, Jr.)

The following computer-based interpretation is derived * * exclusively * * from the structural data of the record and does not include consideration of the sequence of scores or the verbal material. It is intended as a guide from whom the interpreter of the total protocol can proceed to study and refine the hypotheses generated from these actuarial findings.

*   *   *   *   *   *

1. The record appears to be valid and interpretively useful.
2. The data indicate that the subject is currently experiencing considerable situationally related stress that has created an important stimulus overload condition. Capacity for control and stress tolerance is both lowered substantially and it is likely that the tolerance is both lowered substantially and it is likely that the overload will cause the subject to be more negligent in processing information than is usually the case. Some behaviors may not be well formulated and/or implemented, and a vulnerability to impulsive-like behaviors is clearly present.
3. This is the type of person who is prone to involve feelings in thinking, decision operations, and most of their behaviors. Such people prefer a trial-and-error approach to problem-solving.
4. This subject does not modulate emotional displays as much as most adults and, because of this is prone to become very influenced by feelings in most thinking, decisions, and behaviors. This is an especially important problem because it relates to the effectiveness of the basic coping skills.
5. This person is much more negative than most. Such extreme negativism often takes the form of anger which can detract significantly from the forming and directing of adaptive responses.
6. This person is experiencing considerable emotional irritation because of strong, unmet needs for closeness that are usually manifest as some experience of loneliness. This is made more irritating because some data suggest a preference for dependency on others.
7. The subject does not have as much interest in others in others as do most adults and older children.
8. This subject tends to focus more on himself (herself) than is customary among adults. This is typical of those with concerns about themselves and one consequence is less attention to the external world.

9. This kind of person tends to over glorify their personal worth and probably harbors many of the features that would be considered "narcissistic." This feature often becomes a major obstacle to forms of treatment that involve uncovering or reconstructive efforts.

10. When this person engages in self examination a tendency exists to focus upon negative features perceived to exist in the self image, and this results in considerable internal pain. This process is often a precursor to feelings of sadness, pessimism or even depression.

11. This subject is very prone to interpret stimulus cues in a unique and over personalized manner. People such as this often view their world with their own special set of biases and are less concerned with being conventional and/or acceptable to others.

12. This person makes a marked effort to organize stimuli in a meaningful and integrated way.

13. This person tends to set goals that may be beyond his/her functional capacities. This often leads to failure, disappointment, and/or frustration. Any or all of these can create a chronic state of tension or apprehension, and, as a consequence, the tolerance for stress is lowered.

14. This person is very defensive about being challenged. He or she often tries to avoid such a stress by an excess of intellectualization, some of which may be very concrete. People such as this is often try to be overly esoteric in an effort to neutralize threats. People like this are often very resistive during early phases of intervention as this tendency toward denial causes them to avoid any affective confrontations.

* * * End of Report * * *

STRUCTURAL SUMMARY

R = 20   zf = 14   ZSum = 43.0   P = 4   (2) = 5   Fr+rF = 2

LOCATION FEATURES	DETERMINANTS BLENDS	SINGLE	CONTENTS	S-CONSTELLATION (ADULT)
			H = 2, 0	NO . . FV + VF + V + FD > 2
W = 12	M.FC	M = 1	(H) = 1, 0	YES . . Col-Shd Bl > 0
(Wv = 1)	M.Fr	FM = 3	Hd = 0, 0	YES . . Ego < .31, > .44
D = 8	m.rF.TF	m = 0	(Hd) = 0, 0	NO . . MOR > 3
Dd = 0	CF.F'C	C = 0	Hx = 0, 0	NO . . Zd > +-3.5
S = 4	CF.YF	Cn = 0	A = 4, 0	YES . . es > EA
	M.FC.FV	CF = 0	(A) = 0, 1	YES . . CF + C + Cn > FC
DQ	m.CF	FC = 1	Ad = 0, 0	YES . . X+ < . 70
· · · · · · · · · · · (FQ?)	CF.YF.m	C' = 0	(Ad) = 0, 0	YES . . S > 3
+ = 6 (1)	CF.m	C' F = 0	Al = 0, 0	NO . . P < 3 or > 8
o = 12 (0)		FC' = 1	An = 0, 0	NO . . Pure H < 2
v/+ = 1 (0)		T = 0	Art = 4, 0	NO . . R < 17
v = 1 (0)		TF = 0	Ay = 2, 0	6 . . . . . TOTAL
		FT = 0	Bl = 0, 0	
		V = 0	Bt = 1, 1	SPECIAL SCORINGS
		VF = 0	Cg = 1, 1	

				SPECIAL SCORINGS		
		FV = 0	cl = 0, 1		L1	L2
		Y = 0	Ex = 1, 0	DV =	1 x 1	0 x 2
		YF = 0	Fi = 0, 0	INCOM =	1 x 2	0 x 4
FORM QUALITY		FY = 0	Fd = 1, 0	DR =	1 x 3	0 x 6
		rF = 0	Ge = 0, 0	FABCOM =	0 x 4	0 x 7
FQx	FQf	M Qual.	Fr = 0	Hh = 1, 0	ALOG = 0 x 5	
			FD = 0	Ls = 0, 0	CONTAM = 0 x 7	
+= 0	+= 0	+= 0	F = 4	Na = 1, 0	- - WSUM6 = 6	
o = 11	o = 1	o = 4		Sc = 0, 0	AB = 1	CP = 0
u = 8	u = 3	u = 0		Sx = 0, 1	AG = 0	MOR = 0
− = 1	− = 0	− = 0		Xy = 0, 0	CFB = 0	PER = 6
none = 0	none = 0			Idio = 1, 1	COP = 2	PSV = 0

RATIOS, PERCENTAGES, AND DERIVATIONS

Zsum-Zest = 43.0 − 45.5	FC: CF + C = 3:5	W:M = 12:4	
	(Pure C = 0)		
Zd = −2.5		W:D = 12:8	
	Afr = 0.82		
- - - - - - - - - - - - - - - - -		Isolate:R = 6:20	
• EB = 4:6.5 EA = 10.5 •	3r + (2) /R = 0.55		
• >D = −1		2Ab + Art + Ay = 8	
• Eb = 7:7 es = 14 •	L = 0.25		
•_ _ _ _ _ _ _ _ _ _ _ _ _ _ _ _•		An+Xy = 0	
(FM= 3 : C' = 2 T = 2) (Adj D = 0)	Blends:R = 9:20		
(m = 4 : V = 1 Y = 2)		H(H):Hd (Hd) = 4:0	
	X+% = 0.55	(Pure H = 2)	
a:p = 5:6	(F+% = 0.25)	(HHd):(AAd) = 2:1	
	X−% = 0.05		
Ma:Mp = 2: 2	(Xu% = 0.40)	H+A:Hd+Ad = 9:0	

SCZI2(1) = 1(1)   DEPI = 2   S–CON = 6   HVI = 0 + 2

CARD NO	LOC #	DETERMINANT(S)	(2) CONTENT(S)	POP Z	SPECIAL SCORES
I	1 Wo	1 FMao	A	P 1.0	
	2 Wso	1 Fu	Ay	3.5	PER
II	3 W+	1 Ma.FCo	2 H, Cg	4. 5	
	4 Do	3 FTo	A		
III	5 D+	9 Mp.Fro	H	P 4.0	
IV	6 Wo	1 FC'o	Bt	2. 0	PER
V	7 Wo	1 FMpo	A	P 1.0	
	8 Wo	1 FMao	A	P 1.0	PER
VI	9 D/	4 mp.rF.TFo	Na	2. 5	
VII	10 W+	1 Mpo	2 Art, (H)	P 2.5	
	11 WS+	1 Fu	Id, Bt	4. 0	
VIII	12 WS+	1 CF.C' F−	Fd,Id	4. 5	
	13 Wo	1 CF.YFu	2 Art. (A)	4. 5	PER
IX	14 DS+	3 Ma.FC.FVo	2 (H), An. Cl	2. 5	
	15 Do	9 Fu	Hh		
X	16 Wv	1 ma.CFu	Ex,Ab		
	17 Do	11 Fo	Ay		PER
	18 Do	1 CF.YF.mpu	2 Art		
	19 Do	6 FCU	Cg,Sx		
	20 Wo	1 CF.mpu	Art, Ab	5. 5	

© 1976, 1985 by John E. Exner, Jr.

Abbreviations Used Above:

DQ:	CONTENTS:	SPECIAL SCORES:	
"/" = V/+	"ID" = Idiographic	"CFB" = CONFAB	"FAB" = FABCOM
	Content	"CON" = CONTAM	"INC" = INCOM

About the Authors

James N. Butcher, Ph.D., is currently Professor Emeritus in the Department of Psychology at the University of Minnesota. He was born in Bergoo, West Virginia and graduated from Stonewall Jackson High School in Charleston, West Virginia. After graduating from Guilford College in North Carolina with a BA in psychology in 1960, he received an MA in experimental psychology from the University of North Carolina at Chapel Hill in 1962. He received a Ph.D. in clinical psychology at the University of North Carolina at Chapel Hill in 1964 and was awarded an honorary doctorate (Doctor Honoris Causa) from the Free University of Brussels in 1990. Dr. Butcher also received an honorary doctorate from the University of Florence in Italy in 2005.

Having maintained an active research program in the areas of personality assessment, abnormal psychology, cross-cultural personality factors, and computer based personality assessment, Dr. Butcher has published more than 50 books and 175 articles in the area of personality assessment, abnormal psychology, and psychotherapy.

Dr. Butcher was a member of the University of Minnesota Press' MMPI Consultative Committee that was actively engaged in a large scale project to revise and restandardize the MMPI. He is the former editor of *Psychological Assessment* and serves as consulting editor for numerous other journals in psychology and psychiatry. An active fellow of the American Psychological Association, he has served on the Board of Trustees of the Society for Personality Assessment and the Executive Committee of Divisions 1 (General Psychology) and 5 (Division of Measurement and Evaluation).

In 1965, Dr. Butcher founded the *Symposium on Recent Developments in the Use of the MMPI* to promote and disseminate research information on the MMPI and continued to organize this conference series for 38 years. Dr. Butcher also founded the *International Conference on Personality Assessment*, a program devoted to facilitating international research on personality assessment.

Sixteen international conferences have since been held, in Australia, Belgium, Denmark, Holland, Italy, Israel, Japan, Mexico, the United States, and Norway.

Dr. Butcher was a co-founder of the Walk-In-Counseling Clinic in Minneapolis, Minnesota, in 1979, a free clinic aimed at providing emergency psychotherapy to clients in need. He has been actively involved in developing and organizing disaster response programs for dealing with human problems following airline disasters. He organized a model crisis intervention disaster response for the Minneapolis-St. Paul Airport and organized and supervised psychological services following two recent airline disasters: Northwest Flight 255 and Aloha Airlines' Maui accidents.

Julia N. Perry, Ph.D., LP is currently the Team Coordinator/Program Manager and staff psychologist for the Mood and Anxiety Disorders Team at the Minneapolis VA Medical Center. She is also an Adjunct Assistant Professor in the Department of Psychiatry at the University of Minnesota

Born in Minneapolis, Minnesota, Dr. Perry graduated from John F. Kennedy High School in Bloomington, Minnesota. After graduating from Hamline University in 1994 in St. Paul, Minnesota with a B.A. in psychology, she earned a Ph.D. in 1999 in clinical psychology from the University of Minnesota.

Dr. Perry has worked as a management consultant for national business organizations, local municipalities, and public safety departments, and has provided a range of organizational development and organizational effectiveness services, including fitness for duty evaluations.

She has written about and conducted research in the areas of personality assessment, treatment planning, abnormal psychology, computer-based personality assessment, and the impact of culture on mental health service utilization.

Dr. Perry has held an Adjunct Assistant Professor appointment at Hamline University and has provided guest lectures and workshops at other post-secondary institutions on various topics in clinical and organizational psychology.

Index

General Pathology Composite (GPC), 117, 120
Graham, John R., 25, 85–87, 103, 107, 162
Grayson Critical Items, 94–95
Greene, Roger, 25

Han, K., 32
Harkness, A. R., 81
Harris-Lingoes MMPI-2 subscales, 98, 100–101
  case history, 101–3
  description, 98–100
  limitations of interpretation, 101–2
Hathaway, S. R., 23
Health concerns, 108. *See also* Exaggerated symptom expression; MMPI-2 clinical scales, scale 1; MMPI-2 clinical scales, scale 3; Physical Malfunctioning (D3) subscale
Health Concerns (HEA) scale, 108
Hilsenroth, M. J., 164–65
Ho scale, 79
Hostetler, K., 103
Hypochondriasis. *See* Health concerns
Hypochondriasis (Hs) scale. *See* MMPI-2 clinical scales, scale 1
Hypomania. *See* MMPI-2 clinical scales, scale 9
Hysteria (Hy) scale. *See* MMPI-2 clinical scales, scale 3
Hysterical conversion. *See* Somatization of Conflict (SOM) scale

Imperturbability, social, 99
Imperturbability (Ma3) subscale, 100
Impulsivity, 71. *See also* Disconstraint
Inconsistent Responding (INC) scale, 117, 118
Inconsistent response scales, 28, 51
Infrequency scale. *See* F (Infrequency) scale
Inhibition of Aggression (Hy5) subscale, 99
Introversion-extroversion (I-E), 41. *See also* MMPI-2 clinical scales, scale 0
Introversion/Low Positive Emotionality (INTR) scale, 83

K (Subtle Defensiveness) scale, 31–32
  interpretation of, as function of social class, 53
  patient attitudes toward treatment and, 52–53
Keane PTSD scale, 80–81
Koss-Butcher Critical Item List, 94–95

L (Lie) scale, 31
  patient attitudes toward treatment and, 52
Lachar-Wrobel Critical Item List, 95
Lack of Ego Mastery, Cognitive (Sc3) subscale, 100
Lack of Ego Mastery, Conative (Sc4) subscale, 100
Lack of Ego Mastery, Defective Inhibition (Sc5) subscale, 100
Lassitude, Malaise (Hy3) subscale, 99
Lie (L) scale. *See* L (Lie) scale
Low Expectation of Therapeutic Benefit (EXP) scale, 117, 119
Low Self-Esteem (LSE) scale, 109, 111

MacAndrew Alcoholism Scale (MAC), 74–75
  predictive research on, 76–77
Malingering, 30. *See also* Exaggerated symptom expression
Managed care, 8
Mania (Ma) scale. *See* MMPI-2 clinical scales, scale 9
Marital Distress Scale (MDS), 79–80
Masculinity-Femininity (Mf) scale. *See* MMPI-2 clinical scales, scale 5
McKinley, J. C., 23
Meehl, Paul E., 129
Mental Dullness (D4) subscale, 98
Minnesota Report, 135
  illustrations, 135–48, 201–3
Mistrust, Paranoia (Pa) scale, 71
MMPI (Minnesota Multiphasic Personality Inventory), 23–24
  books on, 24–25
  reasons for broad acceptance of, 24–25
MMPI-2 (Minnesota Multiphasic Personality Inventory-2). *See also specific topics*
  abbreviated forms, 46–47
  books on, 24
  BTPI and, 124, 125, 191–205
  case analyses, 181–84, 191–95, 199–203
  code types and treatment-related hypotheses, 64–72
  content interpretation, 93, 113
    critical item approach, 94–97
  content scales, 93, 107–11, 113
    research on, 111–12
    treatment planning with, 112–13
    unreliability of brief measures, 97
  content subscales, 98
    rationally derived content subgroups. *See* Harris-Lingoes MMPI-2 subscales